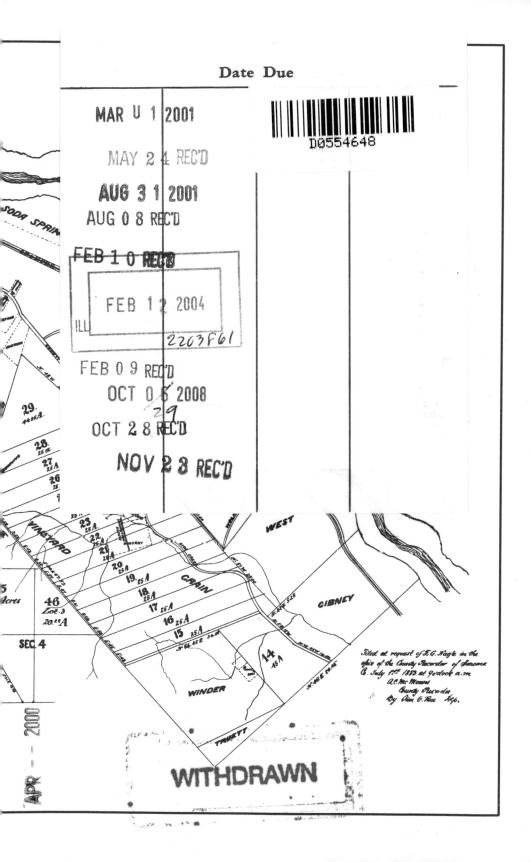

Legacy of a Village

Also by Jack W. Florence, Sr.:

A Noble Heritage
The Wines and Vineyards of Dry Creek Valley
The fascinating story of one of California's premier grape-growing regions
from the days of Mexican occupation in the early 19th century to 1992.

Legacy of a Village

*The Italian Swiss Colony Winery
and People of Asti, California*

Jack W. Florence, Sr.

Raymond Court Press   Phoenix, Arizona

Cover design by Marge Gray
Book design by Jeannine Gendar

Please address orders, inquiries, and correspondence to:

Raymond Court Press
P.O. Box 50673
Phoenix, AZ 85076

Publisher's Cataloging-in-Publication
(Provided by Quality Books, Inc.)

Florence, Jack W.
    Legacy of a village: the Italian Swiss Colony
Winery and people of Asti, California / Jack W.
Florence. – 1st ed.
    p. cm.
    Includes bibliographical references and index.
    LCCN: 99-93378
    ISBN: 0-9673081-0-0

    1. Italian Swiss Colony (Winery) 2. Wine and
wine making–California–Asti–History. 3. Asti
(Calif.)–History. 4. Vintners–California–Asti
–Biography. I. Title.

TP557.F56 1999
641.2/2/0979418   QBI99-1124

for Anne

Contents

Anne Matteoli
1917–1998

We Will Not Forget

GOLFREDO MATTEOLI ARRIVED AT ASTI shortly after the turn of the twentieth century to work for the Italian Swiss Colony winery. His wife, two children and their wives all worked at the Colony at one time or another. Son Lilio had been working at the Colony close to twenty years when he married Anne Toniatti in the little church at Asti in 1950. By 1988, Anne had worked at the Italian Swiss Colony winery for 33 of her 71 years.

The extent of the involvement of the Matteoli family with ISC was not unusual, but Anne's love for the years she spent at Asti most certainly was. For Anne never quite got over the closeness of the families living there, or the subtle ways Asti reached out to those in her midst. She never forgot the lunchtime strolls with fellow workers to the Villa, eating grapes, an orange or possibly a fig picked along the way.

But most of all, Anne loved the Asti church, Madonna Del Carmine. Nicknamed El Carmelo, the tiny chapel tugged at her heart
strings, the pull growing ever more powerful as the church collapsed
onto its foundation. Anne worked with every fiber of her being to
somehow save the church from the tractor blade, and when that
battle stalled, she directed her attention to the Cloverdale Historical
Society and their effort to build a museum to house the archives of
Cloverdale and Asti. While just about everyone had given up saving
the church at Asti, Anne could never let go. She encouraged me, and
in her subtle way implored me, lest they forget, to write the story of
her beloved El Carmelo.

We will never forget Anne, just as she never forgot Asti. Anne
wrote in 1988, just a few months after ISC shut down forever: "I was
going to retire in April of 1988, but I realized things were going to
change, so I stayed on. Several of us were on lay-off up until the
Italian Swiss Colony closed down. We cleaned out our desks on the
last day, and it was a tearful farewell.

"I hope to see Beringer Winery and its parent company replant the
vineyards, fix up the building, keep the gardens lovely, have the
Villa glistening in the sunshine and the Little Church in the Vineyard
repaired.

"A big part of my life was spent at Italian Swiss Colony, Asti, California. As I look back, I couldn't have spent it at a better place."

We were all saddened when Anne unexpectedly passed away on
May 22, 1998. We had lost a friend, and I faced the bitter realization
that I hadn't completed this book project before her death. Be at rest,
Anne. If not in bricks and mortar, El Carmelo will live in the pages of
this book. There is no way to know how often these pages will be
turned, but every once in a while for the unforeseeable future, some
scholar or possibly someone whose family name ends in "i" will pick
up this book and Madonna Del Carmine will live again.

A Special Thanks

Legacy of a Village took over three years to research, write and go through the process of publishing. Other than enormous satisfaction, a book of this nature cannot hope to earn a return for those who invest time and money in its creation, and it is thus all but impossible to get a history such as this into the hands of interested readers. It is for this reason that so many rich and important stories of the people who went before us are never told. Midway through the three-year period, Dr. Kevin Starr, California State Librarian and preeminent historian, urged me to see this effort through to its publication. That this has happened is due to the unbounded efforts of many and to the generosity, wisdom and concern of two wineries, Beringer Wine Estates and Wattle Creek Winery.

Beringer Wine Estates

Beringer Wine Estates, under president Walter Klenz, has earned the gratitude of all of us for the winery's care and concern for the rich history of the defunct winery property it acquired in 1988. They have undertaken the unprecedented policy of cataloging and preserving the artifacts of the Italian Swiss Colony winery. But Beringer has done more than just store artifacts. They also maintain the Villa and the historic grounds in pristine condition even though the winery is not open to the public. My special thanks also to Jim Barfield, who directs Beringer's community affairs, and who recognized the importance of this project. And to Beringer's Bill Knox, to whom the people of Asti owe a special thanks, I add my deepest gratitude. Bill provided unflagging support to me as well as the last Colony employees as they undertook the sorrowful task of closing the pages on a hundred years of life and work at Asti, California.

Wattle Creek Winery

In 1881 Andrea Sbarboro and his friends found an Asti that was little more than wilderness, with untamed hills covered only by grazing sheep and sporadic oak trees. One hundred years later, Asti was home to a major winery. Vineyards surrounded the buildings although the hills, once planted to vines as far as the eye could see, had returned to grazing lands.

What of Asti in 2081? None of Asti's present stewards will likely be around then, but Asti will still be there. Much of how Asti looks then will be influenced by the people of the area as we approach the year 2000.

The people of Asti in 2081, the folks of Sonoma County, indeed the countless numbers not yet born but destined to walk the shores of the Russian River just south of Cloverdale will be grateful for the presence in 1999 of Chris and Kristine Williams. Owners of Wattle Creek Winery, their love for the area will serve to protect it. Andrea Sbarboro brought grapevines to Asti from the old country just as the Williamses have done. The only difference: in 1881 the vines came from Italy, while at the turn of the 21st century the Williams's vines arrived from their country of birth, Australia. They grow only the best fruit and produce extraordinary wines. Chris and Kris are the new breed of Asti-area stewards. Asti is fortunate for their presence and I am fortunate for their support and encouragement.

Preface

EACH YEAR, THOUSANDS OF CHILDREN receive their first cameras. Bursting with enthusiasm, they rush to share their photos of family adventures with eager friends. In so doing, of course, the kids have unwittingly become historians and their friends have demonstrated a passion, albeit a juvenile one, for history. But the educational system soon destroys the enthusiasm of many of these nascent historians, suffocating their natural interest under a blanket of bore, memorized lists or pasteurized renditions of the past. History is more than dates, events or a sanitized past.

History, to be meaningful, must be the record of those who went before us, of their deeds and misdeeds. History must focus on the effects of such actions in order that we who follow might benefit from the telling of their story. The sentiment is not new. Fourteenth-century philosopher-historian Abd-er-Rahman ibn-Khaldun observed, "History has for its true object to make us understand the social state of many i.e., his civilization; to reveal to us the phenomena that naturally accompany... life..."

I have attempted to tell the rich story of Asti, a tiny village in northern California's wine country, as a people story—for that, after all, is what it is. In an attempt to give the story the depth provided by human experience, I have, in a few instances, created entirely fictitious moments and dialogue. These "creations" should be readily evident to even the casual reader. In no instance do I attempt to alter historic fact or present a revisionistic view of the struggles, failures and successes of the wonderful people whose story is told in the pages of this book.

In writing the story of Asti, I was struck by the swirling currents that, in the course of human events, swept over and around the tiny community. Indeed, the life of man is always in turmoil. Society lives on a battlefield, the combatants God and the Devil, order and chaos, the spirit and the flesh. To this mix, man has added another source of societal tension, economic devils. For the entrepreneurs of Asti, fortunes were made and distressingly lost. Competition begot sleepless nights. For the workers, jobs were created then taken away. Surely there was joy in the community at the prospect of new work and sadness among all when jobs were taken away. The prospects for the Colony, the presence of good and bad bosses, all helped to color life at Asti. But while the entrepreneurs came and went, the people endured. Babies were born, children grew to adulthood, got married and gave the older generation grandchildren.

The last seven owners of Italian Swiss Colony, stewards of Asti over a period covering 58 years, are still in business. While they operate in cities around the world, few of their managers have ever heard of Asti, California, or even of Italian Swiss Colony. But the families of Asti are around, for the most part living out their final years within a mile or so of the village that used to sit along the Russian River. Their numbers are declining, and memories dim. In time their story will fade, and like footprints in the sand, be lost forever. Thus this book.

Asti is a story of glorious success and abject failure. It is a story of America's free enterprise system at its best and at its worst. The thoughtful reader might notice that the craving for society's larder at the top seems to have brought less satisfaction than those efforts should have attained, while at the lowest economic level, where aspirations were more modest, life tended to be fulfilled and perhaps even happy. But one needs to be cautious in rendering sweeping judgments in describing human behavior, for behavior is a continuum. Also there are many exceptions to any general conclusion and one can find happy, commercially successful people just as misery abides in the middle and lower economic levels of society.

One of the more telling influences on America's society is the lust for material possessions. It is a lust that stands as a major pillar supporting America's economic system, and it does seem to bring comfort to people. Somehow the people of Asti seem to have missed this driven need for more. And while the folks at Asti likely didn't think about it, there are those who have considered societal greed. For this they are treated disdainfully by society or simply ignored. Economist

Robert Kuttner, in his book *Everything for Sale*, expressed his views as follows: "The collective message of all the advertising is that material consumption will lead to happiness. Consumption is doubtless pleasurable, and nobody minds a high material standard of living. But at their extremes, commercial values crowd out other values." Certainly Christmas is a good example of this phenomena.

In a nation that revels in the days of California's forty-niners, readers may be somewhat chastened by the words of Hubert H. Bancroft, California's legendary historian. (From *Quarterdecks and Spanish Grants* by C. Raymond Clar)

> First the Golden Age, and then the Age of Gold.
> How different! And yet between the end and the
> beginning of a decade California gives us a specimen
> of each, which brief period presents two episodes of
> society the history of the world cannot parallel. Both
> were original, both phenomenal; and so closely upon
> the heels of one followed the other, that for an instant
> both were on the ground at the same time.
> It was when the gold-seekers came that this golden
> age of California was destined to be alloyed with brass;
> for not the age of gold was California's true golden
> age. The age of gold was the age of avarice....
> More nearly resembling the euthanasia of the ancients
> was the pastoral life preceding the finding of the
> Sierra treasures.
> —*H. H. Bancroft, California Pastoral*

There were seekers at Asti and there were those for whom contentment could be found in the vine-cloaked hills of the place. Do the lives of the people of Asti, and the observations of Hubert Bancroft, hold a message for the rest of us?

Someone wrote that history is written by winners. Were there winners (and losers) in the story of Asti? The author leaves this question for the reader to ponder.

The reader is encouraged to read the Notes section. The section contains many "nuggets" that add appreciably to the story.

The Greater San Francisco Bay Area

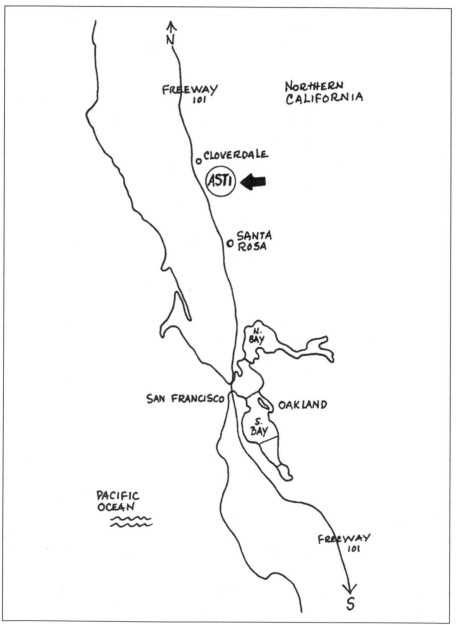

The senator says the territory of California is three time greater than the average extent of the new States of the Union. Well, Sir, suppose it is. We all know that it has more than three times as many mountains, inaccessible and rocky hills, and sandy wastes, as are possessed by any State of the Union. But how much is there of useful land? How much that may be made to contribute to the support of man and of society? These ought to be the questions. Well, with respect to that, I am sure that everybody has become satisfied that, although California may have a very great sea-board, and a large city or two, yet that the agricultural products of the whole surface now are not, and never will be, equal to one half part of those of the State of Illinois; no, nor yet a fourth or perhaps a tenth part.

—*Senator Daniel Webster,* June 27, 1850.
Senate debate over admittance of
California into the Union

1

The Way It Was

The Indians' preservation of the land and its products for the ten thousand or more years of their undisputed occupancy was such that the white invaders wrested from them a garden, not the wilderness it salved their conscience to call it.

—Kroeber and Heizer

THE MOUNTAINS RISE STEEPLY from the icy, crashing sea. A bone-chilling fog carries cold drops of the Pacific Ocean across the shore to shroud the forested slopes one-half mile inward. About sixty miles north of San Francisco Bay, the Russian River sneaks under the fog and twists its way through the dense redwood forest before emptying into the Pacific. In the summer the river struggles to sustain itself, its white stony bottom drying in the long summer sun. But in winter the river surges, taking down trees, creating new banks while destroying old ones before disgorging its brown, foaming waters into the sea. Indians called the Russian River Shabaikai, or snake. Californios called it San Ysidro. By 1843 the river was called El Rio Ruso.

The Russian River is a major waterway within the Coastal Range of northwestern California. Starting in Redwood Valley north of Ukiah, the river flows south to Healdsburg before turning westward toward the Pacific Ocean. About halfway down its eighty-mile route, the river reaches Cloverdale, and then the Alexander Valley just four miles further south. The northern end of the valley is little more than a mile wide. Low-lying hills border the western edge before climbing to two thousand feet and then plunging nearly straight down to Dry Creek on their western side. Early settlers living on Dry Creek looked up at the nearly barren ridge and called it Impassable Mountains. To the east, the valley was bordered by the rugged Mayacamas Mountains and a ridge alive with geothermal steam.

The valley was a wonderful place. It almost never snowed and although winter nights could dip below freezing, the ground never experienced a hard freeze. The winds of spring blew from the north, but they brought little bad weather. While there was no rain during the summer half of the year, there was ample rainfall in winter to support dense forests that included nature's tallest creature, the coastal redwood. Several varieties of oak thrived in the area, the leaves of the magnificent black oak adding red and yellow color to the forests in the fall. Grasses, willows and occasional cottonwood trees prospered along stream edges. Grapes, blackberries, raspberries, strawberries and huckleberries together with mushrooms and a variety of acorns contributed to the pantry for the local wildlife.

The land was the unfettered domain of countless numbers and species of wildlife. Deer and elk were everywhere in forests they shared with mountain lions, wildcats and black bear. California quail led their broods through grassy meadows. Eagles and condors soared on thermals in the crystalline sky. Robins, bluebirds and meadowlarks spent winters in the area. Each spring, thousands of fat salmon returned from a sojourn that took them nearly to Japan before making their final trip up the Russian River. This was nature at steady state, the equilibrium disturbed only by the occasional drought or flooded streams and rivers.

Archaeologists debate the details of man's arrival in North America. For years, the prevailing theory has been that people crossed the

Bering land bridge from Siberia less than 12,000 years ago. Recent discoveries in South America suggest that the Asians might have passed through California centuries earlier. About 5000 B.C. a band of North American Indians began a migration north,[1] and by 3000 B.C. they had settled in the vicinity of Clear Lake approximately thirty miles northeast of Alexander Valley. From there, they migrated west through the mountain passes to the Russian River. Once there, the early settlers spread north and south through the string of valleys along the course of the river.

For almost five thousand years, they enjoyed the isolated splendor of the place. Like most central California people, they depended more on vegetable than animal foods. Over 3500 years two events significantly changed the Indian way of life. About 500 B.C. the people switched from seed grinding to acorn processing for their dietary staple. Now, like the bears, they looked forward to fall, the season when the acorns filled the oak trees. About one thousand years later, around 500 A.D., the bow and arrow were developed and animal meat became an important source of nutrition for the Indians. But these events were fine tuning of a stable, harmonious lifestyle in northern Alexander Valley, thousands of years ago.

The people of the area were the Makahmo Pomo Indians. Their five villages formed an independent, self-governing group sharing a common language, territory and culture. The Makahmos or Cloverdale Pomos spoke Southern Pomo, a language related to those of other tribes in the area. Closest to the people of Cloverdale were the Mihilakawna, the Dry Creek tribe of the Southern Pomo people, who occupied Dry Creek Valley along the southwest border of the Makahmos. The Wappo Indians occupied what is now Geyserville and the rest of Alexander Valley to the south. Each tribe occupied sufficient land to make it independent. The self-sufficient nature of society in the region allowed the various tribes to live in peace with each other. They would visit, sometimes to trade, share ceremonials or even attend marriages between tribe members.

The first Europeans to visit northern California were Spanish traders and explorers. In 1542, Juan Cabrillo visited the coast of Mendocino

County, and in 1579, Sir Francis Drake landed his vessel, the *Golden Hind,* on the shore just north of San Francisco. Neither had significant contact with the Indians. It was almost two hundred years later, in 1775, that Juan Bodega Quada came ashore to trade for goods with the Indians. It is unlikely that any of the Indians of northern Alexander Valley encountered these early visitors to their land.

But the Spanish exploration by land ended their isolation. Now interested in colonization, the Spanish government in Madrid encouraged the Franciscan missionaries in their search for souls in the lands north of Mexico City. By 1776, the missionaries reached San Francisco and founded Mission Dolores. While Americans to the east were gaining their independence, the Indians of the Pacific were about to lose theirs.

The Indians of northern Sonoma County likely first encountered Europeans a few years after the turn of the nineteenth century. In 1812, the Russians established Fort Ross on the Sonoma County coast about twelve miles north of the Russian River. Occasionally the Russians would explore up the Russian River to forage, hunt and trade with the local Indians. Relations with the Russians, who were interested in trade—not the backs of the Indians—were cordial. There were even occasional marriages between Indian women and Russian sailors.

By 1820, rumors were circulating at Mission Dolores of Englishmen infiltrating the territory north of San Francisco. In 1821 an expedition was formed and the Spanish military went north to Calistoga at the top of Napa Valley, then west onto the Santa Rosa plain. This journey marked the first known visit of Europeans, other than the Russians, to central Sonoma County. In July 1821, Spain was forced to accept the Treaty of Cordoba, freeing Mexico from Spanish rule. This made little difference to the lives of the Pomo but by the early 1830s, Mexican pressure on the Pomos was intense. At the time, the Cloverdale Pomos numbered between six and nine hundred persons, living in five villages. The principal town was Makahmo with a population somewhere around four hundred. It was located along the Russian River, about where the river passes through Cloverdale. The other leading town, Amako, was situated southeast of Cloverdale, east of the Russian River. It had a headman of equal rank to the headman at Makahmo.

After five thousand years, the Cloverdale tribe faced an entity that threatened and ultimately destroyed their people as an economic and cultural force in the area. Perhaps nature had treated the Pomos with too much beneficence. The Pomos of the 1830s, their fathers and their fathers before them, had for thousands of years lived in harmony with the natural forces around them. They seldom knew hunger. They never faced life-threatening winters or failed crops. The Pomos, for generation after generation, were born, lived and died in a world of peace, the latter disturbed only by occasional skirmishes with neighbors.

As a consequence, the Pomos developed no leader in the mold of the chiefs of the Plains Indians. The Pomos may have had altercations with neighbors but they had no wars and thus no warriors. But it fell to the Indian generation of the early 19th century to face for the first time a threat to tribal existence. In a move to face these forces, the two principal towns of the Cloverdale Pomos joined together under the leadership of the Makahmo headman, Musalacan. But the forces set in motion in faraway Europe, by people Musalacan would never meet, were not to be stopped. There would be no pitched battles. The Pomo had no fighting force, but that didn't matter. White man's illnesses destroyed them. By 1833, an estimated 70,000 Indians had been swept away by smallpox. The northern California Indians from Fort Ross to Clear Lake and into the Sacramento Valley were thus eliminated as a force to resist Mexican encroachment. By 1835 the Missions had been secularized and taken over by civilians. Now the Indians were viewed as cheap labor and in some instances as virtual slaves. With the Indians vanquished, peace returned to Sonoma County if not to the Pomos. Now the military emphasis became slave hunting and retaliatory raids against hungry Indians who had taken to stealing livestock from the Californio ranchos.

On July 9, 1846, the USS *Portsmith* sailed into the harbor of Yerba Buena (San Francisco). The presence of Old Glory flying from the mast was a reminder to the Mexicans that the United States was there to protect its citizens and the nation's interest in the troubled land. A member of the crew was Lieutenant Joseph Revere, grandson of American hero Paul Revere.[2] Revere could see about half a dozen buildings housing less than an estimated one hundred inhabitants on the slopes of Yerba Buena.

There was little military activity that summer and Revere was free to explore the region. Later that summer, he was assigned to the Mexican outpost in Sonoma, where he found time to lead an expedition into the country to the north. His mission was to explore Clear Lake and to observe the Indian populations in the Napa Valley, Clear Lake and the Russian River areas. His group traveled north through Napa Valley and returned by way of Hopland, then south along the Russian River.

Arriving in the area of Cloverdale, Revere came upon the "site of an old rancheria, in a beautiful and celebrated spot by the river's side, which we distinguished by the raised earth where its lodges had once stood." Revere's Indian guide informed him that "the Spanish had killed or carried to captivity all of its inhabitants." Did their shadows fall that day on the bleached bones of Musalacan? Before returning to Sonoma, Revere visited the Dry Creek Rancho of the Piña family and the Sotoyome Rancho belonging to Henry Fitch.

Treatment of the Indians by first the Mexicans and then the Americans provoked Indian retaliation. Innocents from both sides suffered tragically. Indian women were raped with official impunity; Mexican and American women were savagely murdered in response. The attitude of the day was expressed by the California governor's first annual address to the state legislature in 1851: "That a war of extinction will continue to be waged between the races until the Indian Race becomes extinct must be expected... the inevitable destiny of the Race is beyond the power of wisdom of man to overt."

Within five years, the government arrived at a solution to the "Indian problem." Between 1855 and 1860, a concerted effort was made to round up the Indians and drive them north to a reservation in Round Valley. Indians remember the relocations as a series of death marches, soldiers on horseback herding Indians—men, women, and children—on foot over the nearly one hundred miles to Round Valley. Joseph Revere would have wondered about the nature of the "Indian problem." A decade earlier he had traveled into the heart of Indian territory with just two armed sailors and a ragtag group of Indian guides and translators. Revere had explained, "As I was bound in a peaceful mission, it was not necessary to take a large force."[3]

Many years earlier, before the Indian wars had started in earnest, and just three years after gaining its independence from Spain in 1821, Mexico passed a colonization law. The new country, while still racked with political turmoil in Mexico City, was anxious to extend its colonization of California. One way to do this was to encourage settlements and developments within the territory. To further development and to make certain that the developers were loyal to the government, a law was passed making large tracts of land available for private ownership. These tracts, or ranchos, would be free to approved petitioners; the grantee had only to pledge his intentions to develop the land.

In 1846, Francisco Berryessa petitioned California governor Pio Pico for a tract of land. The tract would include all of present Cloverdale and extend south to within a mile of Geyserville. The piece was roughly rectangular, measuring up to two miles wide and a little over eight miles long. It was a prime piece of the Russian River Valley, tracing the river as it emerged from the hills of Mendocino County until reaching the Tzabacco Rancho of Jose Piña. The latter, which took in all of Geyserville and most of Dry Creek, had been granted to the fourteen-year-old protégé of Mariano Vallejo in 1843. The land carved out by Berryessa totaled 8,866 acres. On April 26 the U.S. declared war on Mexico. Six days later, on May 2, 1846, Berryessa's grant was approved. Its name: Rincón de Musalacan.

2

The Search

"... to buy and sell agricultural lands for colonial purposes, to cultivate the same, to manufacture, buy and sell wines and spirits, to deal in the products of said lands, and all matters and things appertaining to the purposes herein specified."
—Articles of Incorporation,
Italian Swiss Colony

S AN FRANCISCO IN 1852 was an untamed, bawdy, frontier town. Only ten years earlier, the city was called Yerba Buena and the population counted less than fifty isolated souls living on the bleak, windswept hills of the peninsula.

Now a wild energy permeated the city. It was a city without law, which made order unthinkable. It was a place of unfettered lust, unslaked by the gold at Sutter's Mill or the ladies of the night along the Barbary Coast. The brawling town was fed by a stream of adventurers coming from all corners of the world. It was a place of blowing dust in summer and ankle-deep mud in winter.

And still they came. Australia shipped hardened criminals, the Sydney Ducks, who wreaked treachery upon the heedless citizens.

Men from America's east coast sailed to Panama, making a grueling trek across disease-ridden swamps to reach Panama City, where they battled one another for passage by ship north to San Francisco. Aboard ship, the passenger found he had paid $300 for a bunk for eight hours each day, the same bunk being occupied by two other men who also got eight hours each.

After fifteen days in steerage with nothing to eat but salt pork and hardtack, thirteen-year-old Andrea Sbarboro sailed into this cauldron of wild men and reckless women. The youngster could think only of fresh bread as he arrived in the city that would be his home for nearly seventy years. But this was 1852. Now he would join his older brother in the grocery business. In those early days, the brothers' grocery business served the saloons and bordellos of the Barbary Coast, filling their primordial need for fruit and vegetables.

All over the world, rainbows led opportunists to the City by the Bay. The year after Sbarboro arrived, a young Levi Strauss was rowed ashore, wharf space having long been consumed by the abandoned vessels of gold seekers. He was seeking opportunities for his family's New York tailoring business. Strauss brought with him bolts of heavy cloth that he figured would make great tents. He hadn't been in the city a whole day when he began accosting men whose bedraggled figures suggested they had recently returned from the gold fields. Strauss was puzzled by the lack of enthusiasm his pitch received until finally he stopped a fellow who was still carrying the dust of the placers on his threadbare clothes. "A tent?" the fellow growled. "Look at me! My pants are so thin my knees stick out, my pockets have holes in 'em and my arse is sunburnt. Make me a pair of pants and you've got a deal." Levi complied, and one day his name would be emblazoned on blue denim pants around the world.

Bankers and hardware stores moved next to saloons and bordellos, and together they shared in the riotous early days of the city. By 1852, San Francisco's population had mushroomed to almost 100,000 people, 75,000 of whom had arrived within the past two years.

Sbarboro represented a new breed of immigrant to San Francisco. The product of an old, stable European society, he sought the riches of the new world tempered by the values of his Italian family up-bringing. Hard work was all he had known in his few years and when his brother made Andrea bookkeeper for the fledging business, he learned bookkeeping. Along with his thirst for learning Sbarboro had a penchant for teaching. This latter drive would one day lead him to lecture Congress and anyone else who would listen on the evils of irresponsible drinking and the natural good inherent in wine consumption.

Early in the 1860's Sbarboro began teaching English to local Italian children. With no suitable primer available, he wrote his own text-book. By the end of the decade Sbarboro ran his own grocery business and had accumulated about $10,000 from his teaching practice and investments in North Beach city lots. At thirty years of age, Sbarboro was well established in the community.

The decade of the 1860's saw continued prosperity in San Francisco. Construction of the transcontinental railroad started in 1862. Tens of millions of dollars in subsidies and low-cost loans were made to Huntington, Stanford, Hopkins and Crocker to build the Central Pacific Railroad from Sacramento to the East. San Franciscans anxiously awaited the completion of the transcontinental railroad and the prosperity it was to assure their city. The railroad was completed on May 10, 1869, but outside the mansions built on Nob Hill with money bilked from the federal government, little wealth found its way to the streets of San Francisco. Quite the opposite occurred. Unemployment grew as commerce in the city suffered from cheap goods brought by the railroad to San Francisco.

Buffeted by wild swings in the economy, problems for the man in the street escalated. A bitter drought in the winter of 1869–1870 devastated farms and ranches. Beleaguered farmers made their way to the city for jobs which suddenly were no longer so plentiful. The situation continued to worsen. A national depression in 1873 sent thousands of unemployed to California. Between 1873 and 1875, over 260,000 people arrived in the state. The completion of the railroad paid another unexpected blow to the economy of San Francisco. Between 15,000 and 20,000 Chinese laborers, their railroad labor done, returned unemployed to San Francisco. Between 1870 and 1875 another 80,000 Chinese arrived from China. The flow of Chinese, started and promoted by the big four railroad builders, could not be stopped with completion of the road.

If the "have nots" struggled, life went on for the "haves." The Bank of California grew overnight to become one of the city's largest banks, thanks principally to the Comstock lode that had been discovered in Nevada in 1859. The bank enjoyed prodigious growth into the mid-1870's, by which time San Francisco was the tenth largest city in the United States. The Bank of California, wheeling and dealing in the world of risky mining investments, ultimately failed, closing its doors on August 24, 1875, bringing down with it many of the city's other banks. The day after closing, William Ralston, founder of the bank and known to many as the father of San Francisco, was asked by the bank's board to tender his resignation. His family now penniless, the disgraced Ralston drowned later that day while swimming in the water off North Beach. The body of the drowned man was examined by the coroner, but whether the death was accidental or suicide was never settled conclusively. Sbarboro remembered that day very well, for on August 25, his first child, Alfredo, was born.

On the morning of October 2, 1875, the bank reopened. That very evening, another Ralston project opened. It was the Palace Hotel, the largest hotel in the Western Hemisphere. By 1875, Mark Hopkins had completed his mansion on Nob Hill. The cable car ran up the hill in 1876 and the mansions of Stanford and Crocker were soon to follow on the hill. All of this took place in a city that just 35 years earlier was a cluster of windswept hills inhabited by a few families growing herbs at the end of the remote peninsula.

Most of the Italian immigrants of North Beach were working, but their meager incomes barely covered the cost of raising a family. Few had ever been inside a bank—those vaulted marble edifices with barred windows and massive doors through which passed the wealthy of the city. Banks had little interest in the immigrants, preferring to do business solely with those who already had money or who had clever schemes to make it. Bargain interest rates at the time were like credit card rates of the 1990's, eighteen to twenty percent. Often, rates reached two percent per month.

In 1875 Sbarboro got an idea that was to shape the rest of his life. At the invitation of a friend, Sbarboro attended a meeting held in West Oakland, where neighbors planned to organize a building-and-loan society. The friend wanted Sbarboro's opinion about the idea. The concept was new to Sbarboro but he soon learned that such societies generally involved two to three hundred families, who were generally neighbors. Each family would subscribe to stock and pay into the society not less than five dollars nor more than fifty dollars every month. Interest would be earned but not paid out unless a member withdrew from the society. The society would collect up to $10,000 each month, the money to be loaned out only to members and only for the purpose of building a home.

Sbarboro had gone to the meeting an observer, but he left sold on the idea. He joined the group, was elected its secretary and on July 21, 1875, the society was formally organized. The scheme was eminently successful. Over the next several years Sbarboro organized and managed the San Francisco Mutual Loan Association, the West Oakland Masonic Hall and Building Association, the Italian-Swiss Mutual Loan Association, and the San Francisco and Oakland Mutual Loan Association. These associations ultimately raised $6.5 million and financed the construction of over 2500 homes in the Bay Area.

The decade of the 1880's would see the seeds planted for America's future industrial might. The decade would also see seeds of another kind start their growth. Several of the nation's leaders during the depression and war years fifty years in the future were born during the eighties, including Franklin Roosevelt, Harry Truman, Dwight Eisenhower, Douglas MacArthur and George Marshall.

March of 1880 marked the beginning of political recognition of the importance of viticulture to the state of California. Responding to growing interest throughout the state and many newspaper articles calling for state-sponsored information, the legislature created the Board of State Viticultural Commissioners. It was one of their reports, published the following year, that caught Sbarboro's attention. The board reported that the average production of grapes in California was five tons to the acre, with production costs typically $20 per acre. Since the average price for grapes was $30 per ton, the report concluded that growers could average profits of $130 per acre. The message was not lost on the Italian banker.

To quote Sbarboro, "At that time, laborers frequently came to my office asking for employment and as they were generally contadini, who understood the growing of grapes, I thought that some of the money of one of my building and loan associations, which we had on hand and could not place advantageously, might be properly invested in buying a tract of land for the association with a view of putting these Italian vineyardists at work."

On the advice from his lawyer that funds then in his various building associations could not be used for purposes other than housing, Sbarboro formed a new association chartered specifically to fund an agricultural investment. Membership would be limited to Italians, but given the closeness of the people living at the border between the two countries, Sbarboro would invite Swiss immigrants to join as well. He would name this new venture the Italian Swiss Agricultural Colony, or more simply, the Colony. Under this new plan, workers would get paid subsistence wages for their labor with a portion of their wage invested in the association. After some years of "buying in," when the business began earning profits, the workers would, like any shareholder, participate in the distribution of those profits. Ultimately the workers, along with the other investors, would receive a prorated share of the association's land and other assets when the association was "cashed out."

Sbarboro was now forty years old, a successful businessman and well known to the leaders in the North Beach Italian community. He sounded out his friend, Dr. Paolo de Vecchi, who liked the idea, and together they found sixty persons interested in investing in the new venture. The leading figure in the group was Marco G. Fontana. Fontana, who once did canning experiments in his kitchen, was president and one of the founders of the California Fruit Canners Association, then the largest canner in the world.

On March 10, 1881, the Italian Swiss Agricultural Colony (ISAC) was incorporated.[4] Capitalization for the Colony was set at $300,000 through the issuance of five thousand shares at sixty dollars each. Stock subscriptions were five shares minimum, fifty shares maximum. At the time of incorporation, 858 shares were subscribed. The remaining shares would be purchased by the workers. There were nine directors of the association whose stated purpose was "… to buy and sell agricultural lands for colonial purposes, to cultivate the same, to manufacture, buy and sell wines and spirits, to deal in the products of said lands, and all matters and things appertaining to the purposes herein specified."

Sbarboro was joined by fellow directors Stephen Campodonico and M. Perata in a search for suitable vineyard land. Wooed by the Central Pacific Railroad, which measured its land holdings in square miles, the trio traversed the entire state. Working with the railroad made sense, of course, since Sbarboro would need to locate where rail transportation was available to ship their harvest. More than forty sites over central and southern California were inspected by the intrepid trio during the summer of 1881.

Finally Sbarboro looked north. A leading wine merchant in San Francisco, Abe Lachman of Lachman & Jacobi, heard of Sbarboro's search. Lachman told Sbarboro of a small winery located approximately one hundred miles north of San Francisco. Lachman had done business with Conrad Haehl, a grower and winemaker in Cloverdale. Cloverdale, just four and a half hours north of the city, was served by the San Francisco & North Pacific Railroad. Lachman would be happy to accompany Sbarboro and his committee to Cloverdale and introduce them to Haehl.

It was late that summer when Lachman, Sbarboro, Campodonico and Perata left on the ferry from the foot of Green Street, bound for Donahue's Landing where they would board the train. Few ferry rides in the world compare to a sail in San Francisco's harbor. Late August can be free of chilling winds, and a glorious afternoon awaited the four as the single side-wheeler ferry named the *James M. Donahue* slipped its pier at 3:30 that afternoon. There once was a morning train to Cloverdale, but it had been canceled the year before. Cloverdale's newspaper, the *Reveille,* [N-1] had expressed the frustration that towns grown dependent on the railroad have always experienced in its October 28, 1880, edition:

> Donahue has played a pretty trick on Cloverdale and Healdsburg now. Hereinafter we are to have but one train a day and that one will not arrive until 8 P.M. [which means 9]. We can rest assured, however, of getting our mail next morning, giving the company all night to make up for loss of time, etc. Two trains will be run as far as Fulton, the first arriving there at noon. If this train was continued on to Cloverdale, and the night train withdrawn, we would not mind it so much.
>
> The company has also advanced the price on freight in several instances. They now charge $23 for a car of grapes from here to Santa Rosa. Ten days ago the price was only $19.

The *Donahue* was 228 feet long and displaced 730 gross tons.[5] The ferry was only six years old and could accommodate up to 870 passengers. It was named after the son of the ferry's owner, Peter Donahue, who also owned the San Francisco & North Pacific Railway.

The *Donahue* passed the islands of the San Francisco Bay as it took a northerly heading. The forested shore of Tiburon passed on the left a little more than one-half hour after leaving San Francisco. Within another hour, the ferry steamed past San Pablo Point and into the large San Pablo Bay. As the *Donahue* headed in a slightly northwesterly direction, the hills began to fade and flat land began to spread out before them. It would be another hour before the vessel began to make its way six miles up the Petaluma River to Donahue's Landing, where the only passenger train that day waited to complete their connection to Cloverdale.

Peter Donahue played a significant role in the ultimate decision to establish the Colony at Asti, since without Donahue's railroad, there would have been no Asti. He was born of Irish parents in Glasgow, Scotland. He worked as a blacksmith in New York before coming to San Francisco as a forty-niner. In 1851, after the passions of the placers had cooled, Donahue established a blacksmith shop in San

Francisco with his brothers. They were very successful and Donahue was eventually elected to the board of directors of San Francisco's Hibernia Bank.

But it was in railroads that Donahue was to make his mark. He was very much like his fellow railroad barons: driven, ruthless in business, and more than a little willing to trade ethics for profits. He was hated by some, but in general was treated with respect by society. In a June 14, 1869, election in Sonoma County, a subsidy was approved for the company that would build a railroad from the Napa County line to Petaluma and then up to Santa Rosa, Healdsburg, and ultimately to Cloverdale, just south of the county line. The subsidy would be five thousand dollars per mile of track and it would expire in June 1872. The subsidy was awarded to the California Pacific Railroad. The Cal Pac took a while to get organized but Peter Donahue didn't. In August 1869, just a month and a half after Cal Pac was awarded the subsidy, Donahue acquired a portion of the right of way belonging to the San Francisco & Humboldt Bay Railroad and began laying line.

Within two months he had laid ten miles of track out of Petaluma and by the end of the year he had reached Santa Rosa, thereby connecting Sonoma County's two major cities. By this time, Cal Pac, using its $5,000-per-mile subsidy, began laying track right alongside of Donahue's track. But Donahue had a plan. On August 13, 1871, he abruptly sold out to Cal Pac. With competition gone, there was an immediate increase in freight and passenger rates. The county's business leaders complained, but there was nothing they could do. Cal Pac meanwhile rushed to finish the line to Cloverdale before the subsidy expired in June of the following year. They just made it. Six months later, in January 1873, Donahue reacquired the railroad and its name once again was San Francisco & North Pacific.

Peter Donahue's memory is honored by a statue, erected by his son a few years after Donahue died in 1885. Bearing the words "Dedicated to Mechanics by James Donahue, in memory of his father Peter Donahue," the truly beautiful work sits in the heart of San Francisco's business district on the corner of Market and Battery streets. Today, over one hundred years later, businessmen hurry by and youths sit on its pedestal, not one with the slightest idea of the identity of Peter Donahue.

One hundred miles north, in the city of Cloverdale, a similar fate awaited Sonoma County's railroad builder. Because of the difficult terrain to the north (and of course there were no subsidies for track laid north of Cloverdale), Cloverdale remained the terminus of Donahue's railroad for fifteen years. Peter Donahue and his wife, Ann, had come to find themselves in Cloverdale on Sunday mornings, and attended Mass at the Cloverdale Hotel with the Irish Catholics in town. It was seven years before the parishioners could accumulate the funds to build a church and Peter and Ann helped considerably in that effort. Donahue paid for all of the new church's furnishings and priest's vestments, and upon her death, Ann bequeathed five thousand dollars to the Cloverdale church. That sum, very large in 1880, was used to purchase the parish rectory. While Catholic churches are named only for Christ or church saints, it was to thank Peter Donahue that the parish was named St. Peter's.

Although the Catholics of Cloverdale and son James acted from their hearts, others provide a more considered judgment of Donahue and his peers. Donahue did bring commerce to previously remote towns and villages, but only for profit. The rights of way were donated to the railroad by folks anxious for the prosperity the railroad would surely bring. Government, at all levels, was always generous with the railroad companies. But the *Press Democrat,* normally an ardent supporter of commercial development, didn't seem too supportive of Donahue. The newspaper reported that Donahue earned approximately $300,000 in county subsidy bonds plus almost that much again in interest. An editorial of the time succinctly expressed the *Press Democrat's* feelings toward Peter Donahue:[6]

> ... none should gain the impression that the men behind the venture sic the SF&NP railroad were altruists. There has been entirely too much hero worship in the past on writers of history. It is well to give proper credit for achievements promoting public welfare but it is never wise to lose sight of motive.

Hero or villain, Donahue did more than leave his name to a small church and a statue in San Francisco. He left a railroad. And it was his railroad that afternoon in late summer 1881 that Sbarboro and his group climbed aboard for the trip north. Prior to completion of the railroad, the stage trip from Petaluma to Cloverdale took two days with an overnight stay in Santa Rosa.[7] Now the ride would take just one and one-half hours. The train stopped at Lakeville, then Petaluma before heading north to the city of Santa Rosa. Once out of Petaluma, the train entered the broad Santa Rosa plain. It would pass four stations where the train would stop only if flagged. About 45 minutes after leaving Donahue's Landing, the train pulled into Cotati, having averaged close to the maximum speed allowed, 30 miles per hour. Twenty minutes later the train pulled into the Santa Rosa train station.

A history of Sonoma County[8] written during that period described Santa Rosa. "Santa Rosa stands on an alluvial plain sloping gradually from the hills. It is surrounded by farms, orchards and vineyards. It is situated on the banks of Santa Rosa Creek and is almost hidden in groves of trees and luxuriant shrubs and flowers."

Santa Rosa at the time was the home of Luther Burbank, who had established his nursery and greenhouse only six years earlier. Santa Rosa was also a wood-and-water stop, so that passengers could get off and stretch their legs. The four businessmen would begin to feel the heat of the August day. It had been warm in San Francisco at three-thirty in the afternoon, but now it was hot as the temperature rose with every mile of their journey into the inland valleys of northern California.

Departing the Santa Rosa station a few minutes after six-thirty, the train passed Fulton one mile to the north where a line branched off to the redwood forests along the Russian River and to Guerneville. Here the train stopped and passengers could make a connecting train on the Fulton and Guerneville line of the SF&NP railroad. Leaving Fulton, the train continued north, passing Mark West, Windsor and Grants and finally arriving in Healdsburg at 7:15 P.M. Shortly after leaving Healdsburg and passing through a series of low, rolling hills, the train broke into the first really flat land since leaving Petaluma.

This was the beautiful Alexander Valley, stretching for fifteen miles to Cloverdale at its north end. Here the tracks ran alongside the Russian River a few hundred yards to the east.

After passing through Lytton Springs, the train pulled into Geyserville, a tiny village that had been settled thirty years earlier. Geyserville was the only village in Alexander Valley. It was the stepping-off place for visitors to the geysers in the mountains to the east. The last ten miles took the train past Truett's Station and finally to the last stop, Cloverdale, at 8:00 P.M. They had traveled ninety miles since boarding the ferry some four and one-half hours earlier. They had climbed from sea level to an elevation of 315 feet and from the coast to a town about fifty miles inland. Sbarboro and his friends rode the coach the few short blocks to the Cloverdale Hotel, where they would spend the night. They were joined that evening for dinner at the hotel by Mr. Haehl.

Cloverdale had been founded by early pioneer James A. Kleiser in 1854. The town was bordered on three sides by mountainous country. To the south, however, Cloverdale opened onto the Alexander Valley. The nearly isolated town grew slowly until the railroad reached it, providing good transportation to major towns in the county. With the coming of the railroad in 1872, Cloverdale became a regional trade center. Daily stage coaches connected Cloverdale to Anderson Valley to the west and Ukiah to the north. Stage connections could be made to such tourist attractions as Clear Lake and the geysers. Cloverdale supported five hotels and a booming business in land speculation during the 1870s. It was an English land investor, Henry Hutchinson, who owned the land that would become Asti.

The following morning, J. W. Ragsdale, a leading realtor in Cloverdale, took the four men in his buggy for the four-mile ride south on the old Redwood Highway. The "highway," which would one day become the 101 freeway, connected Cloverdale to Santa Rosa and Petaluma, the latter city fifty miles south. For twenty years before the rail line was completed, a stage coach made the trip daily, bringing passengers and mail along the scenic route. For unknown years before that, the route had served as an Indian trail. By late

The barn and Colony House as Sbarboro saw them in 1881, looking south down what would become the Old Redwood Highway. The "view hill" topped with trees rises behind the barn and house. Barn was replaced in 1894. The cookhouse was located to the left, just out of sight in this photo. Courtesy of Cloverdale Historical Society.

August it had not rained a drop for several months in the Cloverdale area and the road was dusty. It was an easy ride, however, almost flat, although low hills began to appear to the west as the road opened into the Alexander Valley. About three miles from town, Ragsdale pointed out the eight hundred acres that were soon to be acquired by the Icaria-Speranza, a French utopian colony.[N-2]

After one more mile they arrived at a beautiful house sitting beneath giant oak trees. The house was situated less than two hundred feet from the road. A driveway went up to the porch and encircled a small garden before returning to the highway. North of the house stood a large barn and a corral. On the east side of the road was a small blacksmith shop and alongside that, a long rectangular building faced the road. A fruit orchard grew next to the long building. A hill rose just to the south of the big house and Ragsdale suggested they climb to the top to get a good view of the parcel that was for sale. On the way up he explained the brief history of the land.

"All of this land was at one time part of the Rancho Rincón de Musalacan, owned by Francisco Berryessa. About 25 years ago Miers P. Truett, a businessman from San Francisco, acquired the ranch. In 1864, Isaac Bluxome, Jr., married Truett's daughter. Truett gave the couple one thousand acres, most of which are now being acquired by the Icaria-Speranza. A few years after their marriage, the couple built this house. Bluxome worked continuously to improve the place. From up here you can see the large barn and corral on the other side of the house. Across the street is the blacksmith shop. Alongside the shop is the bunkhouse (or cookhouse, as it came to be known). Bluxome employed full-time workers to tend the orchards and livestock, which consisted mostly of sheep. There are ten acres of land in barley, another ten acres in corn and twenty acres in wheat. Next to the bunkhouse you can see the orchard. The orchard is about 2.5 acres, with apples on 1.5 acres and peaches on the rest."

Ragsdale couldn't tell them about Truett's and Bluxome's background because he didn't know it.[9] Both men were merchants who met while serving on the Committee of Vigilance, an organization of San Francisco residents who were driven by the lawlessness in the city to take the law into their own hands. As "Secretary 33," Bluxome signed documents of the vigilante committee directing the arrest, expatriation or even execution of lawbreakers. Had Bluxome's identity been found out, his life expectancy would have been measured in hours. It is no wonder that Bluxome invested so much in the peaceful confines of Alexander Valley.

From the top of the hill, the group could see for miles in all directions, although trees tended to block the view north toward Cloverdale. The parcel for sale included the house and buildings and stretched primarily from north to south. It was a land of wooded hillsides and open pasture where Bluxome's sheep had grazed. To the west, the property was bordered by heavily wooded wild terrain that stretched beyond view. Looking to the southeast, the group could clearly see Mount St. Helena, its broad shoulders rising above Calistoga some thirty miles away in Napa County. Turning more to the east, the men faced the Alexander Valley, bisected by the Russian River as it flowed from the north towards Healdsburg. Through the trees they could see the railroad tracks they had traveled over the evening before. And through the trees to the southeast, roughly a mile from where they stood, the men could just catch a glimpse of the one-room schoolhouse. It was on the railroad's edge and was a key frame of reference that morning, since the school marked the northern border of the parcel they were considering. Between them and the school were two parcels that were not for sale.[N-3]

The three investors said little that morning on top of the hill. They were, after all, businessmen contemplating a significant investment. The real-estate broker droned on about the perfect location for grapes. Several wineries already prospered in Cloverdale. The Geyser Peak Winery in Geyserville had started making wine the previous year and the group had undoubtedly seen the Simi Winery as the train left Healdsburg. Grape prices had never been higher. But he needn't have bothered with a sales pitch, for the three San Franciscans had been emotionally transplanted to the rolling hills of Piedmont, home of Asti, in Northern Italy. All that remained to create a new Asti on the brown hills south of Cloverdale were vines in the ground.

They expressed cautious optimism, but they would have to report to the full board of directors. The board did approve, with the proviso that the 123-acre piece in front of the school be included in the sale. Hutchinson agreed, a deposit was taken, and the wheels to change ownership were set in motion. On November 8, 1881, the deal was closed.[10] In addition to the house and outbuildings, the initial purchase included 1497.46 acres. The price was $25,000, with $10,000 to be paid down. The balance was payable at $1,000 per month for fifteen months. By the following spring, the necessary papers had been signed and returned from England. Title to the 123-acre parcel, that part on which the winery would be built six years later, was transferred on May 8, 1882. The two parcels totaled 1620.94 acres.

Sbarboro wasted no time. Preston Davis was hired to survey the property and prepare a detailed map (see map inside front cover). Not only did the board want a good picture of what they had acquired, but Sbarboro needed a map when he made his presentation to the workers who would ultimately buy into the grand scheme. From the beginning the place was called Asti, and the name appeared prominently on the new map. Sbarboro named two creeks after his sons, Alfredo and Romolo. Another principal creek, the one running through the Lucca Ranch, he called Aida Creek after his oldest daughter. A director and member of the search team, M. Perata, got a creek named after him, but nowhere does the name of Campodonico, the third member of the team and also a director, show up. The name (Tommasso) Meineri, a significant ISAC shareholder, shows next to an existing house on Viola Avenue at the southeast corner of the property. Viola Avenue, once part of the main "highway" as it made its way north, still exists as a gravel driveway.

In preparation for his employee buy-in scheme, Sbarboro laid out twenty 25-acre parcels and another 22 parcels of varying sizes with nine of them at forty acres. The grand scheme had been set in motion.

3

A Winery is Born

The fullness of life is in the hazards of life,
And, at the worst, there is that in us which can
turn defeat into victory.

—*Edith Hamilton*

S BARBORO WAS ECSTATIC. He had devised a win-win plan: the
investors would profit handsomely and some of the unemployed
in North Beach would be lifted from their poverty. They would
do what their fathers before them had always done, work the soil.
Flyers were posted throughout North Beach and notices were sent
out to the community. Newspaper notices were printed. Any Italian
or Swiss who was a citizen of the United States, or had declared an
intention to become a citizen, was invited to a meeting to discuss an
opportunity for work and membership in the Italian Swiss Agricultural Association.

Andrea Sbarboro was in his element as he and Dr. Paolo de Vecchi
entered the meeting room. The room was smoky and the aromas of
the city seeped in through the open windows. The young men, bury-
ing their unease, talked and laughed loudly to their friends across the
room. Their spirits were high in anticipation of a chance to work, to

leave behind the depression that was their daily existence. Sbarboro's reputation preceded him, and in spite of his slight stature, barely over five feet, the room quieted before the compelling figure. For a while, Andrea Sbarboro held the men captive. His words about an opportunity to work in the fields and vineyards as they and their fathers had done in the "old country" got their attention. Warming up as he went, lecturer Sbarboro finally got to the best part. The men could assure their financial future with this opportunity to buy into the venture. Sbarboro must have seen the expressions of his listeners begin to darken, their eyes hardening. But in his enthusiasm, Sbarboro assumed that his message was seeping in. Once again he showed them the map and the parcels that they would own in the future.

Just as he had done for hundreds of home buyers in his building-and-loan associations, he showed them the receipt book. Each worker would have his own receipt book, in which his monthly payments would be recorded. Sbarbaro pointed out the places for recording interest charges on late payments. It was a book designed by one of San Francisco's leading bankers. It was complete and up front. Sbarboro thought they would be impressed. An hour ago they wondered how to get money for tomorrow's dinner, now they were discussing plans to buy a piece of America! It was a dream come true. But it was Sbarboro's dream and he was mistaken. When at last the talkative Mr. Sbarboro finished and asked for questions, he got his rude awakening. These men had come to America where the streets were paved with gold. They hadn't seen the gold and now they didn't see the opportunity before them. The questions flew, but they all amounted to the same thing. You want us to give up $5 per month (it would have been nearly 15% of their wages) for records in a book that might, someday, give us a piece of land worth some amount of money? You gotta be crazy, Sbarboro!

They didn't understand. Sbarboro explained it again. They would earn $35 per month plus room and board and sufficient wine for personal consumption. Their needs would be nil; they could easily afford to pay into the association five dollars a month toward the purchase of five shares with a paid-in-full value of three hundred dollars. In just five years they would be paid up and own a part of the company. They would own their own land, actually become part of the American dream. But the men did not share Sbarboro's dream. It was the right message, but the wrong time and place. The men turned Sbarboro down.

Convinced that the time was right for investing in vineyards and excited over the prospects offered by the land at Asti, Sbarboro convinced his investors to change the original charter and to go ahead as a simple, straightforward business investment. Dr. de Vecchi at once rounded up a dozen friends to pledge funds "with the Cavaliere." Paolo de Vecchi, commenting on the mood at the time, said, "I can't say we felt we'd be running into a bonanza. Still, it seemed a reasonable venture. The wine trade was flush, and the commonest grapes were worth thirty-five dollars a ton."[11] The original massive capitalization plan was scaled down to 2250 shares for which subscribers would pay one dollar a month per share until such time as the venture returned a profit. The new plan was approved; additional shares were subscribed and money began to flow at the rate of $2250/month. Fontana was named president and Sbarboro became secretary.

With the site acquired, Sbarboro moved quickly. Giant valley oaks and live oaks, many with trunks several feet thick at shoulder level, would have to be removed. The manzanita, scrub oaks and brush would need to be cleared. The rainy season was due to hit any time and forty inches of rain could be expected to fall over the next four months, leaving the beautiful Asti of summer a cold, soggy, muddy Asti of winter.

Sbarboro hired Luigi Vasconi, a man who had worked all his life in the vineyards of northern Italy, to be superintendent. The workers arrived at Asti during the winter of 1881–82. They moved into the bunkhouse and the main house. Both houses had kitchens. Food and supplies could readily be shipped up from San Francisco. Additional housing existed at the southern end of the Colony property. These houses, which would eventually make up the Lucca Ranch,[N-4] named after the village in Italy, were situated almost two miles from the main house, or as it was soon named, the Colony House.

Under Vasconi, the men set to work. They worked six days a week, ten hours a day. It must have been a help to Vasconi and his crew that there were few distractions in their midst. Today the olive trees growing alongside the old highway are the last remaining vestige of the work of those men one hundred and fifteen years ago. Sundays were spent repairing shoes and clothes. Some caught up on washing not done during the week. A few went to Cloverdale to attend Mass, but most spent Sunday hunting in the wilds of the area or fishing in the Russian River. In February 1882, the *Cloverdale Reveille* reported: "The Italians now on the Truett Ranch are quite frequently seen on our streets; they trade here, but few know anything of the English language."

The lack of wives and women further served to focus the group's efforts; however, Andrea Sbarboro was sympathetic to the workers' plight. A student of the British social reformers Robert Owens and John Ruskin, Sbarboro was a social philanthropist at a time of unbounded social exploitation. Accordingly, another burden was placed upon the driven crew, that of building quarters for the families of the married men. It was a long winter. Mud covered every inch of skin and clothing. Rope-burned hands and aching backs healed at night only to be assaulted the next day. On sunny days spirits rose but dreams of spring were smashed each frigid morning, when frost melted by the rising sun soaked gloves and tormented fingers.

While Sbarboro admired hard work he also loved to party, and he knew his men deserved a party. He had a fine excuse for a celebration as winter ended and spring began, for on May 8, the Italian Swiss Agricultural Colony would close escrow on the second piece of land purchased from Hutchinson. And so, in the fullness of springtime at Asti, Sbarboro threw his men a party. The April 15, 1882 *Reveille* reported: "The Italians on the Truett Ranch will give a grand picnic on May 6. A brass band is to be brought up from the city and an immense time in general is looked for." It wasn't yet "Asti" to the *Reveille*, but it was to be the first in a grand series of parties at Asti that would stretch over the next one hundred years.

The choice of vines and acreage devoted thereto was initially a function of local conditions. Although Sbarboro was concerned with planting top-quality vines, little if any thought was given to the cultural suitability of the varieties to be planted. To do so would have been to put too fine an edge to the matter, for the red grapes ultimately went into one tank and the whites another at the winery. The wine, when it reached the consumer, would be a blend chosen from many vineyards by the wine merchants in San Francisco. One could, however, expect that Sbarboro consulted with the pioneer grape grower in Sonoma County, Isaac DeTurk, and other statewide leaders in the industry. In 1882 DeTurk was king of the Sonoma County wine industry. He had planted grapes in 1862 and in fifteen years his was the biggest business in Santa Rosa. The winery took up a full block and produced one million gallons of wine per year. His principal product was claret which he made from Zinfandel. DeTurk rose to such esteem in the industry that he was appointed to the original Board of State Viticultural Commissioners in 1880.

Luigi Vasconi would have been influenced by the planting choices made by growers in Cloverdale. He could also look to his neighbors to the south. For close to twenty years, wine grapes had been grown in Geyserville, just six miles down the road toward Healdsburg. It was from neighbors that Vasconi would get his first cuttings to plant.

Throughout the winters of 1881–82 and 1882–83, a broad variety of grapes were planted, including Charbono, Mataro (now called Mouvedre) and White (Johannisburg) Riesling. Vasconi would also plant what was to become by far the most intriguing wine grape in California, Zinfandel. Already a widely favored wine in the state, Zinfandel would continue and indeed expand its position as California's own varietal. The state's love affair with Zinfandel was not shared with the nation during Prohibition, when nearly all of the Zinfandel grapes were sold in San Francisco, while two decidedly

Andrea Sbarboro surveys his pride and joy, circa 1890. Photo by Alfreda Cullinan, courtesy San Francisco Historical Society.

less distinctive varieties were shipped east: Carignane and Alicante Bouchet. The latter's sole purpose was to give color to the lack-luster Carignane.

Zinfandel was the most widely planted wine grape in northern California. Zinfandel is from the species *vitis vinifera,* the species of all the great vineyards in Europe. It was *vitis vinifera* vines that were shipped from Europe to establish California's wine industry. Yet Zinfandel, at least by that name, is unknown in Europe. Nearly one hundred years after arriving in California, the precise origin of Zinfandel remains unknown.

Historians, by tradition, believe that wine grapes were first planted in California by Father Junipero Serra, who brought cuttings from Spain to his San Diego Mission in 1769. The Mission grape was widely planted in southern California and plantings continued in the north as Father Serra established missions up the state. The Mission grape period extended through 1850, when significant changes began to accrue in California demographics. The gold rush of 1849 brought not only miners, but miners who stayed on after the rush and returned to their original calling—farming. While grape growing was established in Sonoma County and Napa Valley by the end of the 1830's, it wasn't until after the gold rush that John Osborne and Fred Macondray brought new wine-grape varietals to Napa Valley from established plant sources on the East Coast. One of those varietals was Zinfandel. Once planted in the warm, dry climate of California, it was evident that something special had occurred. The Zinfandel grape, of uncertain origin, had found its home. It was a marriage made in heaven for the grape of "divine origin."

By 1860, Zinfandel was widely acclaimed in California newspapers. Mariano Vallejo's winemaker called for everyone to grow Zinfandel. The *Alta California* noted that "a grape called Zinfandel is declared to be best for producing claret and there is a great demand for Zinfandel cuttings." In 1869 Zinfandel wine brought seventy-five cents a gallon, while Mission paid just forty cents a gallon. By 1884, forty percent of all vines in California were Zinfandel. A directory of growers and vintners, compiled by the Board of State Viticultural Commissioners in 1889, shows Zinfandel as easily the most widely planted varietal.

By 1883, the Colony had 150 acres planted to Zinfandel, 20 acres to Charbono, 35 acres in White Riesling, and 15 acres each of Black Malvoisie, Grenache and "Burgundy." A half-dozen other varieties, planted in ten-acre or smaller plots, brought the total acreage to 293 acres. Notable by their absence were the Italian varieties, but this would soon change. Cuttings sent from Italy by Dr. Giuseppe Ollino arrived at Asti in 1885. By the end of the decade, Nebbiolo, Grinolino, Barbera and San Gioveto grapes were thriving at Asti. The San Gioveto (Sangiovese) varietal was to become the most important of the Italian varietals at Asti as it would become the predominant grape in the Colony's world-famous Tipo Chianti.

The vineyards were cultivated in the timeless fashion of the old country. The vines themselves were head-pruned with two bud spurs growing from the head of the vine. No trellis system was used. The trunk would be allowed to grow about two feet high. From its head, canes grew out in every direction. The fruit, large heavy clusters of grapes, hung from the canes. In the winter, with the leaves gone and the vine dormant, the canes would be cut off, leaving two node spurs from which next year's canes would grow.

The vines were "domestic rootings," not grafted to a different varietal root stock. They were planted at seven to eight-foot spacings, in both directions. After every thirty vines, an avenue was placed to allow access. The avenues were essential, since by summer, the vines would spread to meet their neighboring vines and wagon passage through them would be impossible. In the spring, the tender new shoots needed protection from the occasional predawn frost. The vineyardists at Asti were proud to brag that ISAC was one of the first to use smudge pots in their vineyards while other growers used bonfires and prayer to ward off frost.

At harvest time, the fifteenth vine in from each avenue was flagged and the picking crew would pick the grapes fifteen vines in from each side of the road. The grapes were not dumped into a tank;

rather, the filled boxes were stacked on the wagon for delivery to the winery. Typically a wagon would haul about a hundred boxes, each holding forty to fifty pounds of grapes. The two horse teams would work about four hours before being given a rest. Harvest went on from sunrise to sunset. Temporary field hands were hired for the harvest. They were joined by every able-bodied person at Asti including mothers followed by youngsters who would play or sleep among the vines. Both the grade school and high school were closed for the six to eight weeks of harvest.

The Asti mothers and their children in the vineyards at harvest were following a tradition that likely stemmed at least from ancient Greek and Roman times. One hundred years after Asti, the harvest tradition continues, only now it is Mexican women and their children joining the men to harvest the California vintages. Who will be next? Likely no one, for mechanical harvest machines are poised to remove this human element from the harvest pageant for all time. Hand harvesting grapes is brutal, dirty, sticky work, but the songs and banter that envelop every crew are a beautiful testimony to the indomitable human spirit.

The Italian ethnicity of the work force at Asti was maintained at the direction of Andrea Sbarboro. It was his love for Italy and her people that had started the Italian influence at Asti, but Sbarboro must have felt some pressure to make changes. Before the turn of the 20th century, the cheapest source of field labor were the Japanese and Chinese. The Chinese existed in large numbers in northern California and they were already working in vineyards and wineries across the state. But Sbarboro resisted. He considered the Japanese unreliable and he flatly refused to hire the Chinese, whose habits and dress reflected their sentiments toward China rather than those of their adopted country. It was Sbarboro, with his passion for America and Italy, who created the small but steady flow of Italians to northern Sonoma County that became a wave in the years shortly following 1900.

Housing construction, land clearing and grape planting went on at a feverish pace during the first few years. By 1884, the community of Asti was taking shape. Vegetable gardens had been planted and several acres of fruit trees were in place. Olive trees lined the highway and the knoll on the northern edge of the property, known to subsequent generations as olive hill, was planted. Two hundred and fifty acres of grain were planted as a cash crop. Another one hundred acres of grapes were in the ground. The industrious Colony was on its way to self-subsistence.

The vintage of 1886 was the Colony's first significant crop. The vines produced about 465 tons, much of it Zinfandel. Most of the crop went to Sonoma County wineries, with about seventy tons shipped to the San Francisco market. But the vast plantings throughout the state over the previous six years were beginning to place excess wine grapes in the marketplace. The large vineyards in southern California, notably the Cucamonga vineyards and those in the San Gabriel Valley, were now in production. By far the largest single grape producer was the Vina vineyard of Leland Stanford.[12] Stanford's vineyards, located twenty miles south of Red Bluff at the northern end of California's Sacramento Valley, totaled 3,825 acres and their production simply swamped the marketplace.

Grape prices fell that autumn from thirty dollars a ton to eight dollars a ton as the harvest reached full maturity. Leland Stanford could survive the low prices, but many growers could not. The negative market forces began to affect the growing breed of vineyardists. The enthusiasm of the early 1880's turned cautious, even fearful, and resentment toward the wine merchants in San Francisco began to surface. The wine merchants were the principal sellers and shippers of wine to markets nationwide. As such, they were the principal buyers of locally produced grapes and wine.

Sbarboro was convinced that the San Francisco wine merchants' control over the wine industry was already showing signs of collusion, and as growers, the Colony was in a precarious position. "I saw ruin staring me in the face, and I was indeed a very disappointed man" he wrote.[13] A determined Sbarboro went to his directors and explained the challenge facing the Colony. Grapes are a highly perishable product and as such provide the grower with little flexibility

Pietro Carlo Rossi, not only heart and soul of a great winery but beloved leader of the people of Asti. Courtesy of Bob Rossi, Jr.

when his crop is ready for market. The San Francisco bunch were taking full advantage of this situation. If future prospects were not dismal enough, eight dollars a ton for grapes was simply not enough even to cover costs.

The Colony would have to make a decision: close down as growers or go forward as vintners. The land had long been paid for, but the stockholders continued to pay one dollar a month per share to cover expenses. There had been no profits and thus no dividends had been paid since the Colony was founded almost six years earlier. Sbarboro, once again relying on the support of his directors and shareholder friends, asked for an assessment of ten dollars a share to build a winery. It was approved immediately and the $22,500 was used to build a winery that was ready for the 1887 crush. It was the 108th winery to be bonded in California.

The winery was a two-story concrete structure measuring 150 feet by 50 feet. On the first floor were nine 12,000-gallon redwood tanks as well as several smaller tanks. On the second floor were redwood fermentation tanks with a combined capacity of about 150,000 gallons. The total storage capacity was approximately 300,000 gallons. A small brandy distillery was set up nearby. Along with the production facilities, Sbarboro, sticking to his colony concept, built additional worker housing. The Colony also added the six-hundred-acre J. P. Whitaker ranch to its 1620 acres, bringing the total to about 2220 acres.

With all the pieces in place, the stockholders waited in anticipation for the 1887 vintage. They were in for a major disappointment. Sbarboro had hired a winemaker from Switzerland, where they had to close the doors and windows of the winery during harvest to get the winery warm enough to support fermentation. When the unfortunate winemaker closed the doors and windows of the winery at the broiling Asti, he was rewarded with a winery filled with vinegar. In their anguish over the wine disaster, one wonders if the directors noticed that the price offered by the San Francisco merchants for wine that year was a meager seven cents per gallon.

Ever the optimist, and refusing to back down in the face of still another significant setback, Andrea Sbarboro brought a university-trained chemist into the fold. It was perhaps Sbarboro's greatest move when he hired Pietro Carlo Rossi to be winemaker. Rossi was born in Dogliani, Italy, on October 10, 1855. His family was rather well to do, and both Pietro and his older brother were college graduates. Pietro received his degree in agricultural chemistry from the University of Torino (Turin). Rossi and his brother came to California immediately after Pietro's graduation.

Young Rossi landed in San Francisco in 1875 after a six-month sailing voyage with some money, his health and much talent. Within a few years he and a partner owned a drugstore on the corner of Columbus and Grant Avenues. Rossi married Amelia Caire, daughter of Justinian Caire, a noted figure in the grocery business in San Francisco. It is probable that Rossi, through his drug business, had come to the attention of Dr. Paolo de Vecchi. The physician, a close friend of Andrea Sbarboro and active in the affairs of ISAC, likely introduced Sbarboro to Rossi. Rossi joined the Colony on a part-time basis. For a while, he maintained his interest in the drugstore.

Rossi provided Sbarboro with a man who knew the chemistry of wine, understood fermentation, and appreciated the need for aseptic conditions and temperature control in the wine cellar. Possibly most important, Rossi was not limited by conventional wisdom. He was quick to innovate. P. C. Rossi was the industry's first wine master to work from a laboratory rather than the wine cellar. In fact, he worked out of the Colony's office in San Francisco, 85 miles distant from the winery at Asti. Sensory evaluations of the wines were accomplished on Rossi's weekend visits to Asti and by tasting samples that were continually supplied to the lab in San Francisco.

The Colony team was now complete: Sbarboro the consummate public relations man and supplier of money, and Pietro Rossi, the technician who would soon demonstrate a remarkable talent for business as well as making outstanding wine. His passion and intellectual ability were to serve Pietro Rossi well as he led the growers and vintners in the battles about to come.

4

At War

You're never too bad to win.
　　　　　—*Tom Elliott*

WITH P. C. ROSSI ON BOARD, the 1888 vintage was a huge success, but life never seemed to get easier for the Colony. There were 130,000 gallons of wine and 4,000 gallons of brandy in the cellar. Once again the San Francisco "wine ring" was offering a ruinous seven cents a gallon for wine that cost twelve to thirteen cents a gallon to produce. In addition, the producers had to pay freight of about two cents a gallon for delivery to San Francisco. The *San Francisco Examiner* added to the growing tension with a series of front-page articles discussing problems in the wine trade. One article was headlined "Wine Is Too Cheap."[14]

A questionnaire sent by the *Examiner* to growers and vintners throughout the state, as well as interviews with local vintners, produced for the most part safe, innocuous responses. The industry's problems were due either to poor-quality wines or to a small consumer base. These arguments, which have always been used to define any problems the industry might have at any time, were nothing more than vague opinions.

Two local vintners, however, had the courage to address the

problem directly.[15] W. W. Waterman, who produced 4,000 gallons of wine each year at his vineyard in Santa Cruz, noted that he was "convinced that there is a dealers' ring working against the growers. A man cannot go to San Francisco with a sample of wine and offer it at one house without its being known all over the city in less than an hour, and the price offered will be the same at every house." Isaac DeTurk, the prominent grower/vintner from Santa Rosa, expressed his feelings more succinctly. Said DeTurk: "There is no real necessity for this depression in the wine trade, it is all brought about by an unnatural condition of the wine market, caused by a combination of dealers. You cannot buy a small bottle of wine in San Francisco of any kind for less than 12.5 cents. That is $1.25 per gallon. Allow six cents per small bottle for glass, labels, packaging, handling and cases and you find that you are paying 53 cents per gallon for the wine. Surely the dealer can afford to pay more than seven cents for a gallon of wine that nets him 53 cents."

DeTurk further opined that for good claret, the gap was even greater, for the consumer paid two dollars to the dealer for wine costing the dealer ten cents a gallon. DeTurk's figures are not complete, but he apparently allows twelve cents a gallon for taxes and the cost to blend and inventory the wine in the merchant's cellar. In addition, he fails to account for the large volume of bulk wine the San Francisco merchants shipped to eastern markets, which sold for considerably less than 53 cents a gallon. But the message is nevertheless clear; the grower/vintners who were forced to sell their wine to the San Francisco wine merchants were being victimized in classic turn-of-the-century "free enterprise."

Rossi and Sbarboro clearly recognized that ISAC could never be profitable, indeed could not survive, selling to the wine ring. Sbarboro was convinced the wine merchants feared Italian Swiss Agricultural Colony and wanted to drive them out of business. However, the reverse occurred. Instead of eliminating Italian Swiss as a formidable competitor, the wine merchants forced Sbarboro to go once again to his board for approval to build a blending and bottling plant in San Francisco. Once again the board supported Sbarboro.

The Colony established its own cellars in San Francisco in time to handle the 1888 crush. From the home office and bottling plant on Battery Street in San Francisco, the Colony now distributed wine to New York, Chicago, Philadelphia and New Orleans, where retailers sold it for between thirty and forty cents a gallon. The wines were good, and so well received that Sbarboro proudly remembered one agent who specified on his follow-up order that they send him the same quality of wine as forwarded before. Elated, Sbarboro wrote that Italian Swiss Colony had at last attained success.

With the profits gained from these sales, operating expenses were paid and more vineyards planted. Others, of course, including Isaac DeTurk, had vertically integrated, but no one had done so on the scale of the Italian Swiss Agricultural Colony. Overnight, the Colony had their cellars operating in San Francisco, opened offices in New York City, and had wine vaults in Chicago and New Orleans as well as New York. The Colony, under the leadership of P. C. Rossi, was fast becoming a force in the California wine industry. Grapes grown by neighboring growers plus the Colony's six hundred acres were turning out more wine than the winery at Asti could hold, but with bulk storage in three major cities, the ISAC was in good shape. By 1890 there were fifty men working in the vineyards and winery at Asti. There were now a total of seven hundred acres planted to grapes. Several Italian varieties had been planted over the past few years. There were also one hundred acres in fruit trees.

The 1891 vintage was huge. A heavy crop hanging on the vines portended a harvest that would swamp the winery. During the summer of that year, the winery capacity was doubled. Two great storage tanks named "the twins" were built. Named after Rossi's twin five-year-old sons, the tanks were two stories high and held over 25,000 gallons each. With additional tanks installed, total storage at the winery at Asti reached one million gallons. The half-million-gallon crush was readily handled by the winery and shipments of Colony wine began reaching to more and more cities along the East Coast and the central regions of the country. Ten barrels of wine were even shipped to Central America.

In 1891, the California Board of State Viticultural Commissioners compiled a directory of growers and vintners. Sonoma County had 736 growers, 118 of which produced wine. Average winery production in the county was about 1,500 gallons a year. The Colony was already a giant among its peers. It was now ten years old. Conceived as a means of providing employment for jobless Italian immigrants, the Italian Swiss Agricultural Colony was one of California's largest wineries, and arguably the largest producer and shipper of premium wines in the country.

When the board of directors met for their annual meeting in 1892, the air was indeed salubrious. Sales were pushing one-half million gallons of wine annually. Major markets were developing in Europe as well as the United States. Few ships carrying wine to the East Coast did not have hundreds of barrels of Colony wine in their holds. Nearly half of the Asti ranch was in grapes, another two hundred acres in grain, and a hundred acres in fruit trees. P. C. Rossi was elected president, and the euphoric board decided they wanted to see their wines entered in important wine competitions in the United States and abroad.

In 1892 the Colony was awarded its first medal, a gold, for its Burgundy at the Dublin Exposition. Gold medals continued to come from competitions both in the United States and in Europe. A silver medal was awarded the Colony in the 1895 Bordeaux Exposition. With Rossi producing fine-quality wines and Sbarboro carrying the flag, things looked good for the Colony.

While the business of the Colony took place at the usual frenetic pace of business in the city, life at the bucolic Asti went on at its own pace. It was an active community, growing grapes, making wine and producing families. The men labored in the vineyards or in the winery and the women gossiped as they hung wash out to dry in the warm sun. The language of the Colony was Italian with one notable exception. As in any immigrant society, the schoolchildren led the way into the new society, because at school they learned English.

The school had been built in 1872, the same year the railroad was opened to Cloverdale. The building was situated just a few yards from the track, in Washington township, on land donated to the county by Miers Truett the year before. As they made their way to school in 1893, the children's daytime dreams may have been momentarily disturbed by the rumblings of the train on its run from Cloverdale to San Francisco, but life for the children at Asti was serene. Of course, conversations at home around the dinner table might have alerted the older ones to the stirrings in their fathers' wine business.

Indeed the adults at Asti couldn't help being aware of the currents and counter-currents swirling about them. In 1893 the vineyard scourge, phylloxera, was making itself known in the Colony's vineyards as well as its neighbors'. And if phylloxera wasn't enough, extensive plantings of the early eighties, particularly in southern California, were producing ever more grapes and wines. On top of the increasing supply, the producers and wine merchants were looking at ever decreasing market prices. Unlike the small growers and vintners throughout the state, the wine merchants weren't worried about payments due on the mortgage. Their concern was riveted on the increasing competition for market share. Large grower/vintners, led by the Colony, were establishing markets in New York, Chicago and other major cities. Wine prices were falling out of control.

That year, Rossi made a trip east to visit the Colony's wholesalers and to check out personally the stories coming back to California. He was appalled by the extent of the price-cutting tactics at play in New York and Chicago. Rossi was well aware of the soft market, but these practices could not be sustained. He had already complained to the Board of State Viticultural Commissioners to censure the wine houses for similar activities in New Orleans. Now, to Rossi's dismay, cutthroat pricing practices were spreading like wildfire. Ultimately the industry would get through the 1893 harvest, but not the 1894. Overproduction combined with a deep national depression forced eruption of seething unrest in the wine industry. The grower/producers moved toward war with the wine merchants.

A segment of the wine industry that ended for good with Prohibition, wine merchants operated in the major markets to age, blend and bottle wine purchased in bulk from producers operating in vineyards around the state. The wine growers or producers were generally small operators whose mentality was closer to farming than the business of marketing wine. In most cases, they were the Mom-and-Pop operations of the 19th century. For wine growers in northern California, the only market for their wines was the wine merchants in San Francisco. Their wines were "field blends," meaning the red grape varieties grown by the wine grower went into the red wine tank, and the white varieties into their own tank. The somewhat different growing clocks for each varietal, together with the uneven impact of the growing season, resulted in different relative yields each year and a somewhat different blend of red and white wine each vintage. The mix was further skewed as new plantings came into (or out of) production.

The wine merchants in San Francisco sorted all of this out with their aging and blending programs. The merchants would either bottle and place their own label on the wine or they would sell it in bulk to merchants in other markets worldwide. The leading wine merchants were big businesses. Most sold over one million gallons of wine each year. The largest, C. Carpy & Company, at one time owned over five million gallons of storage capacity. While many of the wine houses also owned vineyards and wineries, they were primarily merchants, because that was where the money was.

One of the most beautiful wineries in Napa Valley is the famed Greystone Winery, home for many years to the Christian Brothers. The winery was built in 1888 by W. B. Bourn, a wealthy San Francisco attorney, and his manager, E. Everett Wise, a small-scale winemaker from Dry Creek Valley. The basement of the Bellerose Winery (now Everett Ridge Vineyards and Winery) in Dry Creek was a part of the old Wise Winery. The Greystone venture was a financial disaster from the start and was offered at auction early in 1893. The two leading bids turned out to be identical. They had come from Carpy and a chief merchant rival, Lachman and Jacobi. At the suggestion of Carpy, the winner was decided by a coin flip. Jacobi won. As the bidders rode the train back to San Francisco, Jacobi asked Carpy if he still wanted Greystone. When Carpy answered "yes," Jacobi said, "Take it." While we can presume that Jacobi had second thoughts about the bidding, he clearly felt his money was better invested in his merchant business than in a three-million-gallon production facility located in the middle of one of California's premium grape-growing regions.

In the spring of 1894, an Englishman named Percy T. Morgan began an effort to organize a "trust" of the wine merchants. Morgan was an accountant whose only tie to the wine business was through the wine dealer S. Lachman & Company, for whom he provided accountant services. But Morgan had a feel for business and in a few short months he had organized seven of the leading and well-known wine firms in San Francisco.[16] They were: C. Carpy & Company, S. Lachman & Company, Kohler & Frohling, Arpad Haraszthy & Company, Kohler Van Bergen, D. Dreyfus & Company, and the Napa Valley Wine Company. In August, these seven wine dealers incorporated as the California Wine Association, or more simply CWA. The seven agreed to pool their assets and immediately they formed two committees, one to estimate the value of the wine each member had on hand, and the other to appraise the property and other assets of each member. The combined assets of the seven members were set at $3,030,700, and each member was given shares in the CWA proportional to contributed assets.

With the merchants established, the grower/vintners shortly followed suit. In November of 1894, the crush now resting quietly in storage tanks, the growers and vintners formed the California Winemakers' Corporation, or CWMC. The CWMC hired John H. Wheeler, former secretary of the Board of State Viticultural Commissioners, to manage the organization. The leaders were P. C. Rossi and Andrea Sbarboro. The Colony facilities at Asti would crush members' grapes and the ISAC sales organization would market the wines. The CWMC members subscribed a portion of their production, grapes or wine, and the members then participated in the corporation's sales on a prorated basis. Given their size, ISAC was the leader in the wine growers' group and Rossi and Sbarboro became its leading spokesmen. The CWMC members felt confident they would now have some options in selling their product in a market that was more and more controlled by a single buyer, the California Wine Association.

The California Wine Association fired its first salvo when it made an offer of six cents a gallon for the 1894 vintage to the winemakers. But the shot fell short when the wine growers refused to sell. The CWA then offered ten cents a gallon but still the CWMC held firm. Finally, in January 1895, the CWMC came of age when it sold one million gallons of wine to the independent merchant, Lachman & Jacobi. The price was twelve and one-half cents a gallon. The California Wine Association, worried over the market share Lachman & Jacobi might capture, then agreed to pay twelve and one-half cents a gallon for four million gallons of CWMC wine. Furthermore, the CWA announced an agreement to purchase five million gallons of wine annually from CWMC winemakers for each of the next five years. The price was to be arranged each year. The CWA further announced that it would lease to CWMC, for the same five-year period, its Carpy wineries at St. Helena (the Greystone), Napa City, and San Jose; Kohler & Frohling's winery at Glen Ellen; the Orleans Hill Winery at Esparto; and the Pioneer Winery at Livermore. The California wine industry was thus neatly allocated, competition controlled, and all parties hoped for peace and prosperity.

But the enmity that existed between the two factions could not be so easily overcome. The obvious hole in the agreement, that they would agree to a new price each year, resulted in predictable disagreement. By June of 1896, the two groups were arguing over a fair price for the 1895 vintage, the very first year of their agreement. The CWMC wanted fifteen cents a gallon. At that price the CWA would buy only a small portion of the agreed-to five million gallons. Thereupon the CWMC requested they be released from the five-year CWA winery leases and CWA agreed. The deterioration of the fragile relationship continued into 1897. On February 10, 1897, the CWA acknowledged they had not paid the interest due on sums owed for the 1896 harvest. Furthermore, they refused to pay the $800 interest that had accrued. If CWMC wanted its money, it had better submit an itemized list of bills dating back to 1895.

At their March meeting, the 150-member CWMC was told their group was holding out for twenty cents a gallon for any unsold wine from the 1896 vintage. Wheeler acknowledged to the members that

Asti railroad station, circa 1900, before Sbarboro built his concrete tower station to serve his family and friends. Sbarboro, top center, appears to be returning to San Francisco with a basket of fruit and vegetables from the garden. Photo by Alfreda Cullinan, courtesy San Francisco Historical Society.

their group had made no attempt to negotiate the price with the CWA as was required by their agreement. Wheeler explained that hits from phylloxera, a severe frost during the past winter, and continuing pressure on profits from the low prices in the marketplace forced the winemakers to insist on the twenty cents a gallon figure. Furthermore, the CWA was in arrears on its interest payments to CWMC. Andrea Sbarboro proposed to sue the CWA for $30,019.24, the sum owed them. Of course, CWA countersued for $171,000, claiming that the Winemakers had reneged on their contract.

The Colony, for its part, was not without resources. In August of 1897, construction began on the world's largest wine tank, a one-half-million gallon behemoth. The Colony announced that the giant tank would be built to help hold the large crop anticipated that fall. Of course the Colony could then hold more wine longer in its battles with the CWA, but that was not mentioned. With typical gusto, the

ISAC men went to work. The concrete tank measured 80 feet long by 34 feet wide. It was 24 feet high and had a glazed surface to prevent contamination of the wine. It took just 46 days to dig the hole and pour the concrete. Upon completion, the tank was covered with dirt and the top decorated by a coronet made of stones from which a sign proclaimed: "World's Largest Underground Wine Tank." When bottled, wine from the tank could fill over 200,000 cases or well over ten million glasses of wine.

The following spring, after emptying and cleaning the tank of its first red wine vintage, Sbarboro invited the elite of San Francisco to a dance at Asti. The president of the SF&NP railroad, reflecting the importance of Sbarboro's business, volunteered a private train for the 215 invited guests. Ever the showman, Sbarboro held the dance, including a ten-piece brass band, inside the tank. The *San Francisco Chronicle* described the party:[17]

> A hundred couples danced in a wine vat at Asti today. Where but a few days ago 500,000 gallons of California Chianti bubbled, two hundred merry-makers whirled in the mazes of a Strauss waltz. There was no great crowding. An excellent orchestra in the center of the novel ball-room made music for the dancers, while onlookers stood about the sides of the tank and enjoyed the fun.
>
> Few, however, lost the opportunity, that might never again occur during a lifetime, to participate in terpsichorean pleasures on a floor which had known the weight of enough wine to fill 4,000,000 bottles, and whose walls were stained a most lurid color by the juice of hundreds of millions of grapes. The dancers were of many degrees and ages. Supreme court judges elbowed San Francisco supervisors, and foreign consuls reversed their steps to avoid collisions with millionaires. There were others too. Men and women who had first tasted Chianti in the vineyards of Italy and Switzerland touched the heels of native sons and native daughters in the grand march.
>
> It was the fete day of the Italian Swiss Colony at Asti and the

officers of the association outdid the most attentive and generous of hosts in their care for the comfort and delight of the hundreds of guests from San Francisco and other cities.

The outside appearance of the mighty receptacle is much like one of the pyramids of Egypt with the top sliced off. The ascent to the top is by concrete steps on four sides. Its roof is a charmingly plotted garden, with pyramids of flowers and gravel walks. In the center is a stone fountain of interesting design which arches the entrance. The opening is three feet in diameter and when the interior is filled, this is hermetically sealed.

Today a winding staircase made descent of twenty-four feet to the bottom easy. Two arches partly divide the reservoir making three compartments thirty feet square. The floor, walls and ceiling are all of cement. Fifty men were employed night and day for forty-five days and 1,000 barrels of the best Portland cement and 6,000 barrels of gravel and fine sand from the nearby Russian River bed were used in its construction. The walls are two feet thick, and glazed to the imperviousness of a glass bottle.

It was first filled on October 15, 1897. Two steam pumps being busied for over a week in the task. It was emptied on March 10, 1898 and wine removed to the 30,000 gallon vats in the cellar proper.

Being about to take into its capacious storage another 500,000 gallons of wine, the Italian Swiss colonists thought it fitting that the great event should be celebrated.

With an hour's siesta, the dancing in the tank began and lasted till the whistle of the train summoned all for farewells.

Legend at the Colony claims the revelers danced for two days and three nights! Such was the comfort of Sbarboro's hospitality.

In May of 1897 CWA started the price war that would prove calamitous to the California wine industry. Both the CWA and CWMC were led by capable, dedicated men. In such a war, it is the side with the greater resources that comes out on top. Firing the first salvo, the Wine Association reduced the price of its wine to twenty-two cents a gallon delivered, to the out-of-state markets. This was a whopping twenty-percent price decrease. By the fall of the year, the CWMC was auctioning its wines in New Orleans for less than fifteen cents a gallon and before the year was over Lachman & Jacobi in San Francisco purchased a million gallons of premium red wine for prices ranging from seven cents to ten cents a gallon. But Percy Morgan and his boys were not done.

Unlike the wine growers, the merchants had the cash reserves and the determination to continue the offensive. Next they attacked the New York City market, offering their wine for less than city merchants had previously paid for CWMC wine. The effect was immediate and it was devastating. The New York merchants, feeling cheated by the growers, no longer trusted the CWMC and stopped buying. In 1897, ISAC possessed the largest acreage of dry table wine vineyard in California. Their winery capacity was three million gallons. But ISAC strength wasn't enough to help the Winemakers. The reeling CWMC then suffered an attack from where it could least afford it, from within its own ranks. The growers and vintners were paid five dollars per ton for their grapes or equivalent in gallonage of wine plus one dollar for every cent per gallon the wine brought CWMC. This was a fine contract, but unless the wine was sold, the growers were left with just five dollars a ton.

The legion of small growers and vintners who delivered their grapes and wine to ISAC for the CWMC program could hold out no longer. They were already seeing their grape yields lowered by the rising incidence of phylloxera and they had nowhere near the resources of the CWA or, for that matter, the likes of Italian Swiss Agricultural Colony. So they sued the CWMC for failure to sell their wine. In splendid array, suits erupted everywhere, including CWMC against CWA and a countersuit filed by the latter.

The Winemakers accused the Merchants of dealing in bad faith, of not paying debts owed, and failing to agree to a fair price for the wine as was called for in the contract. The Merchants, for their part, accused the Winemakers and in particular ISAC for failure to provide wine to the association in accordance with their contract because the

CWMC wished to become merchants rather than producers. The breach-of-contract suits were eventually found in the CWA's favor and CWMC had to pay $100,000 in damages. The California Winemakers Corporation went down rapidly as it lost effectiveness in the market. In 1899 the CWMC was dissolved.

In 1898, the Colony seemed under attack from every quarter. Its distributors in the eastern markets were unhappy, members of CWMC were suing, and the CWA was bent on crushing the CWMC and the Colony itself. Yet Sbarboro and Rossi continued to be optimistic. Still, it is difficult to read their mindset when, on June 11, 1898, they acquired the old Turner ranch (see Note 3). The ranch was now owned by Giuseppi Ginocchio, a major Colony stockholder who had been elected to the ISAC board of directors in 1883. Ginocchio had built a greenhouse on the property to grow vine stocks and tropical plants. For several years after he sold the property to the Colony, Ginocchio grew exotic plants for Sbarboro and Rossi in the nursery.

At the turn of the century, ISAC, although bruised and battered by the war with CWA, was a successful operation, steadily growing in stature under the artful leadership of P. C. Rossi and Andrea Sbarboro. By the summer of 1900 it had been nineteen years since Sbarbaro climbed the hill for his first view of the lands of Asti. It is unlikely that the sixty-year-old would have climbed the hill behind the superintendent's house that summer to view the accomplishments of ISAC, but Rossi, at the age of 44, might have made the climb. If he did, Pietro likely swelled with pride at the vista before him. From the trees lining the Russian River to the east, to the mountains bordering the rolling knolls to the west, all was Colony land. Although his view would have been partially obstructed by hills and trees, most of what he could see to the north and south were also Colony lands. Immediately below him, at the very foot of the hill, was the beautiful, porticoed Colony House.

Across the street was the cookhouse, where forty single men slept, ate and occasionally sent letters home to faraway Italy. Behind the cookhouse was the bakery, where Barelli baked his Italian bread, so treasured by everyone at Asti. The blacksmith shop stood just north of the cookhouse, across Bertoli Creek. Back on this side of the road, on the other side of the Colony House, a large barn housed the sixty or so horses that worked the vineyards.

Just below and to his right was a two-story house with a wrap-around porch on the second floor. The families of the winemaker and cooper shared the house. Two more houses sat between the creek and the winemaker's house, and on this side of Old Redwood Highway, at the foot of the hill, were still more houses for married workers. The winery itself looked huge, indeed out of place, in the middle of the bucolic setting. Beyond the winery, against the river, he could vaguely see the little schoolhouse, its single room soon to be filled with noisy children. Rossi wondered if Miss Geohegan, the Irish schoolteacher, had arrived yet to take up her school-year residence at Asti.

Of the colors, only tans and greens were used, some vivid, others muted in the shimmering waves of sunlight coursing over his shoulder from behind. A puff of dust coming up the Redwood Highway from Geyserville signaled an approaching wagon. It was still a speck in the distance and seemed to be the only thing moving in the still life before him. The summer house belonging to Dr. Paolo de Vecchi was partially visible through the trees planted to shield de Vecchi from the Asti sun. De Vecchi, Rossi's friend of twenty years and the man responsible for Rossi's being on that hill that late summer afternoon, was thinking of retiring and moving back to New York.

Turning a little further toward the west, Rossi could gaze over the gently rounded hillocks that made up the biggest part of the ranch. He could not quite see the little cluster of Lucca Ranch buildings that served as home for the vineyard hands. Turning now to the west and shielding his eyes from the reddening sun, he could see the wild hills bordering the ranch standing black against the sky. There was uncertain terror in the business world, Rossi mused as he returned down the hill, but life at Asti was good—good people, good values, good earth. Pietro felt refreshed even though the setting sun was still hot.

Even as Rossi walked toward the superintendent's house, another immigrant from Dogliani, Italy, headed for his home some three miles south of Asti. His name was Edoardo Seghesio and, at forty years of age, he had lived and worked at or within walking distance of Asti for fourteen years. For Seghesio, life in the promised land was everything he had dreamed.

Edoardo had worked for the Rossi family in Italy. Recognizing him as an ambitious worker, Pietro Rossi had invited Edoardo to join the new-world Asti adventure in 1886. After a journey of more than half a year, the 26-year-old arrived at San Francisco, penniless and friendless, save for Pietro Rossi. Rossi promptly took Seghesio to Asti where they were met at the station by Luigi Vasconi, the superintendent. The walk from the railroad station to the cookhouse where Edoardo would live was about half a mile through the Colony's vineyards and orchards. For Edoardo it felt as if time failed to exist, that somehow the threesome arrived at the cookhouse instantaneously. Seghesio could remember, as the years passed, that walk into his new life. He could remember the hills, the vines and the dust at his feet that puffed into tiny clouds with each footfall.

Edoardo couldn't wait to begin. He fell into step immediately with life's rhythms at the cookhouse. The cookhouse was a wooden building, fifty feet wide by one hundred feet long. It had been built years earlier by Isaac Bluxome as a bunkhouse for his sheepherders and ranch hands. Cots at either end of the building slept fifteen to twenty men. The middle of the building served as the dining room and kitchen. Here sat long tables at which the men enjoyed "back home" cooking.

While Cloverdale shops provided some of life's necessities, the men of Asti worked to make the Colony independent. A beautiful vegetable garden thrived in the deep loam outside the cookhouse. This was a northern Italian garden. Tomatoes and garlic were planted but much space was given to zucchini, chicory, basilico and eggplant. The greatest planting went for Italian beans, the wide-pod vegetable that was a staple of their diet. Sacks of corn flour for polenta, tortellini and pasta arrived by train from San Francisco.

Wild game was plentiful in the area and the cook never lacked for

Edoardo Seghesio and Angela Vasconi on their wedding day, June 12, 1893. Courtesy of Eugene (Pete) and Rachel Ann Seghesio.

venison, rabbit or even wild pig. With each meal the men were served wine in keeping with a lifestyle enjoyed by countless generations, and consistent with Sbarboro's strongly held belief that wine with meals was not only a natural adjunct to good eating, but served as a constraint to alcohol abuse. Years later Edoardo would wistfully re-call the ten-hour workdays, six days a week. Now that he had moved up in the world and owned his own vineyard, it was twelve-hour days and at times the work week was seven days.

Seghesio was well aware of the big-time battles going on in San Francisco, but his world was much smaller; if he could just get one year ahead, enough money to pay his costs one year into the future, he would feel secure and be happy. Farmers the world over seek that economic security, but few achieve the goal. For Seghesio, facing growing needs for a growing family, that level of security would always be a goal, never a reality.

He had worked hard, very hard. Upon arriving at Asti, Seghesio had made a deal with the ISAC whereby his wages would be held by the Colony for three years. At that time he would receive his accumu-lated pay, less charges for room and board and with the surplus he could afford a trip home to Italy. But after the passage of the three years, Seghesio found the sum wasn't enough and so he continued the arrangement for five more years. Finally, after eight years, he had the money to return to Italy and marry the girl his family had long ago picked out for him.

When his boss, Luigi Vasconi, learned of Seghesio's plans, he of-fered another suggestion. Why spend all of that hard-earned money on a trip to Italy? And why lose all that time and over a year's pay? Vasconi had an idea. He also had a young niece living at Asti who was eminently available. Seghesio understood the logic in Vasconi's plan. He stayed at Asti and one year later, on June 12, 1893, Edoardo Seghesio and Angela Vasconi were married.[18]

Now, married for seven years, Seghesio was the father of a six-year-old daughter, Ida, and a one-year-old son, Arthur. He owned his own home and a 56-acre ranch. Asti had been good to Edoardo and he to Asti.

Edoardo likely didn't think of it, but as he walked the vineyard avenue toward his home, he was immersed in the very heart of the wine industry, the grapevines. While city merchants might scurry for advantage, and businessmen in fancy suits might meet around polished tables, while lawyers everywhere argued before learned judges, it was all about this, these plants sitting in the sun of Asti. These were not simple, everyday plants; these were plants with a pedigree. The Sangiovese vines that watched Seghesio pass that afternoon were direct descendants of vines that for centuries had grown along the banks of the Tanaro River in Piedmont. Like a family pet, these faithful vines asked for little and gave much. In Seghesio's vineyard, each vine produced an average of ten pounds of grapes each season. Yet they received no irrigation during the long hot summers of Asti and no fertilizer.

As growers everywhere have always done, Edoardo walked with his head down, searching his vines for any signs they might hold out to him. It was getting close to harvest and in his hand he held a cluster of grapes to be tasted during the walk home.

A grape grower's work is set in a rhythm established by the natural forces around him. There are moments of arduous effort and there are mini-deadlines set by nature, but the whole is guided by just one timekeeper, harvest. Then, for six weeks, the growers find little sleep. Will the fruit ripen before the rain? Rain? Don't even think about it. Try not to picture wet clusters, their grapes bearded with rot, a year's work wasted. Will there be labor enough on the days we pick? And what about yield? How much money will the crop bring?

Suddenly it's over. A stillness prevails across the vineyards although the lights burn all night in the wineries. Now it's time for other things. The roof needs to be fixed before it rains. Wood must be cut for winter fireplaces. For ten months Momma and Papa have told imploring children to "wait until after harvest when we get the grape money." It's the message they've told each other since last winter's rains. And so it goes—no need for a calendar to remind the grower's family that another year has passed.

5

Dawn of the 20th Century

For yesterday is but a dream and tomorrow is
only a vision. But today well lived makes every
yesterday a dream of happiness and every
tomorrow a vision of hope...

—Author unknown

T HE 19TH CENTURY BEHIND HIM, the vanquished Rossi faced
the new century with a heavy heart. The war with CWA had
been a no-holds-barred struggle and Rossi had thrown himself
totally into the conflict. It was Rossi and Isaac DeTurk who had proclaimed their case against the CWA in newspapers across the state.
For thirteen years, Rossi had fought with every fiber of his being for
the Colony and its independent growers in their battle for independence from the San Francisco merchants.

It had been a war and Rossi had lost. The CWA had destroyed the
CWMC and now the CWA controlled wine sales in all of the important eastern marketplaces, particularly in New York. Rossi knew that
the Colony could not stay in business competing with CWA. Once
again, it was either close down ISAC or approach CWA with a white
flag and try to make a deal. Abe Lachman, their old ally who had

helped Sbarboro find the site that became Asti, agreed. Neither Lachman & Jacobi nor ISAC could take on the CWA in the market-place. Hat in hand, the two warriors approached the CWA.

Rossi's twin sons, who were fourteen years old at the time, never spoke of the agony their father must have endured that year.[N-5] As the seasons passed and talks dragged on, it became clear to Rossi that the CWA was not going to share their hard-won market with the vanquished Colony. Indeed, Rossi realized that an independent Italian Swiss Agricultural Colony was not to be. On November 14, 1900, the CWA reported to its shareholders that they had accepted propositions for membership from two firms, ISAC and Lachman & Jacobi.[19] Each applicant would swap one half of its capital stock for CWA stock, the latter at par value. No cash changed hands. A new company, Italian Swiss Colony (ISC), was formed to manage the business of the new partners. The deal was remarkable in that ownership of Italian Swiss Colony was split evenly between ISAC and CWA. No joint managing board was created, no CWA representative sat on the board of ISAC. Rossi and his management team remained intact and operated with almost no input from CWA. The company letterhead dropped the word "Agricultural" but significantly, the CWA name did not show on the new letterhead or on any wine labels. It was almost as if nothing had changed. But of course there was a significant change. From then on, one half of the Colony's profits went to CWA. From then on, Rossi had to provide CWA with a copy of the Colony's monthly financial statement. For the emotional Pietro Rossi, it was a crushing defeat, administered monthly.

Before the year was over, the last remaining major independent merchant, C. Shilling & Company, was "accepted for membership" in the CWA. The wine trust was in place. The CWA now controlled both the marketplace and the price of grapes. It was a remarkable achievement. In two years they had gained control over two-thirds of all California wines. CWA was a classic trust. Technically it operated in violation of the Sherman Antitrust Act. However, enforcement of the Act was lax, and trusts were left alone as long as they operated outside of public attention. CWA proved masterful in avoiding the press.

Not once during the entire year of 1900 did news of the ISAC-CWA talks appear in the press. Although the partnership began operating in January 1901, it was not until March that the news appeared in the newspapers of San Francisco.

It was control of the marketplace that lay at the heart of the unique CWA corporate structure. They didn't need fifty-one percent ownership of their subsidiaries; fifty percent was sufficient. And they didn't need CWA people on their subsidiary boards, not as long as subsidiary board members or company managers realized that a word from the nearly omnipotent CWA to wine wholesalers could put a recalcitrant subsidiary out of business, and make their tangible assets available to CWA at deep discounts as well.

The Wine Association ran their empire with remarkable constraint. Their brands competed freely with each other. In many instances the makers of competing brands were not even aware that each was a part of CWA. To avoid the possibility of internecine warfare, CWA would bring Claus Shilling and Pietro Rossi to their board of directors. Rossi was elected to the board at the January 1904 shareholder's meeting.

The effect of the new partnership arrangement was evident at Asti almost immediately. Having joined forces with the company that controlled well over one half of the California wine industry seems to have changed the attitude around Asti. The Colony had gone from fighting a desperate war to a period of peace with a confident view of the future. 1901 marked the beginning of a buying spree, starting with two small wineries, the Cloverdale Wine Company and the Sebastopol Winery. Between the two, they added one million gallons to ISC's storage capacity. By the time of the 1902 vintage, the Colony had a total storage capacity in California of almost ten million gallons.

The promise of the 20th century went beyond the wine business of the Colony. Within two years of each other, Sbarboro and Rossi built homes at Asti that will likely outlast the most durable winery building. Sbarboro's concrete monolith, Villa Pompeii, sits essentially unchanged as it approaches its 96th birthday. The Rossi house, Buen Retiro, has remained in the family 94 years with no change in sight.

Picnic at Asti—Andrea Sbarboro second from left, Mrs. Romilda Sbarboro second from right, circa 1900. Photo by Alfreda Cullinan, courtesy San Francisco Historical Society.

During that time, the successive Rossi generations have watched ownership of ISC change thirteen times. (See Figure 1, p. 290)

In 1900 Sbarboro traveled to Europe to be present at the Paris Exposition, where the ISC collection would be awarded a silver medal. On this trip he visited the ruins of Pompeii, the ancient Roman city that was destroyed by lava flow when Mount Vesuvius erupted in 79 A.D.[20] For more than 1500 years, the ruins lay undisturbed beneath ashes and cinders. In 1748 archaeologists began excavation at the site. The excavating has gone on ever since, save for periodic interruptions for war. Shortly before Sbarboro's visit, the completely intact villa Casa dei Vetti was uncovered. Sbarboro was enthralled. The Vetti were wealthy tradesmen. Their name was discovered on bronze seals found in the house in the ashes of Pompeii. The house was not the biggest, nor the most splendid in the city, but among the houses of the merchants, the Vetti had the most lavish decorations. The house was noted for its miniature frescoes showing cupids at target practice and racing chariots. Scenes of commerce depicted florists, goldsmiths, fullers, bakers and vintners.

The leader of the excavating team, Professor Lembo, presented Sbarboro with a copy of the Vetti plans on file in the archives of Pompeii. Sbarboro brought the plans back with him to San Francisco. He had the perfect place to recreate a nearly 2,000-year-old Italian villa. In 1902 Sbarboro built an exact replica of the Casa dei Vetti 8,000 miles distant from the original. Sbarboro named his dream house Villa Pompeii. The Sarno River was replaced by the Russian River and the setting was certainly different, but Sbarboro had arranged his version of a marriage between the nations he loved.

From a distance the concrete structure looks strange, indeed out of place in the bucolic setting of trees and vineyards. But proceed down the palm-lined avenue, away from the intrusions of the winery and folks working around the plant, and the villa will extend its greetings. If it could talk, the Villa Pompeii would likely be grateful for its rescue from the dark, quiet ash of Pompeii, but bemoan a new kind of quiet in the full light of the California sun. In recent years the Villa has been quiet, its lights dark each evening.

But it wasn't always so. For its first twenty years the house pealed with the voices of Sbarboro's guests. A new people had replaced the Pomos at nature's banquets at Asti. Sumptuous dinners were served using fruits and vegetables grown in the garden; venison and quail, nurtured in the nearby fields and hills, served as centerpieces to the gala occasions. And every table was graced with wine nurtured from vines that knew both Astis. The villa served the Sbarboro family as a vacation home and weekend retreat until 1941 when it, along with the winery, was sold to National Distillers.

Banquets and winery-related special events were celebrated regularly at the Villa during the 1950's, '60's, and '70's. A hall for hire during the '80's, the Villa hosted young lovers breaking bread for the first time as husband and wife with family and friends.

From the moment of completion, the Villa became the center of Andrea Sbarboro's days at Asti. Few visiting dignitaries to San Francisco

Villa Pompeii, Andrea Sbarboro's replica of the Casa dei Vetti. The original building was built before 79 A.D. at Pompeii, Italy. Courtesy of Cloverdale Reveille.

could pass up a Sbarboro invitation to visit Asti. It was a delightful ferry ride to Sausalito, then a comfortable train ride through beautiful Marin and Sonoma Counties before reaching the little stop at Asti. For the passenger riding through the Alexander Valley there was a sense of enclosure, but it was a comfortable enclosure. Defining the valley to the west was a ridge of tree-covered hills, while to the east the 3,457-foot Geyser Peak stood atop the ridge that paralleled the train's route.

The hills were softened by luxuriant tree cover or grassy patches. Towering redwood trees and massive Douglas firs looked down on the scene from their hillside perches. Greens and tans were everywhere. Just four miles before reaching Asti, the train passed through Geyserville, its neat wooden houses looking like they, too, grew from the fertile soil. And everywhere, vines. Green in their summer

Portal to the Villa, the vine-encrusted lintel bears the name "Villa Pompeii" inscribed in the solid concrete. Courtesy of Cloverdale Historical Society.

garments, the vines changed to yellow and red in the fall. Stripped of their leaves, the gray trunks stood aligned in neat patterns in winter fields of grass or spring's yellow mustard flowers.

At last the train would stop at Asti. For Sbarboro's guests there was no waiting room or wooden boarding platform typical of turn-of-the-century railroad stations. Instead, a concrete-pillared lintel greeted the disembarking visitors. Across the lintel, fashioned in the concrete, were the words *"Villa Pompeii."* To the right was Sbarboro's idea of a waiting room—a Roman tower. Also made from cement, this waiting room was a cylinder standing on end. It measured fourteen feet in diameter and stood almost twenty feet high. Its single window was a small opening in the wall so that one could look down the tracks to see the approaching train. Access to the inside was through an opening facing north. While there was no door, this

The author standing in front of Sbarboro's ivy-covered Roman tower railroad waiting room. Photo by the author.

arrangement protected Sbarboro and his family from the broiling summer sun as they waited inside for the afternoon train back to San Francisco.

With all the trees and lumber surrounding the area, most builders might have been inclined to elect the easy way and put a wooden roof on the cylinder. But not Sbarboro. Just as the Romans had done centuries before, he had a concrete conical ceiling put on the tower. Sbarboro's Roman fantasies didn't stop with the building. This was, after all, a waiting room, and a bench was necessary. Standing outside in brightness, one can see three ornately carved benches in the deeply shadowed interior. But these benches are entirely of concrete, the effort of a master mason. Wood suggests warm softness, comfort. Concrete, used extensively in Europe after the forests ran out, is cold, but represents strength and endurance. If Sbarboro had chosen wood for these structures in the early days of the 20th century, they would likely be only memories as we approach the 21st century. But he chose concrete, and as a result, we can enjoy his structures just as he did when the concrete had barely dried almost one hundred years ago.

In the early days, guests were met at the train by a horse-drawn carriage and transported the hundred yards down the avenue to the Villa. The carriage would draw up alongside concrete steps onto which the ladies could gracefully alight from the carriage before stepping down to the grass. A second platform, toward the rear of the house, served for offloading baggage. Immediately to the right as passengers alighted from the carriage was a large elliptical concrete "vasca." Roughly 15 by 21 feet, the shallow saucer held about one foot of water. In the center of the saucer stood a 36-inch concrete statue of a Roman legionnaire. Sbarboro's initials were placed in the wet cement the day the saucer was poured. In front of the Villa was a second vasca, similar to the first but considerably larger. This one was circular and measured approximately twenty feet in diameter. A beautiful statue of a nude by William H. Rinehard, an American who spent most of his life in Italy, graced the center. This valuable work which was sculptured in Rome in 1869 is now kept in the winery office for safekeeping. Its spot on the vasca is currently occupied by a concrete sculpture of a girl holding a cluster of grapes. Around the vasca were planted colorful flowers including petunias, zinnias, dahlias, and in the winter and early spring months, violets. Between the caretaker's house and the Villa were hydrangeas that created a sea of blue and lavender.

Everywhere there were fruit trees: pears, peaches, apricots, cherries, apples, figs, plums, walnuts and almonds. Each spring a variety of citrus trees lent their sweet fragrance to the whole. Pear trees lined the roadway as it made its way around the house. Two enormous fig trees thrived in the deep, loamy soil alongside the caretaker's house just a few dozen yards north of the Villa. Alongside the house, outside the kitchen wall, there was a plum tree given to Sbarboro by Luther Burbank.

Sbarboro would later recall with pleasure that a decade before building the Villa, he had his men plant oranges, lemons, pomegranates and olives around Asti. His next-door neighbors, the Icarians, were skeptical of Sbarboro's choice of plants. To quote Sbarboro[21] who paraphrased his neighbors, "… we were laughed at by the colony of Missourians who had ranches immediately adjoining. They exclaimed, 'See what those crazy Italians are doing! They are setting out oranges and other tropical trees that will never grow here.'"

Among the early plantings of citrus was a small (something over one acre) grove of oranges planted between the Colony House and horse barn. For years the thriving block of orange trees provided fruit for the elaborate Colony displays at Cloverdale's Citrus Fair. A few of the trees still produce fruit, over one hundred years since they were planted.

Mr. Giampaoli, the Villa's caretaker, grew a full vegetable garden and all summer crates of tomatoes, peppers, beans, potatoes, corn, peas and herbs of all kinds would be shipped via Railway Express to Sbarboro and his family in San Francisco. Mr. Giampaoli was careful to ship the fruit and vegetables slightly underripe so that they would last a little longer in Sbarboro's pantry.

Sitting on the bank of the Russian River, the building offers little charm. Instead, the visitor is moved by the palpable antiquity of the place. Front steps took visitors onto the breezeway. Upon entering, guests first walked over a mosaic terrazzo embedded in the concrete floor bearing the initials "A. S." A second terrazzo a few feet further on bore the word "salve," Latin for welcome. To the right was a door leading to the living room, while a dining room opened on the left. In the floor, a few more feet into the breezeway, was a concrete slab, eighteen inches square, showing a guidon, or small flag such as was carried before marching Roman legions. The banner bore the letters "SPQR," Senatus Populusque Romanius, the "Senate and the People of Rome." Along each wall of the breezeway were beautifully colored frescoes in yellows, blues, whites and reds. The frescoes featured a beautiful peacock, a favorite bird in the gardens of Italian royalty. (The frescoes, chipped and generally in poor condition, were ultimately painted over by house painters at an unknown time.) Above the breezeway was the Sbarboro master bedroom.

Walking through the breezeway the visitor entered the courtyard. To the left was a large kitchen, while four bedrooms occupied the wing to the right. A door connected each bedroom and the bedrooms also opened onto the courtyard. A fountain graced the center of the courtyard, while concrete pillars bordered covered walkways along each side. The walkways met in a curved pathway that marked the end of the courtyard.

Passing through the courtyard the visitor was at once embraced by the hospitality of the cavaliere and the delights of the backyard. In a screened room beneath the huge grape arbor Sbarboro entertained his guests. Close by was a stone grotto within which five hammocks hung, the feet nearly touching, the heads fanning out like spokes of a wheel. The whole was covered by a concrete ceiling which protected the occupants from the sun. The center hammock hung from a concealed hook which, when pulled by the weight of the occupant, opened a valve admitting water to flow on the roof. A strategically placed hole in the ceiling allowed the water to pour down on the unsuspecting occupant of the hammock. It would provide a cool shower for the victim on hot summer afternoons and lots of laughs

Sbarboro and friends enjoy dinner in the Villa backyard. Sbarboro is fourth from end on the right. Mrs. Sbarboro is on end closest to the high chair vacated probably by a grandchild. While positive identification is impossible, the lady at left side of the table, arm on table, is probably Amelia Rossi; Pietro is next to her and next to him is likely Marco Fontana. Circa 1910. Photo by Alfreda Cullinan, courtesy San Francisco Historical Society.

for Andrea and his guests. The hot, dry summers of Asti would dry the wet clothes well before the train trip home.

But Sbarboro didn't stop with the rigged hammock. A small concrete enclosure called the meditation chamber stood several feet from the hammocks, in full view of Sbarboro's dining table. Every first-time visitor to the Villa would step in through the small opening to take a peek inside. Once inside, the curious would step on a concealed, pressure-activated valve, and a shower resulted. It was a red-faced guest who would emerge to the laughter of the guests watching the whole time. An enclosed aviary housed unusual birds that splashed among numerous fountains. Sbarboro's water system was modeled after the famous hidden springs of Pegli at the Villa Palavioini near Genoa.

Sbarboro was a generous host and lavish lunches and copious amounts of Asti wines were served. The beneficence of Asti was evident at Sbarboro's table. Freshly picked peaches soaking in Colony red wine were often served for dessert. After lunch, guests could enjoy a game of bocce or play tennis on the immaculately tended tennis court.

During the years leading up to World War II, Sbarboro's five children and their families would visit Asti for long weekends or week-long vacations. For their longer visits they would generally bring along their own cooks and servants. Alfredo, the oldest son, was always the quiet, respectable banker. Guido Musto, husband of Romilda, the youngest of Sbarboro's children, was different. Guido was a fun-loving, would-be opera singer who would sing at the top of his voice at all hours of the night at the otherwise silent Asti. Sometimes Musto would be joined by Father Tocci, pastor of St. Peter's Church. Musto was a child of the roaring twenties. He drove late-model Lincolns and loved to push his cars as fast as they could go when he reached the country roads of Sonoma County. With predictable frequency he collected speeding tickets. Musto naturally got to know the highway patrolmen along the northern reaches of the Old Redwood Highway. Once he invited four of them, motorcycles and all, to the Villa. They got drunk and spent the night at the Villa.[22] The

Meditation chamber behind Villa Pompeii. A hidden pressure valve inside drenched curious visitors. Courtesy of Beringer Winery, ISC Archives.

Sbarboro family's association with the Villa ended in 1941 when they sold the property to National Distillers.

Not one hundred feet from the Villa Pompeii sat the old Truett house. It had been there since the 1860's, when Truett built the house for his family. Now it was occupied by the Villa's caretaker. It was a fine house, built for the large families of the time. In 1919, there were two bedrooms and a bathroom with a tin bathtub upstairs, and two bedrooms, a dining room, kitchen and two pantries downstairs. The Giampaoli family, hired as Villa caretakers, moved into the house in 1919. Some years later, Mr. Giampaoli set about enlarging the earthen cellar. He uncovered several bottles of Colony champagne hidden away for a future use that never happened. Anxious to make amends for the wasted opportunity, Giampaoli opened the unlabeled bottles of unknown vintage. Giampaoli pronounced them perfect. The Truett house burned down in 1970, but the Villa stands virtually untouched by time. Sbarboro's concrete monolith sits unchanged a few years short of its hundredth birthday. The building and setting have changed little since Sbarboro and his guests walked its breezeway 97 years ago.

There would be no Villa Pompeii for Pietro Rossi. Rossi was a courageous, and at times daring, businessman but almost always cautious. He was once asked by a reporter from *Pacific Wine and Spirit Review,* "What was the most important thing that happened to you in your evolution from immigrant boy to your position as president of Italian Swiss Colony?" Rossi would answer: "My first experience in the stock market shortly after I arrived in California, for it cured me once and for all of ever hoping to get rich overnight."

Rossi had been caught up in the speculation fever that did not exist in Italy but swirled everywhere around him in San Francisco. For months he listened to his customers in the drugstore talk about opportunities to strike it rich in the wildly speculative mining stocks. Finally he gave in and invested heavily in a stock a friend was sure would make them both rich. Of course, the mine went broke and Rossi lost his entire investment. It was an experience that stayed with him. From then on his achievements would be the result of intelligence and hard work.

The Rossi villa, built in 1904. The landscaping in 1999 remains much as shown in this early photo. Courtesy of Cloverdale Historical Society.

By the winter of 1904, Rossi was ready to build his place at Asti. In February of that year, ISC sold 9.96 acres to Amelia Rossi (Pietro's wife) and the Rossis began construction of their Asti vacation house. Rossi's intentions went a little further than vacation; the father of a growing family named his dream house "Buen Retiro." This was no grand recreation of an ancient relic. This was a California house, made of wood, yet made to last. The house was located with no neighbors save his friend Dr. de Vecchi, whose house was across the road a hundred yards to the north.

The Rossi house was sensibly situated on the highway yet close enough for just a short walk to the winery. Most sensible of all, Buen Retiro was a long way from the Russian River, with its attendant threats of flooding each winter. The house was U-shaped like the Villa Pompeii, with a massive living/dining room occupying most of the house across the front. The bedrooms, all ten of them, occupied one wing. There were only two bathrooms, but washrooms containing a lavatory connected the bedrooms in pairs. The kitchen was adjacent to the dining room in the other wing. But it was in the backyard that Pietro followed Sbarboro's lead, for here Rossi built an immense covered porch, perfect for feeding his large family or guests on summer evenings. The house occupied 9,400 square feet, including the outside dining room.

With the pressures of the wine wars behind him, Rossi and his family were able to spend summers and long weekends at Asti. Rossi was 49 years old and Amelia turned 43 the year they built Buen Retiro. Unfortunately she got little time to spend on the veranda facing the rolling vineyards of Asti. She had given birth to fourteen children, ten of whom had lived, including one set of twins. The other four had died as children, at ages ranging from two to six years. Three of the first four died over a span of four years, providing Amelia and Pietro with enough agony to last a lifetime.

That first summer at Asti, her third and youngest son, Carlo, was just five years old. The girls were a blessing. Maria, the oldest, was nineteen, and a big help. But the leader of the kids was Esther, just fifteen that year, for it was Esther who "mothered" baby brother Carlo and was big sister to young Eleanor, then just seven years old. Amelia and Pietro were proud of their children. They would grow up to ·
become successful adults. Three of the children would dedicate their lives to the Church. With one third of their children taking religious orders, it is clear that Pietro and Amelia led a very religious family. The three who entered religious life were not the only children to inherit their parents' faith. Third-generation Edmund Rossi, Jr., used to tease his slow-driving father that the only time he drove fast was on his way to church. The Rossi house has remained in the family for 95 years with no change in sight. During that time the successive Rossi generations have watched ownership of ISC change thirteen times.

The community at Asti went to church in Cloverdale until 1893, but Rossi wouldn't be happy until the families had their own church at Asti. They had a school which was a suitable place for a priest to say Mass and hear confessions. Rossi went to the pastor of St. John's Church in Healdsburg and suggested that, since the priest went right through Asti on his way to Cloverdale, couldn't he stop for an hour so that the many families who lived at Asti could attend Mass in their own community? In fact, there would likely be just as many Italians attending Mass in Asti as there were Irish and Germans in Cloverdale. The Rev. John Meiler agreed to get up an hour or so earlier and bring Mass to the flock living at Asti, Chianti and the Lucca Ranch. And to his people, Rossi promised that the schoolhouse was a temporary arrangement; one day they would have "a real church."

The school was located south of the winery, close to the Russian River. It was about one mile from the superintendent's house and the cookhouse, but it was only one-half mile from the Lucca Ranch to the west. For the ladies of the Colony, the schoolhouse church was heaven-sent. Now they could walk to church and they wouldn't have to miss Mass on weekday holy days, when the men were working and transportation to Cloverdale was unavailable. Besides, now they could linger after Mass and talk to their friends from the Lucca Ranch who, while still on Colony property, were too distant for convenient visiting during the week. And the walk back home through the vineyards on Sunday morning was a pleasant time to gossip and talk about the church they would one day build at Asti. They knew that if P. C. Rossi had promised them a church, it would happen. In the meantime, delicious anticipation.

6

El Carmelo

A baby is God's opinion that life should go on.
—*Carl Sandburg*

OR FOURTEEN YEARS, the Colony's families went to Mass in the schoolhouse. Rossi and his family now spent many weekends at Asti. Each Sunday, Rossi was reminded that attending Mass at the schoolhouse was not like going to church at home in San Francisco. It was certainly convenient for the Rossi family, whose house was just up the road from the schoolhouse, but the 0.3-mile walk home after Mass could be a problem since most of it was up a pretty steep incline.

But the hill wasn't Rossi's problem. The problem was that no schoolroom could ever substitute for a real church. There was just no feel to it. The schoolroom could never elicit the comforting warmth surrounding the glow of the sanctuary lamp forever burning in the quiet dimness of the altar. There was no altar and no altar rail. There was no tabernacle, no stations of the cross. It was obvious to Rossi, who by now ran the Colony in all matters save public relations, the latter being the reserve of Andrea Sbarboro, that Asti needed a church—and Rossi figured how they could get one. The Colony did not need

Madonna Del Carmine, known to parishioners as El Carmelo, in her prime. Citrus trees guard entrance to the church, vineyards thrive on both sides. Courtesy of ISC Archives, Asti, California.

the conservatory where Mr. Ginocchio grew citrus trees and rare tropical plants for the Colony. It would make a fine church, although only a person with Rossi's vision could ever have pictured the little greenhouse as a house of worship.

The conservatory was in a perfect location. It was next door to the cookhouse, where the church would serve daily to remind the single men of their Sunday obligation. The greenhouse was close to the Colony House and alongside most company housing. The building measured 36 feet by 22 feet. It had a concrete floor with concrete walls rising two feet high, enclosing the floor except for a doorway on the west side. The walls and roof were continuous, rising in a curved fashion up from one side and down to the opposing concrete footing. Wooden structural members held glass panes throughout the walls and ceiling. This was a typical design at the time for green-houses. In fact, the conservatory looked very much like Luther Burbank's greenhouse in Santa Rosa, which had been built in the 1870's.

The simple conservatory wasn't a stable in Bethlehem, but the greenhouse too would serve a far more noble purpose. It would be a church for the people of Asti. As in Italy, the church would also serve as a social center around which the community could coalesce. The only details that remained were the money to build the church and the land upon which the church would stand, since the Archdiocese of San Francisco required that the Catholic Church hold title to the land. Rossi had no problem with that. On September 2, 1907, the Colony deeded the 0.3-acre site to the Archdiocese for ten dollars. Funding was not a problem either, although no records exist concerning the feelings of partner CWA toward the generosity of P. C. Rossi.

The story goes that Rossi approached a crew working in the vine-yard. He told them of his plans to build a church and how every employee would have the chance to make a small "donation" that would be deducted from their pay. Furthermore, the men's assessment would be matched by the Company, so that their burden would be light. While the single men needed prodding, the families were eager to contribute to the building fund. Although attendance at Mass was somewhat less important to the men, for the women the Church was everything. Together with their children, attendance at Sunday Mass was a vital part of their lives. The community buzzed with excitement. Joe Lyle, a builder from Cloverdale, was given the job of changing the greenhouse into a house of worship.

The design called for two dormer windows on either side of the church. A ten-foot vestibule would be added at the entrance end of the rectangle, or nave, and an apse added at the other end for the altar. A six-foot by six-foot space extended beyond the apse. This room, which was behind the altar and thus screened from the congregation, served as the sacristy.[N-6]

There wasn't much work accomplished that first winter, but 1908 was devoted to tearing down the greenhouse and building the new roof. The church had nineteen pews or benches, ten aligned on one

Proud parishioners at inauguration of El Carmelo Catholic church at Asti,
May 1909. Credit: ISC Archives.

side of a center aisle and nine on the other side. Space was reserved
for the small organ located at the back of the church. A small bench
and a confessional box occupied the back wall on the other side of
the center aisle.

In September 1908, Sbarboro sailed to Italy to attend a Colonial
Congress in Rome. Before returning to San Francisco, he toured Sic-
ily. His first stop was Messina, from where he traveled by train to
Taormina,[23] a town situated on a beautiful hill in sight of Mount Etna.
He lodged that night at the ancient St. Domenico monastery, which
now served as a hotel. The proprietor had maintained the facility
exactly as it had existed when the building served the holy friars.
The guests slept in cells that had once been occupied by the monks.
On the door of each cell was the name of a different Madonna, reflecting the Madonna chosen by the cell's occupant. The monk who
had occupied Sbarboro's cell favored La Madonna Del Carmine.

Moved by his experience in that remote Sicilian monastery, Sbarboro
later urged that the new church at Asti be named Madonna Del Carmine. His wish was granted in May 1909 when the new church was

formally dedicated. (The name was later anglicized for the successor church built in 1960. That church is called Our Lady of Mount Carmel.) The name of the little church was eventually shortened by parishioners to El Carmelo. The pastor was Father Maurice Barry, who continued to serve both the Asti and Cloverdale churches from his parish in Healdsburg.

When the bells pealed that morning in May 1909, calling the faithful to the 8:30 A.M. Mass, the immigrants had a special beam on their faces. They knew they would never return to Italy, but now a little more of the old country was brought to Asti, California. The congregation came from the families living at Asti, Geyserville and Chianti, the tiny community just south of the Colony's vineyards.* The unique nature of this congregation is evident when one considers that of the nineteen families noted below, six still go to Mass at Our Lady of Mount Carmel, ninety years later, and at least two thirds of the families have descendants who are members of the church at Asti or nearby St. Peter's in Cloverdale.

Asti tingled with unusual excitement that Sunday late in the spring of 1909. The little church was filled to overflowing. Establishing a custom that would endure for many years, the Sbarboro family occupied the front two pews on the left, Pietro and Amelia Rossi and their family of ten children filled the next two pews, and behind them sat the Baiocchi family. Schoolchildren sat in the front pews across the aisle from the Sbarboros. The choir occupied the back pew, adjacent

---

* Among the proud families making up the church community in 1909 were:
Mr. & Mrs. Pietro C. Rossi, President & General Manager of ISC
Mr. & Mrs. Andrea Sbarboro, Secretary and Founder of ISC
Mr. & Mrs. Jules Alleghrini, Winery Superintendent
Mr. & Mrs. Francisco Baiocchi
Mr. & Mrs. Nello Baiocchi
Mrs. Katerina Carazzo
Mr. & Mrs. Gioelle Del Sarto
Mr. & Mrs. Giuseppi Mazzoni
Paulo Pellegrini
Mr. & Mrs. Edoardo Seghesio
Mr. and Mrs. Abramo Trusendi
Other families that made up the congregation included Berezzi, Brignoli, Coppo, Domenichelli, Moscardini, Pigoni, Teldeschi and Vasconi.

El Carmelo—her distinctive shape suggested a wine barrel to tourists, but the curved sides and roof merely reflected her origin as a greenhouse. Circa 1919. Courtesy of Cloverdale Historical Society.

Inside El Carmelo. The circular stained-glass window, donated by the Rossi family, looks down from above the altar. Courtesy of Cloverdale Historical Society.

to the pump organ. With the people in place, the little church was about to join the family of Roman Catholic communities the world over in their celebration of the Eucharist.

A small bell sounded and the low buzz in the excited congregation stilled as the people rose to their feet. Father Barry, preceded by solemn altar boys, moved to the altar. At that very instant, somewhere in the far reaches of the world, other priests came to an altar to lead their parish families in the timeless ritual of the Holy Mass. The congregation outwardly retained a respectful silence, but within their breasts, hearts pounded.

After Mass, the entire congregation spread out before the church for the first of "a million" photos of Madonna Del Carmine.

The new church with gleaming altar, perfect benches and sparkling clean windows not yet dirtied from the vineyard dust outside had her slip showing that morning. Along both sides of the crowded church, the younger children sat on the planking that covered the concrete ledge that rose two feet from the floor, and although it was partially covered by their squirming posteriors, the wall was a stark reminder of the origin of this latest house of God.

It may have been an obscure little church, but the appeal of El Carmelo was too great not to be shared. Literally millions of outsiders would visit the church over its 53 years of service. Tens of thousands of visitors took photographs of the little wine-barrel-shaped church. Millions of postcards bearing the likeness of El Carmelo were sent around the world. With the exception of St. Peter's in Rome, the little church would one day be possibly the most photographed church in the world. The church was always open and the faithful, as well as the tourists, were free to visit.

On summer Sundays, artists sat beneath nearby oaks with their easels, paints and brushes, intent on capturing the image of El Carmelo. Uncountable photographs captured every detail of the little church in the vineyard for the folks back home. Visitors generally thought the little church was made from a wine barrel. It wasn't, of course, but the idea added to the aura of El Carmelo. Eighty-seven years ago, the young church was described by Ernest Peixoto, a writer visiting

ITALIAN SWISS COLONY.

CAPPELLA

EXTRA-MELLOW CALIFORNIA
RED TABLE WINE
ALCOHOL 13% BY VOLUME
MADE AND BOTTLED BY ITALIAN SWISS COLONY, ASTI, CALIF.

The church label—El Carmelo graced this
line of red wines during the 1960's.
Courtesy of Anne Matteoli & Alex Carrey.

Asti for *Scribners* magazine, as "the quaint church, La Madonna Del Carmine, where they sing Gregorian chants on Sunday."[24] He was the first writer of note to be captivated by El Carmelo. Scores of writers and painters followed. She was special, Madonna Del Carmine, made more so by the uncomplicated love expressed in her being by the people who built her.

❦

The tiny pink face lay almost buried in the sea of white: white dress, white cap, and somewhere among it all, white booties, the whole wrapped in a newly knit white blanket. Her eyes closed, she ignored the whole thing—possibly she was listening to the angels she had left only a few days earlier. Now the baptismal water coursed over the few strands of thin black hair. She frowned and then, after crying out her unhappiness at being disturbed, she returned to her angels. Moments later, cradled in her godmother's arms, she left the tiny church and emerged into the bright sunlight, a new child of Asti about to play her lifetime role in the little community.

7

Cleric on Horseback

The real hero is always a hero by mistake... he
dreams of being an honest coward like everybody else.
                              —*Umberto Eco*

F OR THE FIRST SEVERAL YEARS at the Colony, the Asti families
traveled to Cloverdale, a distance of some four miles, to attend
Mass. The Catholic congregation in Cloverdale could trace its
roots to a time just fifteen years before the Italians arrived at Asti; the
faithful in 1866 consisted of twenty or so Irish families. In 1864, the
Smith family arrived from Ireland. In 1866, they purchased the
Cloverdale Hotel with its three guest rooms from the Sullivans. The
Smiths led the move to bring the celebration of Mass to Cloverdale
and offered their hotel as a place that their Catholic brethren could
gather for Mass. Mass was first celebrated at the Cloverdale Hotel
in 1866.

The first Mass was offered by Father Louisiana,[25] a Mexican friar
who traveled barefoot among the growing Mexican enclaves in the
remote outposts north of San Francisco. Father Louisiana had been
bringing the sacraments to the Mexican settlement in Hopland since
1863. Father Louisiana did not speak English. That wouldn't have

concerned the Smiths and their fellow Irishmen in Cloverdale, since Mass was celebrated around the world in Latin. Father Louisiana's lack of English did, however, eliminate the sermon. History doesn't record how the Irish felt about that. Father Louisiana made the hilly, fifteen-mile trip from Hopland to Cloverdale occasionally or when the weather was good for a period of seven years.

In 1872 the Friar's visits were augmented with occasional visits by Father Kaiser, a German priest who had immigrated to San Francisco to minister to German-speaking Catholics in the area. By this time there were roughly twelve Irish families in Cloverdale and eight German. It is likely that Father Kaiser spoke little or no English, and so the Smiths and Sullivans and their Irish neighbors still had no English-speaking priest.

Cloverdale was situated at the far reaches of the diocese of San Francisco. It was the northernmost town in Sonoma County, only a few miles south of Mendocino County. Mendocino County was served by the Marysville Vicariate in Yuba County, some eighty miles to the east. Bishop O'Connell of Marysville had agreed with his boss, the Archbishop of San Francisco, to provide a priest from Mendocino County to serve the City of Cloverdale. Subsequently Bishop O'Connell arranged for a priest who lived in Mendocino City on the coast to bring the sacraments to Cloverdale's Catholics.

One wonders if either bishop had ever traveled to Cloverdale. From San Francisco, the trip to Cloverdale was roughly ninety miles and consisted of a very pleasant ferry ride, and after 1872 a train that went right into town. From Mendocino City or Marysville, on the other hand, there was not only no railroad, there was no road. The trip from Marysville to Mendocino could only be made on horseback, over Indian trails that wove their way over the mountains that divided Yuba and Mendocino counties. While only a little over one hundred miles west, the climate and topography of the coast might as well have been a continent away. Because of the difficult terrain, the priest assigned to Mendocino City was required to visit the tiny villages of the remote county once a month. He would need to cover only the southern half, since a priest from Round Valley could assist with the widely separated villages in the redwood forests of northern Mendocino County.

It was to Mendocino City that young Father Thomas Petit was assigned early in 1873.[26] Father Petit was ordained in All Hallows College, Dublin, Ireland, in 1868. The young cleric was immediately assigned to the Marysville Vicariate in northern California, halfway around the world from the life he knew in Ireland. Fr. Petit fairly burst with pride and burning ambition when he put on his Roman collar each morning and anticipated the life that lay ahead. He had plenty of time in which to anticipate; the journey from Ireland to California took at least six months. There had been letters sent back to All Hallows from priests who had made this one-way trip before him. They were filled with stories of adventure and of the opportunity to bring Christ to souls whose life in the remoteness of California had deprived them of a priest. Petit was going to join Father James Callan, whose letter to the seminary had inspired so many seminarians, including Tom Petit. Petit could almost repeat from memory the last paragraph of that letter.

> Whole counties, some of them almost as large as Ireland, are without a single priest. Is there a month scarcely that I don't hear a cry from young and old as they write to his Lordship, asking for some holy youth of All Hallows to come out and dwell amongst them? There is the mining town of Reese River over in Nevada, having a population of five thousand, and not a single priest to bring to the dying the bread of life. From Yreka in Siskiyou county to the seacoast not a priest! Oh, if the generous sons of Old Ireland, and the fair daughters of St. Patrick knew the spiritual distress of their countrymen and countrywomen, were they possessed of but one shilling each, they would give the half to support a priest from All Hallows, that those poor souls for whom Christ died, might be reached from the Evil One, from the torments everlasting.

Arriving late in the year, Father Petit was assigned to assist Father Callan in the mining towns around Forest Hill, Michigan Bluff and

Iowa Hill in Placer County. Early the next year, Father Petit was transferred to Oroville, where he served for four years. Petit was likely pleased when, after four years at Oroville, he was relocated to beautiful Mendocino City along the Pacific coast. Mendocino City was wet and cool, even a bit green. Father Petit's fellow priests told him it was a little like Ireland.

Father Petit must have amazed friends and family back in Ireland with tales of his duties. Once a month he would depart Mendocino City, travel on horseback (or if the weather was good on a buggy) sixty miles southeast to Cloverdale, then head north, stopping in Hopland and Ukiah before reaching Willits, forty miles north of Cloverdale. The priest would then travel west to the coast, a distance of thirty-five miles, arriving at Fort Bragg, which lay twenty miles north of Mendocino City. It was a round trip of over one hundred fifty miles through some extraordinarily beautiful and hazardous trails, and it would take about a week, most of it in the saddle, before he would return home.

It was a trip that would have given the young cleric plenty of time to consider his vocation. Departing Mendocino City, Father Petit would travel treacherous mountain trails where danger lay in bears, rushing streams and steep trails, all of it frequently cloaked in dense, gray fog. The weather would be cold, winter or summer, the fog wetting everything, carrying the chill clear to a man's bones. If it was summer, the weather would warm as Father left the coastal mountains for the inland valleys. By the time he reached Cloverdale, the priest would be suffering from sweltering heat which would easily be over 100°F, some forty degrees warmer than the temperature when he had left home on the coast.

After hearing confessions, celebrating Mass and possibly performing a baptism, Father Petit would mount up and head north, roughly following the Russian River. Now his trail went through desolate, hot country, dry in summer, impossibly wet and muddy in winter. The terrain was sometimes easy along flat valley bottoms, but at times the trail narrowed to passes knifing through the hills that lay everywhere in the county. Now he would be occupied keeping his horse from missing a step and falling into a deep ravine, throwing a shoe or breaking a leg on the rock-strewn paths. At Willits, his rump sore from almost a week in the saddle, the good priest faced the trip west. The rock slides and rattlesnakes were behind him as he once more trekked the mountains to the soggy coast. Petit must have felt expiated from any past transgressions upon his return to Mendocino City.

Father Petit comforted the ill, buried the dead and said Mass monthly at the Cloverdale Hotel until 1879, when a church was built on the corner of Broad and Main. There was no rectory since there would be no priest living in Cloverdale. At the time there were about twenty families in the parish, roughly two-thirds Irish and one-third German. Within two years, a third ethnicity would be added. Like seeds planted on congenial soil, the Italians would flourish to become the principal group of Catholics in the Cloverdale area. But now, seven years after the railroad was built, it became convenient for a priest from Santa Rosa to make the 45 minute trip by train to Cloverdale. With a tip of the clerical hat to Father Petit, the San Francisco archdiocese reclaimed Cloverdale. Now Father Conway came from Santa Rosa to say Mass and administer the sacraments to the growing Catholic population in Cloverdale.

Father Petit was transferred to Reno, about two hundred miles east as the crow flies from tiny Mendocino City. Reno, settled in 1858, had grown into a prosperous town with the discovery in 1859 of the nearby silver deposits, known around the world as the Comstock lode. Upon arriving at Reno, Father Petit made a discovery of his own. As pastor of the Reno church he was required to serve Surprise Valley, the tiny northeast corner of California separated from the rest of the state by the Warner Mountains. Now Father Petit would travel two hundred miles each way, over almost uninhabited land, to reach Surprise Valley from Nevada.

The church in Cloverdale was built by the Irish families in town. Among the principal movers when the church was built were the McAlarney, Menehan, Perry and Smith families. Significant contributions were made by Peter and Ann Donahue, Irishmen who didn't even live in Cloverdale. This is the same Donahue who was owner of the San Francisco & North Pacific Railroad.

A captain of industry, a peer to the robber barons of the 19th century, Donahue played by the same shady and sometimes illegal rules as his fellow railroad magnates. He was buying and selling railroads at the time Father Petit was making his lonely trips on horseback through the remote regions of Mendocino County and Pietro Rossi was a high-school student in Dogliani, Italy. Peter Donahue has a church named after him and a beautiful statue dedicated to his memory graces Market Street at a busy corner in downtown San Francisco.

Pietro Rossi's name lives on only in his family, and Father Petit's only in arcane Church records. Father Petit toiled in obscurity for the people of Mendocino County and the Irish of Cloverdale. He faced mortal danger, alone and unnoticed in service to others, his pay the clothes on his back and an occasional meal with another man's family.

Pietro Rossi earned great sums of money but suffered two breakdowns in his battle for good over evil. Rossi spent his life working from his office in San Francisco not only for the owners of ISC, but for the people at Asti. Both Rossi and Fr. Petit are obscure, and likely to remain so; both were devoted to their faith but neither has been proclaimed a saint, or had a statue dedicated in his name.

8

A Look Back

… This beautiful spot in Sonoma county (Asti)
which thirty years ago was considered a barren waste…
—*Pietro Rossi to Governor Gillette, 1910*

O N OCTOBER 10, 1907, Rossi turned 52. He had been accumulating honors for years but one recently awarded was particularly treasured. "In recognition of your charities and kindnesses extended to your countrymen," King Victor Emmanuel III conferred upon Mr. Rossi in 1907 the title of Chevalier of the Order of the Italian Crown.

The demands on his time as CEO of California's largest (and growing larger) winery were enormous. Wags would ask how Rossi found time to father fourteen children. But Pietro was a passionate man who loved his family as he loved his work. And now in 1907, his oldest sons, the twins Edmund and Robert, would graduate from St. Ignatius College. The college, a Jesuit institution, would later become the University of San Francisco. Plans called for the twins to take Master's degrees in Fermentation Science at the University of California at Davis, after which they would join their father at Italian Swiss Colony. And Rossi could use his sons at the Colony. The

ISC/CWA partnership now owned over two thousand acres of vine-yards throughout the state. The winery's storage capacity exceeded ten million gallons, including storage at wineries at Madera, Cloverdale, Fulton, Sebastopol and Fresno, and depots at San Francisco and New York City.

During the early days, ISAC business was conducted out of Andrea Sbarboro's office at 518 Montgomery Street, San Francisco. But when the Colony went into the wine business, this changed. In 1888, the company established offices in San Francisco that included storage facilities for wine and a laboratory for Rossi. The office was staffed with eight people. Ten years later, new offices were established at 719 Battery Street, between Pacific and Broadway. This facility was big. It stood four stories high and could hold four million gallons of bulk wine. Three years later, the Italian Swiss Agricultural Colony became the Italian Swiss Colony. The wine war was over and the Colony built grand new headquarters at 1265 Battery, on the corner of Battery and Greenwich streets in San Francisco. This was a three-story, square building that measured 137.5 feet on each side. It had storage facilities for two million gallons of wine. It was a good location for a storage and shipping facility. Rail tracks ran inside the ground floor and the building was only a few blocks from the wharves in the harbor.

As they were digging the basement, construction crews uncovered a spring which was then developed as a water source for the building. When the San Francisco earthquake struck on April 18, 1906, water lines beneath city streets were broken, rendering fire hydrants useless. Fires, unchecked, ravaged the city for days. Ten million gallons of wine stored in various CWA vaults in the city were lost when their depots burned to the ground. As the blaze approached the vaults at ISC headquarters, Sbarboro, P. C. Rossi and his twin sons mounted a defense. They had an enormous advantage over the rest of the city, for their water supply was unaffected. The three Rossi men slept on the floor of Pietro's office. With electric power out, the men started up the building's steam generator. Using a steam-powered pump and wine hose, they pumped water from the basement to the roof. They created a lake on the flat roof to protect the building from flying ash. Edmund Rossi described the event: [27]

> The brick building at Battery and Greenwich, extending back to Sansome St. was built shortly before the earthquake and fire on April 18, 1906 by the Italian Swiss Colony, under the direct supervision of my father. It was a very substantial building and went through the earthquake without any damage.
>
> I remember my father telling me that he attributed its wonderful condition to the fact that he insisted repeatedly with the contractor that the bricks before being laid should be thoroughly soaked.
>
> Though army officials dynamited practically all buildings in the neighborhood in an effort to prevent the spread of the fire to adjoining areas, my father succeeded in persuading the army to spare the I.S.C. cellars, because it contained a deep water well.
>
> The water from the well was used to inundate the flat roof of the buildings, which prevented the big fiery cinders from setting fire to the roofs. Thus, the cellars were saved.
>
> The well served as a source of water supply to the neighborhood for days after the fire....

Sbarboro also remembered the fight to save the Colony's building, but he recalled the threat from neighboring buildings. In 1910 Sbarboro wrote: [28] "We fought unceasingly for three days and three nights. The last night, while the building was being kept saturated with water, the heat from the fire in the vicinity was almost unbearable." Sbarboro found a hose crew pumping water from the bay a few blocks away and convinced them to spray the burning houses close to the winery. "... The powerful stream was played on the houses which were burning near our own building and immediately the atmosphere was cooled. The crew continued to play that stream all night, and thus our building, with its million and a half gallons of wine, was saved from the destructive flames." Sbarboro also described how several Italian residences, lacking water, were saved when blankets, soaked in wine, were used to cover the roofs of their houses. After the fires,

Asti vineyard workers sometime before 1910. The roof of the original Colony House shows above the trees in the center. The end of the cookhouse is barely visible beyond the Colony House. The horse barn is on the left below Olive Hill. An orange grove lies in front of barn. Finley Collection, courtesy of Gaye LeBaron.

Roughly the same view as previous photograph. The barns are gone. Olive Hill is now planted to grapevines. The site of the head-pruned vines where the workers posed is now a one-year-old vineyard about to be trellised on wires. Photo by the author.

the Colony well became one of the few sources of fresh water in the city. People came from all over to fill buckets and (wine) barrels with precious water. The winery at Asti was not damaged by the quake, but the half-million-gallon tank cracked. Repairs left the tank in three sections, with the capacity reduced to 300,000 gallons.

Rossi was delighted that, with the wine wars over, he no longer had to worry about marketing his wines. Marketing wasn't his long suit and now, in 1907, Rossi had a major viticultural problem facing him and the Colony. While the industry had been in denial for years, those with courage recognized that they faced a challenge that imperiled the very existence of California's wine industry. During the middle of the 19th century, French plant scientists studying powdery mildew on grapevines imported grapevines from America. With these vines, the French had unknowingly imported—and the Americans, equally unknowingly, had exported to France—one of the deadliest scourges of the *vitis vinifera* grapevine, *dactylasphaera vitifoliae shimmer* or, as it is known to growers around the world, phylloxera. The French could find no cure for the deadly aphid which, in its larval stage, attacked the vines' roots and which, by 1900, had destroyed 75% of the centuries-old vineyards in France.

By the turn of the 20th century, a cure for phylloxera had finally been realized, just in time to save the French wine industry. Researchers found that phylloxera is native to the soils in the Mississippi valley. But as anyone who lives in the region knows, wild grapes thrive in the soils of the area. It was these humble grapevines, growing quietly in the midwestern United States and impervious to phylloxera, that saved the world's wine industry. Today, the French vineyards and most of the *vitis vinifera* vineyards worldwide are planted on phylloxera-resistant rootstock.

While the European vineyards were being decimated, California growers anxious to capitalize on the problems in Europe frantically planted the same *vitis vinifera* grapevines directly in the ground in California, thus inviting the inevitable disaster. But not all the growers lost their heads. By 1907, Georges DeLatour of Beaulieu Vineyards and others were turning out tens of thousands of resistant rootstock, nearly all Rupestris St. George. ISC was one of the belated leaders in the move to replant, and thousands of Colony acres were now being replanted with vines budded to St. George rootstock. As the 20th century draws to a close, St. George rootstock is still being used in new plantings. Although resistant to the new strain of phylloxera (Phylloxera B) moving against California vineyards, St. George has mostly been replaced by a wide variety of new rootstocks that offer other viticultural advantages in addition to phylloxera resistance.

Rossi always kept an eye on developments in the wine industry in Europe. Of particular interest was the research being done in France with yeast strains. Wine had always been fermented using the yeast that normally grew on the grape clusters in the vineyards. But this was not a reliable process, as the wild yeast produced wines that differed from batch to batch. Too often there were stuck fermentations, in which the fermentation would not go to completion because the yeast stopped working. Wines were produced with off flavors. Sometimes the result of even the most careful winemaker's effort was vinegar. ISC was producing millions of gallons of wine from grapes grown all over California, and the risk of poor fermentations was both real and potentially costly. Rossi decided to visit France and learn more about the yeast research project firsthand. He arranged a trip to Europe for the summer of 1908. The twins, with degrees in fermentation science behind them after just one year of study at U.C. Davis, joined their parents on a "trip of rest and pleasure" to Europe.

The senior Rossi had much more on his mind than a vacation. They were gone three and one-half months, mixing business and pleasure. Rossi visited France, where they were experimenting with a process of adding potassium metabisulfite to the crushed grapes (the must). The metabisulfite released sulfur dioxide (SO_2) into the must, killing off the wild yeasts. A purified yeast of known fermentation characteristics could then be added to the must to produce a desirable and controllable fermentation. Rossi was sold on the idea although there was a problem using this technique in the United States, where the FDA was against (but had not banned) the use of SO_2. The process of using minute quantities of SO_2 is almost universally in use in the wine industry today. Highly improved sanitary conditions and the use of SO_2 account for the ability of today's wineries to produce consistently high-quality wine.

In addition to the use of SO_2, Rossi was concerned with fermentation carried out in hot climates. The Colony had wineries in Madera and Fresno, and both places were hot in the fall, when fermentation took place. The Rossis visited Algiers, where an extensive wine industry had existed for centuries in a climate much like that of California's Central Valley. Here they talked with winemakers who were using refrigeration to control the temperature of fermentation. Refrigeration, now in general use in California wineries, was introduced to the state and ISC wineries by Rossi as soon as he returned from Europe. Because of the prevailing sentiment in the U.S. against the use of SO_2, Rossi was more circumspect where it came to use of purified yeast strains. One winery at a time, he carefully introduced the new technology. It would be a few years before he told Sbarboro about his use of SO_2. Temperature-controlled fermentation and pure yeast strains were used in Rossi's wineries by 1911, yet these techniques were used only sporadically in the California wine industry as late as the 1950's. By this time, under urging from enologists at U.C. Davis, California vintners began widespread use of SO_2. Temperature-controlled fermentation and pure yeast strains are almost universally employed in the California wine industry in the 1990's.

Rossi was also interested in the production of champagne. He had been producing champagne for several years, always working to develop an outstanding sparkling wine. The line was called Montecristo champagne, but it had not reached the level of quality that P. C. desired. Rossi decided he needed to know more about the ancient craft of champagne production and one way to do that was to find a job for Edmund with a French champagne producer. But the champagne makers did not want to train an American in their centuries-old craft, and no position could be found. While looking to purchase equipment for producing improved Montecristo champagne, Rossi met an equipment manufacturer who introduced him to Charles Jadeau.

Jadeau was from Saumur, on the Loire River, where he made sparkling Saumur Mousseaux wines, produced in the same fashion as their more famous brethren from the Champagne district in France. Since he couldn't find training for his son in France, Rossi decided to bring France to Asti in the person of Charles Jadeau. Although he was an Italian living in America, P. C. spoke fluent French and he made a favorable impression on Jadeau. Jadeau accepted an invitation from Rossi to visit Asti to develop and then direct production of a superior line of ISC champagne.

When news of Jadeau's leaving France to assist an American champagne producer was announced, a veritable firestorm of protests broke out. *LePetit Journal of Paris* echoed the sentiments of the French people in this following article, which fairly drips with biting sarcasm.[29]

The Americans are wrong when they think they can do everything better than anyone else, and that nothing is impossible for them. The fact is that there are still in the world many, many things which they can never achieve. For example, they have not been able to manufacture Champagne or even produce a sparkling wine that suggests the Champagne of France.

It is true they have left no stone unturned to wine success. Their most eminent wine-makers have spent months, even years in Champagne at the expense of their firms or their Government. They have studied our methods of cultivation and wine-making on the ground with the attention, zeal and patience of which they have the secret. They have received the best instruction in wine-making and secured the choicest vines and the most selected yeasts.

Armed with all these advantages and voluminous files and bundles of paper, they have started for California, an admirable country, where the sun shines just as gloriously as in France, inducing specialists from the Champagne district to go with them by spanning the ocean with a bridge of gold. Then they announced to the world that it was all over with the French monopoly. "A few years more," they said "and the California Champagne, the best on earth, will dethrone the French product."

Built and equipped in 1910 for about $300,000, the often-photographed champagne building still stands, its use now limited to storage of seldom-used items. Courtesy of Beringer archives, Asti, California.

Oh, the fine bragging! But despite all this blare of trumpets, the Champagnes of California have turned out to be frightfully sour wines, only fit for German troopers. The Americans themselves—I speak of the discriminating connoisseurs—were the first to cast them aside. Alas, the imitators of Champagne had forgotten one important thing, the soil of France with its subtle sorcery. To be sure this important feature would not be an easy thing to carry away, even if it were possible to agree upon a price.

At the time of his trip to Europe, Rossi was not certain that Sbarboro shared his enthusiasm for expanding the Colony's champagne business. Rossi hoped to learn enough from the trip to France to help him convince Sbarboro that ISC could produce champagne at Asti equivalent to the greatest being produced in Europe. He was eminently successful. Within a few months of his return, the board authorized an investment of $300,000 for equipment, a new building to produce sparkling wine, and funding for the consultant, Charles Jadeau. In February, less than six months after the Rossis had returned from Europe, construction of the new champagne plant was well along.

On February 19, 1910, California governor James Gillette visited Asti for lunch and a tour of the winery and vineyards. When the governor arrived at the station at Asti he was given an enthusiastic reception by the schoolchildren and residents. An elaborate luncheon was served at the Colony House, where the Governor had an opportunity to taste Colony wines. In the afternoon, he was driven over the 2,500-acre estate (1,750 acres in vines) and then inspected every department of the immense winery and storage vaults. The governor was especially interested in the new, two-story, reinforced concrete building, which measured one hundred by one hundred feet and was nearing completion. This was the new champagne plant.

While the Colony for years had produced sparkling wines, they had made this branch of the industry only a side issue. But now that Congress had adopted a new tariff protecting native sparkling wines, it was their intention to manufacture champagne on a large scale. Some years earlier, Governor Gillette, then a representative in Congress, had shown his loyalty to the California wine industry by working hard for a tariff that would protect California wines from European imports. This prompted Mr. Rossi, when they were examining the vaults on the lower floor, to remark: "Governor, you are in a way responsible for the erection of this building, for if we had not been encouraged by the favorable new tariff of Congress on wines, we never would have dreamed of putting more of our time and capital into the development of this costly champagne."

P. C. Rossi, in one of his few public speeches, later addressed the governor and visitors:

> Governor Gillette. We cannot let this auspicious occasion go by without inflicting on you a little formality as we want to express our appreciation of the honor you have done us in visiting Asti today.
>
> It gives us great pleasure to have you as our guest in this beautiful spot in Sonoma County which thirty years ago was considered a barren waste, fit only for grazing purposes, supporting only a thousand sheep and offering little encouragement for future development. Today we will have an opportunity to show you what a wonderful transformation has taken place in this brief span of thirty years. If the industry is properly encouraged, there is no reason why similar results could not be achieved in many parts of California where millions of acres could be utilized in the growing of wine grapes.
>
> By hard work, patience and perseverance, the Italian Swiss Colony has succeeded in clothing these barren hills with a mantle of flourishing and productive vines which now give employment to hundreds of laborers, support hundreds of families, and produce choice wines which have added materially to the prosperity of the country and helped to advertise the wonderful resources and possibilities of California throughout the United States and Europe.
>
> We feel proud that we have succeeded in producing dry wines which European and American connoisseurs have pronounced equal, if not superior, to the foreign product. But while we have had cause

to rejoice at the success we have achieved, we have always felt that our mission was not complete unless we could produce a sparkling wine that would rival the world-famous French champagne.

Our hard-earned dry wine victory has made us forget the countless drawbacks and discouraging obstacles that marked our pathway for many years. But we did not feel that we have reached our goal yet—for there was still another field for us to conquer. We have been constantly asked why California, which produces as fine dry wines as are to be found anywhere in the world, did not also produce a champagne that would equal the French sparkling wines. We did not answer that question, but simply made up our minds that we would try to capture the immense market in the United States as soon as we could surmount certain difficulties.

While we may forget the people who have attempted to ostracize our legitimate industry, we will never forget our friends. You may be assured that the residents at Asti district and especially the little schoolchildren who welcomed you this morning, every one of whom are native sons and daughters, appreciate the honor you have done them by coming into their midst and noting the progress they have made.

Hoping you will come again, I ask everyone to rise and drink to the health of the governor.

If the focus that winter of 1910 was on building, by May it had turned to rebuilding. On Sunday, May 15, 1910, the Colony House burned to the ground.[30] Officials attributed the blaze to a fire in a chimney flue. T. M. Malesani, superintendent of Asti, was in Madera at the time, but his wife and children were at home. No one was seriously injured, but Mrs. Malesani and the children, still in their pajamas, were moved to the Rossi house. The neighbors mounted a bucket brigade and saved the barn. The loss was estimated to be $7,500 to $10,000.

The loss of the Colony House was more than economic. The house had been built during the 1860's by Isaac Bluxome, Jr. Bluxome had built the beautiful home and established a farm on the Rancho Rincón de Musalacan only twenty years after the land had been claimed by Francisco Berryessa. The *Alta California*[31] had described Bluxomeville

The cookhouse in its heyday, circa 1915. Courtesy of Cloverdale Reveille.

as "a handsome cottage, nestled in the shade of monster oaks... surrounded by choice shrubbery and beautiful flower beds. The house was situated close to the county road and was approached from the railroad by a carriage-way laid out by Bluxome." The carriage-way still exists, well over a hundred years later, but now it is a nondescript avenue in an Asti vineyard.

An orchard was planted in front of the house under the direction of Thomas H. Selby, who would later be elected mayor of San Francisco. Bluxome built housing for his workers, who were employed the year around. That workers' housing became the Colony's first cookhouse. Bluxome's barn and blacksmith shop would serve the Colony for many years. The Colony House had been headquarters, living quarters and entertainment center for Italian Swiss Colony since the very beginning in 1881.

The *Pacific Wine and Spirit Review*[32] wrote the following after the fire:

> Among the distinguished people entertained there were diverse ministers, university presidents, and even royalty. Count Luigi of Savoy, son of the late King of Spain and cousin to the present

King of Italy, visited the Colony in 1896 with a suite of ten officers, in the party being Count Cagni with whom Luigi went to explore the Polar regions. Ferdinand of Savoy also enjoyed the hospitality of the Colony in 1905, with Count Marenco di Moriendo and his suite of officers. So delighted were the royal parties with Asti that they remained there several days and the members were profuse in their expressions of genuine admiration.

In the summer months it was customary to entertain visitors to dinner out of doors, in a green arbor just off the dining room. Not long ago, Mrs. T. M. Malesani, wife of the popular superintendent of the Colony, transformed this beauty spot into a bower of golden oranges in honor of the visit of Governor James Gillette. Unfortunately, however, it drizzled the morning of his arrival and dinner was served indoors instead.

The loss of the Colony House was only temporary. Work began immediately to build another house, much like the first one, on the same site. And the beat of driving nails and rasping saws continued, since at the same time Rossi had his men build a new cookhouse. The Colony House would be in use, as beautiful as ever, into the 21st century. The cookhouse would serve until 1945. It was demolished with all traces gone in the summer of 1998.

In March 1910, Jadeau arrived and began tasting wines for selection in the first cuvée. After tasting a large variety of wines, he chose Johannisburg Riesling, French Colombard, Golden Chasselas and Pinot Noir for the champagne cuvée. The blend was in the bottles by spring of 1910. The first cuvée amounted to 150,000 bottles of champagne and 100,000 bottles of sparkling burgundy. The champagne was named Golden State Extra Dry. The sparkling red wine would be labeled Asti Rouge.

The sparkling wines were released for sale on July 15, 1911. The timing couldn't have been better. It was the height of America's love affair with French champagne. That year Americans spent more than $12 million on imported French champagne. In 1911, the freight and duty on a case of French champagne was approximately twelve dollars.

9

Tragedy Strikes

I would willingly stand at street corners,
hat in hand begging passers-by to drop
their unused minutes into it...
            —*Bernard Berenson*

W HILE THE ROSSIS were in Europe in 1909, they received word
that four senior people at the San Francisco office had quit or
been fired. It was important enough news to make them leave
for home immediately. Among the four were Giulio Perelli-Minetti,
the winemaker for ISC, and his brother Carlo. It was their brother
Antonio, an ex-ISC employee, who enticed the two and their friends
to leave ISC.

A great many men who later became leaders in California's wine
industry spent a part of their early careers at ISC. One of the most
notable was Antonio Perelli-Minetti. Perelli-Minetti was born in 1882
near Milano, Italy. His father was a leader in the Italian wine industry. The senior Perelli-Minetti wrote several winemaking books and
was a noted wine judge. His sons, including Antonio, were educated
at the Royal College of Viticulture & Oenology of Conegliano. The

senior Perelli-Minetti was president of the wine jury at the Exposition of Turin in 1898 and a wine judge at the Paris competition in 1900. In those capacities he played a part in awarding ISC a Diploma of Honor at Turin and a silver medal at Paris two years later.

Mr. Perelli-Minetti had also met Dr. Ollino, one of the founders of ISC. Perelli-Minetti was impressed by the people from Asti and their wines. He was also convinced that the future for his sons was in America. As each son graduated from college, Perelli-Minetti sent him to San Francisco to work at the Colony. Giulio was first, followed by Antonio. Andrea Sbarboro's niece taught Antonio English. Antonio was bright and motivated. He was also brash and impatient. It would not be long before he took off on his own. While working at Asti, he learned that the few Americans on the payroll were paid better than the Italians. In fact, Perelli-Minetti found that the fellow he had replaced, an American, was earning $125 per month, $50 more than he was being paid. Perelli-Minetti went to Rossi for an explanation. Rossi explained, "You know he is American, and if we don't pay them good wages they criticize us."[33] "I (Perelli-Minetti) said to myself, I am in the wrong church. I'm getting $75 per month because I am Italian and the other fellow's getting $125 per month because he is American." The explanation didn't sit well with Perelli-Minetti. He decided he must work for Americans, since they paid Italians better than Italians paid Italians.

During the winter of 1902–03, Mr. & Mrs. Percy Morgan and Mr. Almond R. Morrow, General Superintendent from the California Wine Association, visited Asti for a tour of the facility. At Morgan's request, Antonio loaned his overcoat to Mrs. Morgan to wear during her day at Asti. Before leaving later in the day, Morgan asked Perelli-Minetti if he could purchase the coat for his wife. Perelli-Minetti refused to sell, instead giving Mrs. Morgan his coat. One week later Antonio was working for the CWA.

A year later, while on his way to visit brother Giulio, who was still working at Asti, Antonio was convinced to leave the train in Healdsburg to help a total stranger finish a batch of wine that had gone bad. That led Antonio to eventually purchase the Frank Schmidt winery in

TABLE I

Wines and brandies produced by the
Italian Swiss Colony from grape cuttings
imported from the different European countries
by the Italian Swiss Colony

CALIFORNIA RED WINES	CALIFORNIA WHITE WINES	CALIFORNIA SWEET WINES
Claret	Hock	Port
Burgundy Type	Riesling	Muscat
Carignane	Gutedel	Angelica
Mataro	Tipo	Tokay Type
Barolo	Chablis Type	Madera Type
Barbera	Pinot Blanc	Malaga Type
Tipo	Sauternes Type	Marsala Type
Cabernet	Sauvignon Blanc	White Port
Malbec	Haut Sauternes Type	Sherry
Pinot	Chasselas	
Zinfandel		

CHAMPAGNE	SPARKLING WINES (NATURALLY FERMENTED)	BRANDIES
Golden State Extra Dry	Asti Special (Sec)	Grape Brandy
	Asti Rouge	(Bottled in Bond)
	(Sparkling Burgundy)	Grappa
		Prune
		Peach

A SPECIALTY

El Carmelo Dry Altar Wine
El Carmelo Sweet Altar Wine
El Carmelito Medium Altar Wine

Healdsburg in 1907. His father, who by now had also immigrated to America, convinced his son to bring his brothers into the winery and make it a family business. Giulio was winemaker for ISC and brother Carlo was also working at Asti. The two, along with California Malati, an ISC salesman, accepted Antonio's invitation to join the fledgling Healdsburg winery.

The only problem was money. They had none. The three decided to keep their jobs at ISC while they worked to get their own winery on its feet. This arrangement worked until the summer of 1909, when Sophus Federspiel decided that he'd had enough of divided loyalty and fired the three. The fourth individual was Mario Tribuno, a top ISC salesman in New York and Rossi's nephew. Tribuno's son Jack later marketed a widely successful secret-formula vermouth through the 21 Brand in New York.

With no money, and with the wages of the partners cut off, the venture soon failed. But not Antonio. He continued to snap up any opportunity that came his way. He got involved in winemaking adventures up and down the state. He spent seven years in Mexico consulting to that nation's wine industry before acquiring land in Delano, California, where he planted grapes and built a winery. At last there was to be a Perelli-Minetti family winery; only the family was his sons, not his brothers. Through the twists and turns of time, the family came to own what remained of the old monarch of the industry, the California Wine Association.

Among the assets of CWA was the brand name Golden State Extra Dry, the loving brainchild of Pietro Rossi. Even more ironic, Antonio was offered the chance to purchase ISC for $115,000.[N-7] Perelli-Minetti spurned the offer. "Asti was a lemon," he said. "The land is bad, it gives us poor yields. In the early days train loads of manure, collected from the streets of San Francisco were shipped to Asti, but the only productive land was along the river and at Chianti." (Time and technology change all things. Today, the "lemon" is a prime Gallo vineyard, valued on the order of $35 million.) Giulio Perelli-Minetti's departure from ISC left a vacancy for young Edmund Rossi, who became winemaker upon the family's return from Europe.

By the end of 1910, ISC had climbed to new heights. They owned seven wineries with a total storage capacity of fourteen million gallons. The Colony owned five thousand acres of vineyards, forty percent of which were prime Sonoma County vineyards, and they controlled another five thousand acres. According to an estimate by wine historian Thomas Pinney,[34] what had started out worth $150,000 was now estimated to be worth about $3,000,000 in 1910 dollars. Colony wines were available throughout most of the world. The explosive growth of the Colony was as much a reflection of the times as it was of superb management. At the turn of the 20th century the United States economy moved with unchecked optimism. It was a time when only speed counted, not the direction. Of course that mentality sped into a wall in 1929.

At the beginning of the 20th century, there was no formal, sophisticated approach to marketing at the Colony as practiced by large companies toward the end of the 20th century. But nimble management, quick to respond to market forces or good ideas, had its benefits. The overnight plunge into the super-premium champagne business was a good example of such visionary and responsive management. Before would-be competitors or imitators could react, the Colony had a major new product in full production and distribution. On the other hand, it is astounding to consider that at this period, ISC offered thirty different still wines, three sparkling wines, and four brandies, which included grappa, and three altar wines, dry, medium and sweet.

At the turn of the century, wineries spread their names through international expositions. Among the most important were those held in Paris and Bordeaux, France; Turin and Milan, Italy; Dublin, Ireland; and those in the United States, which included Chicago and San Francisco. For Rossi, the 1911 competition at Turin had special significance, for Turin was the city of his youth. Turin held that special place in his heart that alums everywhere reserve for their college days. Of course, Turin was not many miles from the town where he was born.

Rossi sent only his finest wines to the Turin Exposition, but in a move uncharacteristic for the conservative Rossi, he included his unproven Golden State Extra Dry Champagne. Rossi had spent several years working to develop a world-class champagne. He had been so excited upon his return from France in 1909 that he had gone out on a limb, exerting considerable pressure, more pressure than even before, to convince Sbarboro and the board to finance production of a champagne that would be the equal to Europe's finest. Now would come the accounting, before all the world. The champagne, having been on the cork for about thirteen months, was released to the market on July 15, 1911.

The Exposition was held the first week of October 1911. Among the judges were some of Europe's most distinguished wine tasters. The highest award was the Grand Prix. After a week of tasting and comparisons, the wine world, especially the Europeans, was shocked when it was announced that the Grand Prix had been awarded to Italian Swiss Colony's Golden State Extra Dry Champagne.

Rossi was at Asti the weekend the results were announced from Turin. Like everyone else at ISC, he worked seven days a week during harvest. Rossi stayed at the Colony House, which had spare rooms for visiting staff or important guests. Sunday morning, P. C. walked the few hundred yards to the little church to attend the 8:30 A.M. Mass. October is possibly the most attractive time of year in Asti. The month is warm, and usually very dry. Inside the little church the air would be cool. There is generally little wind in October, but the aromas of crush would make their way over all of Asti. Creeping in through the open windows, the soft fragrance would envelop the congregation. The priest, saying the Latin Mass in vestments and language used the world over, completed the timeless scene.

Walking back to the Colony House after Mass, Rossi was joined by the stable master, Pietro Sani, who suggested that P. C. might like to try out a new horse in the stable. After breakfast, Pietro went to the nearby stable, where the new horse was hitched to the Rossi buggy. Sani drove with Rossi sitting alongside. The horse was skittish, but that was understandable, given its new surroundings. After leaving the stable, they turned in the direction of the winery. One hundred yards down the road, not even to the church, Rossi, frightened by the behavior of the horse, made ready to jump. Sani urged him to hold on, but Rossi felt the horse was about to bolt. Rossi did jump. His head hit a rock and P. C. went still.

Two calls went out immediately, one to Dr. Grant in Cloverdale, the other to Father Maurice Barry from Healdsburg. Doctors from Healdsburg and Geyserville arrived later in the morning. A telegram was sent to Andrea Sbarboro, who left immediately for Asti by auto. With him were Dr. Lawrence A. Draper and son-in-law H. J. Sartori. Mrs. Rossi was in Santa Barbara at the time and she headed for home immediately upon receiving her telegram. Sbarboro and his team reached Asti shortly before three o'clock that afternoon.

The seriousness of the injury was obvious, and in a desperate attempt to save the dying Rossi, the doctors operated. It was to no avail. At 3:30 that afternoon, October 8, 1911, P. C. Rossi died at the Colony House. It was a tragedy of immense proportions, for when great men die, they leave great voids. Colony historians profess uncertainty as to Rossi's having heard the results from Turin before his death but a letter to the *Pacific Wine & Spirit Review*[35] makes it clear he had heard. In his letter, Sophus Federspiel, second in command to Rossi at the San Francisco office, explained: "It is of great satisfaction to the associates of our late president, Mr. P. C. Rossi, that his life was spared until the news had reached California that Italian Swiss Colony's new brand of champagne, Golden State Extra Dry, had been awarded the Grand Prix at the Turin International Exposition in Italy." One must wonder how *LePetit Journal of Paris* covered the news.

Pietro Carlo Rossi died just two days before his 56th birthday. He left a wife and ten children, the youngest just eleven years old.[N-8] The girls would marry well and leave a string of doctors and lawyers in their wake. The twins would spend their lives building an industry their father had started. Pietro Rossi would have been proud of all of them, but three would have given him special satisfaction.

Daughters Aimee and Olga took religious orders. Both sisters earned Ph.D.'s and became nuns in the Order of the Sacred Heart. Aimee founded the San Diego College for Women. The college eventually combined with a men's college to become the University of San Diego. The youngest child, Pietro Carlo, Jr., also devoted his life to the Church his parents loved. Carlo earned his Ph.D. at the University of California and became a Jesuit priest.

Taking a vow of poverty upon entering the priesthood, Carlo contributed his money to a fund that built the Jesuit retreat house in Los Altos, California. The retreat house, named El Retiro, is also known as the Rossi Chapel. Nephew Bob Rossi still attends a retreat at the chapel once each year. Pietro Rossi left another living legacy, the people of Asti. Allowing for the writing style in the early years of the 20th century, the reader almost one hundred years later must smile yet appreciate the following description of life at Asti at the time of Rossi's death.

> Many bright and happy children, belonging to the laborers' families, have been born there and attend a school of their own. There is a Catholic church, recently erected, a post office and telegraphic communication. A complete electric light plant, which furnishes not only Asti but the surrounding country with light and power, is a part of the equipment. Asti is without a doctor or druggist—there is no business for them there. Pure wine and outdoor life keep health abloom, and with it comes happiness for all. (Writer unknown)

10

Life Goes On

Change alone is eternal...
—*Arthur Schopenhauer*

W HILE THE FAMILY DEEPLY FELT the loss of their husband and father, the Colony also suffered greatly from the loss of P. C. Rossi. At Rossi's death, the Colony owned eight wineries in addition to the Asti facility. These facilities were located at Madera, Lamar, Kingsburg, Selma, Fulton, Cloverdale, Sebastopol and Clayton. They totaled over ten million gallons of storage capacity in addition to Asti's four million gallons. Italian Swiss Colony owned five thousand acres of vineyards and controlled another five thousand acres. In addition to San Francisco, where the Colony had storage vaults that held two million gallons, vaults in New York City held one million gallons of bulk wine. Smaller storage facilities were located in Chicago.

Most local wineries in the Geyserville/Healdsburg area sold wine to the Colony. At the turn of the century, Dry Creek Valley alone had over a dozen wineries shipping all or a part of their production to Asti. Because of the grade on Canyon Road as it climbed out of Dry Creek Valley and descended into Alexander Valley, the wine was shipped one puncheon (one hundred twenty gallons) on a wagon pulled by one horse. But it took two people to haul the load, one to stay on the wagon and hold the brake while the helper placed chocks at the wagon wheels in case traffic caused the wagon to wait in line on the downward slope into Alexander Valley.

While most producers at that time sold their wine in bulk to independent blenders and bottlers, under Rossi the Colony was already bottling a significant percentage of its wine. Rossi had taken this unusual step to protect the Colony's premium wines from adulteration by unscrupulous blenders. The top-of-the-line dinner wine produced at Asti was Tipo Chianti. Tipo was a blend of Italian grape varieties, principally Sangiovese, although by the 1950's, under Ed Rossi, Jr., Tipo contained a large portion of Zinfandel. Both the red and white blends were named Tipo Chianti.

In 1906, the Colony registered the word Tipo (the word means "type"), and the word Chianti was dropped from the label. By 1910 the name had once again been changed. Now the premium table wines were called Tipo Red and Tipo White. To assure its quality, the Colony had begun bottling Tipo before the turn of the century. Rossi saw to it that Tipo was bottled by the Colony's own agents in New York and Chicago as well as at Asti. By contrast, James Lapsley[36] notes that as late as the 1930's, eighty percent of California wine was sold in bulk to out-of-state bottlers, who blended, cellared, bottled and labeled the wine. In an article appearing in *Wines & Vines* in 1938, Edmund Rossi wrote:[37]

> In pre-Prohibition days, Tipo was very considerably advertised in New York and Chicago markets, and had received fine acceptance, particularly in New York, where it was being sold at a price equal, if not superior, to the imported Chianti.
>
> Italian Swiss Colony today has reestablished and even enhanced for Tipo the reputation of pre-Prohibition days. It is this wine that in previous years established the reputation of Italian Swiss Colony wines. It is sold only in Chianti flasks. This wine is never sold to the trade in bulk. Today it is available on all diners

The Rossi clan—family reunion at the Rossi villa, April 14, 1979. Note Pietro and Amelia's children sitting in the third row from bottom. Courtesy of Bob D. Rossi, Jr.

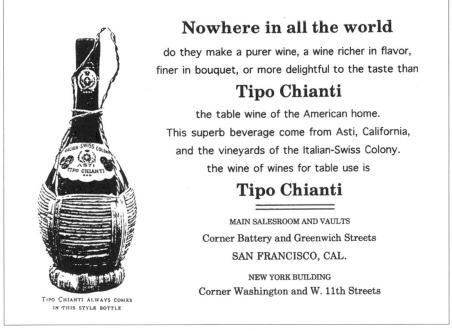
A Tipo Chianti ad circa 1910. Courtesy of ISC Archives.

and buffet cars of the Pullman Company and on the diners of
most of the major railroads.

Unlike the Italian Chianti, the grapes for Tipo Red before fermentation are stemmed as they have enough astringency without the additional amount that might come from fermentation
and contact from stems. Also because of a sufficiency of tannin
and color, we do not find it necessary to induce a second fermentation after the first fermentation is finished by the addition
of fresh grapes of high color. Tipo is bottled when about four
years old; sometimes five years old. This possibility is older than
the age of the Chianti bottled in Italy, because the Italian population as a whole likes a fresher wine.

ISC was the largest winery in the world. One out of three bottles of
California wine came out of ISC. The original investment of $150,000
was now worth an estimated $3,000,000. But Prohibition changed

Marco Fontana: From shining shoes for a living in New York City, Fontana became one of California's wealthiest men. He was the financial strength behind the Colony prior to Prohibition. Courtesy of Beringer archives, Asti, California.

everything, and we can only guess how P. C. would have reacted to that adversary. Andrea Sbarboro was 71 when Rossi died. P. C. had run the Colony for 24 years. Sbarboro was deeply fond of Pietro and he trusted Rossi implicitly. In his remarks to a businessmen's group a few weeks after Rossi's death, Sbarboro said, "No one mourns the death of Mr. Rossi more than I do, for I had known him almost from the day he landed in San Francisco, and for 25 years we met nearly every day. You can readily understand how I shall miss him, for since I knew him longest and most intimately, I naturally loved him best." No one could fill Rossi's shoes for Sbarboro, but rather than personally stepping in to fill the void left by the fallen leader, Sbarboro drifted away.

On November 9, 1911, just one month after Rossi's death, CWA's executive committee met to discuss the situation at ISC. As half-owners, CWA had a lot of stake in the Colony. They agreed that, with P. C. Rossi gone, CWA needed one of their men to run the Colony, and they asked Marco J. Fontana if he would take on the job. Fontana was 62 years old, had already amassed a fortune, and had little desire for added responsibilities. But he was the perfect choice, the one man who would most likely be acceptable to Sbarboro and the others at ISC. Fontana agreed to take the post but told the committee he could devote no more than an "hour or two each day to the job."[38] Thereupon an employee, Mr. Kittrege, was made Fontana's assistant.

Fontana assumed Pietro's job as president of ISC. Bob Rossi became a second assistant to Mr. Fontana and Edmund Rossi continued as general superintendent of Asti. ISC had new management. There was no talk of conferring with Andrea Sbarboro or the ISC stockholders, although Fontana, Sbarboro's friend for over thirty years, would certainly have kept him informed. Sbarboro should have been the logical successor to Rossi, but Andrea had never shown a desire to run operations at Italian Swiss Colony.

With Fontana in control, CWA felt it had solved the management problem at ISC. Mr. Fontana had enjoyed an enormously successful career. He was a founder and president of the California Fruit Canners Association, the largest canner in the world and the company that eventually became known to millions as Del Monte. It was Fontana who built the cannery on San Francisco's Fisherman's Wharf shortly before the turn of the 20th century. As the 21st century approaches, millions of visitors to San Francisco visit the shops and restaurants of The Cannery and enjoy magicians, jugglers and comics on Fontana's patio.

Fontana served as a director on numerous boards, including Sbarboro's Italian American Bank. He served on the San Francisco board of supervisors from 1897 through 1899 and was a member of many prestigious clubs and societies in San Francisco. But he was never far from the management of ISC. He was the first president of ISAC and served in that capacity until the appointment of his successor, P. C. Rossi. Fontana, likely with the encouragement of Rossi and Sbarboro, became a shareholder in CWA in 1905. By 1910, he was CWA's largest stockholder and that year he was elected to the CWA board of directors. In February 1911, Fontana was appointed to the executive committee, from which post he had a more direct hand in managing CWA and of course ISC.

Fontana would travel to Asti every weekend in the years following Pietro's death to meet with Edmund Rossi and discuss the week's events. Young Edmund enjoyed the visits from his boss and his reports never failed to satisfy Fontana. For his part, Fontana loved the trips to Asti. The man who, as a youth, used to shine shoes to support his mother, now loved the automobile. At first he would drive a big Stanley Steamer, his wife, Nellie, by his side. Fontana was immensely proud of a later car, a great red roadster. It had a gasoline engine and was possibly the first gasoline auto to travel the Redwood Highway in the northern reaches of Sonoma County.

WHILE MANAGERS WORRIED about managing, the men of Asti and Chianti lived their simple lives. The work crew, living together in the cookhouse, labored for about one dollar per day. Work during the long, hot summer could be brutal, but it really wasn't so bad. They had each other, and of course their sweethearts, wives and children were always with them, if only in their memories.

Winter was the time for life's highs and lows. Cold, rainy days left the men with nothing to do but mourn the absence of family and loved ones. On days when there was no rain, the men worked from sunrise to sunset. The early hours were brutal, frozen fingers barely able to grip ice-cold pruning shears. Pruning always started at the Colony House and worked south toward the Lucca Ranch. As the morning wore on, jackets came off and frozen fingers came back to life under the warming sun. At noon, a big pot of soup brought down from the cookhouse kitchen was served for lunch. The men sat among the vines enjoying the soup, the sun and each other. Nearly one hundred years later the scene would be repeated, only this time the diners were yuppies with BMWs parked under the nearest oak tree.

For the Rossi family, the healing process after P. C.'s death was a slow one. Mother and her ten children would need time to decide their future without Father. The family shares in CWA were not voted in the stockholders' meeting in January 1912.[39] But in February 1912, Andrea Sbarboro asked CWA for a sixty-day option to purchase the CWA shares in ISC. The price offered was $1,125,000, and the option was approved. We are left to ponder this move by Sbarboro. Like the dying man who suddenly shows exuberant signs of health only to be gone a few days later, did Sbarboro's interest in ISC simply flare up? In his seventy-second year did he suddenly wax nostalgic for the old days? Possibly he had been wrestling with the idea since P. C. Rossi's death four months earlier. Sbarboro was a banker and a successful businessman. He had been battling the prohibitionists for over five years. He'd been before Congress several times. He must have sensed at least the possibility that Prohibition could come to the country. Whatever Sbarboro needed to have happen in those sixty days didn't happen. Or perhaps his exuberance died as quickly as it had flared. Whatever it was, Sbarboro never exercised the option.

One year later, in February 1913, CWA prepared for a period of significant expansion. At the shareholders' meeting, the capital stock authorization was increased from ten million dollars to twenty million dollars and an increase of bonded indebtedness from two million dollars to seven million dollars was approved. Some weeks later, on March 17, 1913, CWA purchased an option from ISAC to acquire the latter's interest in ISC. The option ran for eighteen months and CWA paid a whopping $100,000 for it. It was expressly agreed that the option cost was not to be applied to the purchase price of $687,500. It was further agreed that ISC would pay no dividends during the option period. Andrea Sbarboro and his son Alfred signed the agreement dated March 20, 1913 for ISC.

In just one year, Sbarboro agreed to accept what amounted to $787,500 for property he had valued at $1,125,000 one year earlier. It would appear that Sbarboro had given in to the premise that Prohibition would soon destroy his beloved wine industry. But for every seller there is a buyer, and in this case the buyer was CWA. They were certainly operating with the same information that moved Sbarboro. Possibly the company that had done so remarkably well since 1894 missed the genius of the accountant Percy Morgan, but Morgan had resigned from CWA in February 1911 due to poor health. CWA, through its wholly-owned subsidiary CALWA, exercised its option to buy the remainder of ISC, and by the end of 1914, the association owned all of Italian Swiss Colony and controlled over seventy percent of the entire California wine market.

11

Such Things Must Change

The old order changeth, yielding place to new…
—*Alfred Lord Tennyson*

T HE EARLY YEARS of the 20th century were years of unbridled optimism for American business, with leaders lusting after ever-expanding control over their respective industries. Beef producers and hard-coal miners were among the large trusts broken up by the Department of Justice but none was as large as the oil trust. The first formal trust, and the most widely known, was organized in 1882 when John D. Rockefeller merged his various oil-related enterprises into the Standard Oil trust. Trusts owned or controlled several companies which maintained their respective brand names, giving the public impression of competition.

Although the Standard Oil trust came under the glare of public scrutiny, typically the individual companies would escape public attention to their trust affiliations. Federal antitrust laws were enacted in 1890 (Sherman Antitrust Act) and later 1914 (Clayton Antitrust Act) to protect the public from these controlled markets in what was supposed to be a free marketplace. But enforcement of these Acts was arbitrary, and the founders of the California Wine Association learned to live with it. They maintained a profile so low that many of the people working for them were unaware of CWA's existence.

Ruth Teiser tells the story[40] of a distributor whose firm had a contract with the CWA-controlled Lachman & Jacobi to represent their wines in New Orleans. As such, the brokers competed vigorously with other brands, including other CWA brands. On a trip to San Francisco to iron out a commission disagreement, the surprised distributor found himself dealing not with Lachman & Jacobi but with Alfred Sutro, chairman of the board of CWA. It was Sutro who settled the matter.

As we approach the 21st century, Americans live in a nation that mandates full disclosure in all things public and strives for wide disclosure in the business world. It wasn't like that at the beginning of the 20th century. The *San Francisco Call* carried a story in its May 8, 1911, edition concerning a real-estate broker's suit for a commission he felt was due him. Mr. Marcellus Kriegbaum had a contract with CWA to arrange the purchase of a certain vineyard. Mr. Kriegbaum sued when, at the last minute, ISC rather than CWA took title, thus depriving Kriegbaum of his commission. The outcome of the suit is lost to antiquity but not the remarks of the frustrated broker. In the *San Francisco Call,* Kriegbaum tells the world that CWA and ISC are the same company and that they are attempting to corner the wine market. Edmund Rossi, in his oral history,[41] remembered the suit but not the details. He did acknowledge, however, that even though the two were major wine companies at the time, few people were aware that CWA owned half of Italian Swiss Colony ten years after the fact.

By 1915, Sutro decided that the time for secrecy had passed. In a letter to Louis Wetmore, General Manager of CWA, Sutro wrote:[42] "The public is misled into believing that there exists competition between the CWA and its subsidiary corporations such as ISC and Lachman & Jacobi. The CWA should of course promptly take steps to dispel any such misunderstanding." From then on, the name CWA appeared on ISC letterhead.

That summer the growing prohibitionist movement began to touch CWA. On August 26, 1915, the board noted that CWA, ISC, and Lachman & Jacobi had operated since January with no profit, and therefore they would "consolidate the above so that like departments, instead of being managed separately, will be brought under the same head."[43] For the first time since its founding 21 years earlier, CWA's subsidiaries would be brought under operational control of the parent company. In a receding market, there was no longer any need for secrecy to protect the trust. CWA was now in a retrenchment mode. Greater market share was the conquest of earlier boards. This board was concerned only with survival.

In the fall of 1915, still more belt tightening was instituted. Many senior executives saw their monthly salaries cut.

NAME	OLD SALARY	NEW SALARY
M. Fontana	300	—
A. Sbarboro	300	300 (Contract)
S. Federspiel	1,000	750
E. Rossi	350	265
R. Rossi	350	265
A. E. Sbarboro	150	150 (Contract)
C. Jadeau	600	600 (Contract)

By the winter of 1916, Marco Fontana had been on the CWA board for six years and a member of the executive committee for five. He was one of the most influential members of the board. But Fontana was 67 years old. He had little need for additional money, and was thinking of retirement. In preparation, Fontana proposed his assistant at ISC since 1911, Bob Rossi, for a seat on the board. Rossi was elected to the board at the February 1916 stockholders' meeting.[44]

Once again, a Rossi was on the CWA board of directors, but the clock was ticking down for CWA as well as Fontana. As the forces of Prohibition grew, the sale of wine dropped. The heady days of expansion, only a few years earlier, were now days of retreat. On November 23, 1916, Edmund Rossi and Sophus Federspiel made a presentation to the CWA urging that they continue the sale of bottled goods. The board agreed and the wolf was stayed from the door a little longer.

In February 1917, Marco Fontana resigned from the executive committee, but not from the board of directors. Fontana's hand-picked successor, Bob Rossi, took his committee seat.[45] Rossi was only 29 years old.

The decline of CWA continued. In April, the executive committee was advised of the large inventory of Golden State Champagne. The pride and joy of Pietro Rossi, the premier champagne that had taken Europe as well as America by storm, wasn't selling. The committee ordered that the inventory be liquidated, and authorized officials to take whatever steps were necessary.

Bob Rossi had graduated from the University of California at Davis in 1909. After a three-month tour of Europe and North Africa, he returned with his family to work for the Colony. For two years, he and his twin brother learned the business beside their father as he built the most successful winery in the world. But fate had dealt the brothers a cruel one-two punch: their father's sudden death in 1911 and the steady encroachment of Prohibition into their world. Nearly all of the brothers' careers had been spent fighting a losing battle against an enemy before which they were helpless. Bob Rossi needed a change. On November 22, 1917, a few months past his 29th birthday, Rossi resigned from the board of directors. America had been at war since April, he was single, and the time was right to join the Army. Brother Ed was elected to fill Bob's seat on the board.

On January 16, 1919, the Eighteenth Amendment became law and the clouds of Prohibition deepened over the wine industry that now had only one year to live. On April 21, 1919, Ed Rossi and Asti superintendent Enrico Prati were requested by the executive committee to make a preliminary study for subdividing the Asti property into tracts "such as would facilitate sale." Ed Rossi, as a director of CWA and general manager of ISC, had an inside seat from which to keep watch on the future of Asti. Prati had never lived outside of Asti. He had worked his way up from field hand to plant superintendent, and now he constantly nagged Rossi as to the state of affairs. Prati, who had married the girl next door, Ida Seghesio, loved Asti and life in the beautiful Colony House. He could not imagine life anywhere else and he surely wanted to be given a chance to purchase Asti when it became available.

On May 19, 1919, the executive committee authorized Ed Rossi to sell Asti for a minimum price of $120,000, over half a million dollars less than they had paid for half of the business six years earlier. CWA wanted a $10,000 deposit and $85,000 in escrow. They would carry the balance of $35,000 for one year. Not included in the deal were the properties owned by Sbarboro, the Rossi family, the de Vecchi property and the 0.3 acre that had been deeded to the Church in 1907. The wine inventory, all cooperage, and other personal property at the winery were also excluded. The boarding houses, but not boarding house supplies, were included in the sales offering.

Prati didn't have the money, but his in-laws, the Seghesios, had a little. From endless conversations over the past year, Prati and his wife, Ida, knew that Ida's mother, Angela Seghesio, shared their enthusiasm for acquiring Asti. Husband Edoardo was not so easily convinced. But Edoardo was no match for the three. Cautious by nature, Edoardo finally succumbed to family pressure and the lure of the land. It is a disease common to all farmers and for years, Edoardo had wanted that Colony vineyard that sat between his ranch and the Russian River.

Whatever the forces, Seghesio gave in and an offer was made to the CWA. Seghesio would pay $127,500 for the property, depositing $10,000 immediately into escrow and paying $65,000 at the close of escrow. The balance would be paid June 1, 1920. The loan was to carry 5.5% interest. The offer was accepted and on June 17, 1919, Edoardo became master of Asti. It was five months, almost to the day, since the Eighteenth Amendment was passed. The deed was signed by M. Fontana, president and A. Sbarboro, secretary. The wheel had turned full cycle. The two who had acquired Asti 38 years earlier were now sellers. It had been a grand ride, but such things as this must always end. Although the name Italian Swiss Colony did not go with the deal, Asti now had its third owner. For a while, there would be no Rossis running Asti.

12

A Nation On The Wagon

God made the vine and then the wine
To be enjoyed by one and all.
Little fools will drink too much
Great fools none at all.

—*Anon*

T HE PANAMA-PACIFIC International Exposition proved the apogee in the early days of the California wine industry. The exposition was held in 1915 as the nation celebrated completion of the Panama Canal. The notion to host such an event in San Francisco was presented at a 1906 meeting of the San Francisco chapter of the California Promotion Committee. The chairman of the committee, Andrea Sbarboro, saw in the idea an opportunity to showcase San Francisco, which had "miraculously" recovered from the quake of 1906.

The man with the Midas touch raised $17.5 million in the effort to convince Congress to approve San Francisco over New Orleans as the site for the exposition. National expositions had always been great venues for promoting wine, so the Californians had an extra incentive. ISC had won gold medals at the Pan American Exposition in 1901, the St. Louis Exposition in 1903, the Lewis and Clark Exposition in 1904, and the Alaska-Yukon Exposition in 1909. An exposition in San Francisco would give vintners an unprecedented opportunity to showcase the state's wines.

The Panama-Pacific International Exposition was awarded to San Francisco, and the state's vintners went all out to capitalize on their good fortune. A great wine display was featured prominently on the grounds, and a large tasting room provided guests from around the world the opportunity to sample California wines. A prestigious panel of nationally recognized wine experts was assembled for a much-publicized competition to be held at the Fair. July 14 was designated Wine Day (coincidentally, it was also Bastille Day, a major French holiday), and on that day results of the wine judging were announced. Consistent with the joyous celebratory tone of the exposition, the judges awarded enough medals to give nearly all competing wineries at least some sort of medal to display at the winery back home. It is amusing to note the inflationary nature of the awards. A gold medal rated third from the top, exceeded by a medal of honor, and top of the line, a grand prize. While winning a medal was not a particularly great feat, the performance of the Colony was noteworthy. ISC took home six medals of honor and four grand prizes, the latter double the number won by any other winery. Among their lesser awards were thirteen gold medals.

Back home, with the exposition over, the applause and triumphs rapidly faded. The wineries faced a bleak future. For several years there had been stirrings about the country from those who abhorred the nation's increasing consumption of whiskey and beer. In the years just prior to the Civil War, thirteen states had prohibition laws. This number went up and down throughout the second half of the 19th century, but gradually the movement took hold. In 1869 the Prohibition Party was formed and in 1874 the National Women's Christian Temperance Union was founded in Cleveland, Ohio. The Temperance Union became a cohesive center around which women would fight alcohol consumption and the occasion of drinking, the saloon.

Italian Swiss Colony Awards and Diplomas
Prior to Probition

GOLD MEDALS

Genoa, Italy	1892
Dublin, Ireland	1892
Columbia World's Fair, Chicago	1893
Midwinter Fair, San Francisco	1894
Bordeaux, France	1895*
Guatemala, C. A.	1897
Paris, France	1900*
Pan-American Exposition, Buffalo, New York	1901
St. Louis Exposition, Missouri	1903
Lewis & Clark Exposition, Portland, Oregon	1904
Alaska-Yukon-Pacific Exposition, Seattle, Washington	1909
Panama-Pacific International Exposition (thirteen medals)	1915

GRAND DIPLOMA OF HONOR

Asti and Turin, Italy	1898
Milan, Italy	1906
Panama-Pacific International Exposition, San Francisco (six medals)	1915

GRAND PRIZE

Grand Prize for Asti Special Dry Alaska-Yukon-Pacific Exposition, Seattle, Wash.	1909
Grand Prize, Panama-Pacific International Exposition, San Francisco (four medals)	1915

"GRAND PRIX"

Golden State Extra Dry Champagne, International Exposition, Turin, Italy	1911

* Charles Sullivan reports these as silver medals.

The group's name was, of course, a misnomer. Legions of Christian women did not share the views of the primarily Protestant women of the Midwest farm belt, and temperance was never an issue. Common sense and compassion were sufficient to make one realize that the nation needed to moderate its alcohol consumption. But it was religious zealotry that led to the cry for total abstinence and the resultant era of lawlessness, poisoned drinks, and corruption across the country. The goal was total elimination of intoxicating beverages from the nation. American society split, the "drys" supporting Prohibition, the "wets" defending their right to drink what they chose. So great was their zeal that the drys applauded the addition of lethal denaturants to industrial alcohol even though they knew people would die, go blind or suffer other horrible consequences from its consumption. Leaders of the dry movement called consumption of industrial alcohol "deliberate suicide."[46]

Prohibition did not come to the nation purely on the zeal of well-meaning women. There was in fact great cause for reform. In the second half of the 19th century, the nation, traumatized by the horror of a civil war, sought increasing solace in the spirits bottle, and alcohol consumption soared to levels not seen before or since. Society was using alcohol recklessly and this societal abuse helped drive the country over the edge. The idea for Prohibition was reinforced when society recognized its need to protect Indians from the abuse of liquor at the hands of frontier traders.

In the battle for Prohibition, centuries of experience from wine-drinking societies around the world were ignored. The drys fought the distilling and brewing industries with unbounded passion. The whiskey and beer people lashed back in a desperate attempt to defend their economic interests. But for all the furor, there was no mention that bat-wielding Carrie Nation ever saw a wine-sodden sot stagger from the saloons she destroyed. And there is no record of a bottle of claret reaching an Indian encampment in some frontiersman's saddlebags. In an emotion-driven state of mind, the nation would ultimately throw out the baby with the bath water.

The ball had started rolling and by the turn of the century it was picking up size and speed. It wouldn't be many years before the gigantic leap from temperance to Prohibition would be possible. The California wine industry was not oblivious to this current gaining swell across the land. Andrea Sbarboro, the Colony's own teacher, set off to show the prohibitionists just how mistaken they were. Sbarboro was in his element; no man had ever spoken an advocacy more from the heart than Andrea Sbarboro.

In 1907 he wrote a pamphlet-sized book entitled "The Fight For True Temperance."[47] Sbarboro's position was that drunkenness was indeed evil, but the way to cure that evil was to drink wine. This, after all, was life as the 68-year-old had lived it since childhood. From his earliest years, his mother had mixed wine with his water at mealtime. His own five children included an architect and a bank president with nary an alcoholic among them. They had been exposed to wine in exactly the same way, and they had grown to be successful citizens in their communities. Sbarboro argued, almost ninety years before medical science caught up, that wine was beneficial to health and a necessary ingredient of the good life. The essence of Sbarboro's plea was that America could achieve temperance overnight by simply switching from whisky to wine.

Sbarboro was not the first to see the merit in wine and the evil in spirits. Thomas Jefferson had professed the same message one hundred years earlier. In a December 13, 1818, letter to his friend Monsieur le Conte de Neuville,[48] Jefferson wrote about the end of the Napoleonic wars and the future of France. But fully half of the letter discusses the prospect of a reduction of United States duties on imported wine. Jefferson's words fairly shout the depths of his angry emotions.

> It (the import duty) is a prohibition of its (wine) use to the middling class of our citizens, and a condemnation of them to the poison of whiskey, which is desolating their houses. No nation is drunken where wine is cheap; and none sober, where the dearness of wine substitutes ardent spirits as the common beverage. It is, in truth, the only antidote to the bane of whiskey. Fix but

the duty at the rate of other merchandise, and we can drink wine here as cheap as we do grog; and who will not prefer it? Its extended use will carry health and comfort to a much enlarged circle. Everyone in easy circumstances (as the bulk of our citizens are) will prefer it to the poison to which they are now driven by their government.

Another of our Founding Fathers, the sagacious Ben Franklin, expressed his joy in wine by composing drinking songs, including these two verses:[49]

> Twas honest old Noah first planted the Vine,
> And mended his morals by drinking its Wine;
> And thenceforth justly the drinking of Water decry'd
> For he knew that all Mankind by drinking it dy'd.
> Derry Down

> From this Piece of History plainly we find
> That Water's good neither for Body or Mind;
> That Virtue and Safety in Wine-bibbing's found
> While all that drink Water deserve to be drown'd
> Derry Down

Consumption of ardent spirits was never far from the minds of 19th-century Americans. Nearly 25 years after Jefferson, another noted American expressed another view of alcoholic beverages. Speaking to the Washington Temperance Society in 1842, Abraham Lincoln offered his thoughts.[N-9] "I believe, if we take habitual drunkards as a class, their heads and their hearts will bear an advantageous comparison to those of any other class."

Many observers saw a religious element in the war to outlaw alcoholic beverages from American society. Lou Gomberg, dean of wine industry consultants, observed:[50] "They made a career out of bringing about Prohibition on the grounds that all forms of beverages containing ethanol were evil, not only from the societal standpoint, but from a religious standpoint too, and should be prohibited. That was never true, it isn't true now and never will be true, because some, as you know, of the greatest figures of history have praised the use of wine in moderation as a major contributing factor in an enriched and fulfilling life... when Thomas Jefferson praised wine, as he did abundantly; when Socrates praised wine as he did abundantly; when Louis Pasteur praised wine as the greatest beverage... These were perfectly sane, highly cultivated people who recognized the value of wine as a beverage of moderation."

Of unknown vintage, the following purports to be the reply of a congressman to a letter from a constituent asking where he stood on whiskey.[51]

> Dear Friend:
>
> I had not intended to discuss this controversial subject at this particular time. However, I want you to know that I do not shun a controversy. On the contrary, I will take a stand on any issue at any time, regardless of how fraught with controversy it may be. You have asked how I feel about whiskey. Here is how I stand on the question.
>
> If, when you say whiskey you mean the Devil's brew, the poison scourge, the bloody monster that defiles innocence, dethrones reason, destroys the home, creates misery and poverty... takes the bread from the mouths of little children; if you mean the evil drink that topples the Christian man and woman from the pinnacles of righteous, gracious living into the bottomless pit of degradation and despair, shame and helplessness and hopelessness, then certainly I am against it with all of my power.
>
> But, if, when you say whiskey, you mean the oil of conversation, the philosophic wine, the ale that is consumed when good fellows get together, that puts a song in their hearts and laughter on their lips and the warm glow of contentment in their eyes; if you mean Christmas cheer; if you mean the stimulating drink that puts the spring in the old gentleman's step on a frosty morning; if you mean the drink that enables a man to magnify his joy and his happiness and to forget, if only for a little while, life's great tragedies, and the heartbreaks and sorrows; if you mean that drink, the sale of which pours into our treasuries untold

millions of dollars, which are used to provide tender care for our little crippled children, our blind, our deaf, our dumb, our pitiful aged and infirm, to build highways, hospitals, and schools, then certainly I am in favor of it.

There was no move on Sbarboro's part to join forces with the liquor industry and combine resources in the fight against prohibitionists. Driven by principle and not economic interest, he propounded his unique cure for the chronic drunk. Every arrested drunk was to be sentenced to thirty days in jail and served light wines with his meals. Upon his release, Sbarboro believed the fellow would be converted to temperance and an appreciation of wine, and would, in future, abstain from hard liquor. Backsliders were to be given sixty-day sentences and the same therapy.

Sbarboro spoke with passionate conviction in his battle to bring the good news to the American populace. In 1908 he picked up the fervor of his campaign. He wrote a pamphlet entitled "Temperance vs. Prohibition."[52] It is a compendium of letters from American consuls stationed in Europe as well as letters from the clergy and others in the United States. The introduction reveals the nature of his argument and the depth of his feelings on the subject:

> That drunkenness is one of the great evils with which the United States is afflicted cannot be denied.
>
> For over fifty years the good men and women of this country have sought a remedy for this curse, but as yet none has been found.
>
> To remove this great evil, to bring to the American people the blessings of sobriety and happiness which prevail in the wine-drinking countries, is the object of this book. It suggests a practical remedy that has stood the test in Europe and can be applied in the United States.
>
> Last year I published a book entitled "The Fight for True Temperance" which was so favorably received and in such demand that the edition is now exhausted.
>
> During the past year at the request of the Grape Growers of

California, I have made further investigations of this great question throughout Europe and I am now pleased to lay before my readers incontrovertible proofs as to the efficacy of the true remedy I suggest, by which the evil of drunkenness may be removed from that part of our people addicted to the use of strong alcoholic beverages.

In my travels through the great grape-growing and wine-producing countries of Europe, I found that every man, woman and child uses wine at meals and the people are free from the evil of drunkenness, whilst in the non-wine-producing countries the conditions are the very opposite.

In order that I might convince the American people of these facts, I made it my duty, in all the principal cities which I visited, to call on our representatives, the American Ambassadors and Consuls, and from them obtained official documents which I now offer in this volume to the American public. Much of my success in obtaining these important letters was due to the kindly introduction supplied me by Governor James N. Gillette, of California, which is reproduced on the next page. I also include a number of striking letters and opinions from noted clergymen, doctors, judges, editors, professors, Army and Navy officers, United States officials and other eminent men of our own country.

To further prove the fact that sobriety prevails only in grape-producing countries where wine is within the reach of all classes of people and can be obtained in large quantities, of good quality and at low prices, I have only to point to England, Scotland and Ireland, where drunkenness exists to an alarming extent not alone among the men but also the women. In these countries grapes do not grow and as wine is not produced, strong alcoholic beverages are used by the people.

When crossing the English Channel on my way home, I could not help thinking I was leaving France, Italy, Spain Portugal, Switzerland, Belgium, Austria and Germany, containing over 200,000,000 wine drinkers where intemperance is practically unknown and I was going to the English Nation where, with a population of about 40,000,000 people, drunkenness is so common. Two days after my arrival, in a copy of the *London Times,* I read that during the past year 270,000 people had been arrested for intoxication in the streets of London, 120,000 of whom were women!

What an object lesson this is for our country.

A hundred years ago one of the greatest men of America, President Thomas Jefferson, who had been minister to France and knew of the salutary effect of wine, remarked: "No nation is drunken where wine is cheap and none sober where dearness of wine substitutes ardent spirits as its common beverage."

Now in England, grapes will grow only in hot-houses. Therefore, wine can never be within the reach of the masses. The United States, on the contrary, although it is not generally known, is the land of the vine. California can produce wine as fine as that of any country in Europe, and when the occasion will demand, in as large quantities as France and Italy. Many other states in the Union also produce very excellent wine and will increase their production when the existing obstacles to its free distribution are removed.

The American people should carefully read these letters of our consuls in the great grape-growing countries of Europe. They are unprejudiced testimonials as to the actual conditions that exist. They prove conclusively that when our people will have become accustomed to the general use of wine at table, the United States will be the largest grape-growing and wine-producing nation of the world. Then drunkenness will be reduced to a minimum and the same conditions will prevail as in those countries where wine is universally used by every family at meals.

Signed: Andrea Sbarboro

Thirteen consular letters from seven countries in Europe responded to his request for their observations on drunkenness in the cities and countries of their posting. They were all similar but one letter best illustrates their responses.

AMERICAN CONSULATE
Palermo, Italy
December 18, 1908
Mr. Andrea Sbarboro,
Hotel Trinacria, Palermo.
Dear Sir:

Referring to our conversation of this morning, I have to say that my experience of many years in Italy and southern France, where the native wines form a regular part of the repasts of the inhabitants, is that drunkenness in those countries is of most rare occurrence. The use of such wines would seem to fill the need felt by many for a light stimulating or fortifying beverage and not to lead to a craving for alcohol or to other baneful extremes. Here in Sicily, while the people no doubt have their faults, it is a pleasure to witness their general temperate habits.

Even the usual place where drinks are publicly sold is more often a pasticceria, cake-shop, or a pleasant cafe, which the most respectable persons, including ladies and children, may freely enter. There are no screens put up, there is no concealment of the interior or the inmates, for nothing takes place there requiring concealment. The drinking saloon in an offensive sense can hardly to be said to exist at all.

I beg to remain,
Very truly yours,
William Henry Bishop

A letter from the consul general situated in Marseilles, France, points out that the seaport city did have drunkenness, which he attributed to the drinking bars where strong liquors were served as much as wine. One poignant response from an "abstainer" in the Canary Islands reported that he gave his children, ages four and six, at "every noon meal a quarter of a glass of wine mixed with three quarters water to give them blood, and myself although an abstainer, have been ordered at present time by my doctor to drink a glass of wine at every meal..."

In the spring of 1908 Sbarboro went to Washington to oppose passage of the Littlefield Bill, which would have prohibited shipment of wine and liquor from a wet state into a dry one. On March 6 he appeared before the Judiciary Committee in a packed hearing room which held a sizable contingent from the Women's Christian Temperance Union. Sbarboro didn't pull any punches. He suggested to the committee that if small children were allowed to drink a thimbleful of wine mixed in a glass of water at mealtime, they would never experience drunkenness and the nation would get rid of that evil. The scandalized ladies needed no more to convince them that Sbarboro was evil incarnate.

Andrea made enemies with equal aplomb among the temperance ladies, the liquor industry, and anyone else who would ban wine from the nation's table. In an article written in 1916,[53] Sbarboro's growing frustration shows through:

> I was interested in seeing the other day that the famous Stanford Vineyard at Vina was being pulled up, and the land to be used for other purposes.
>
> Mr. Stanford, as we all know, was a great man for California. Among his industries he went into the raising of grapes, expecting to produce a fine wine as those produced in Europe, but whilst he understood all about the building of railroads and transportation, evidently he knew nothing about grapes, so he took the advice of some supposed vineyardist, who knew still less than he did, and set out the immense vineyard at Vina on level land suitable for irrigation[N-10] and the result was that those grapes could not be used to make light table wine, but they were used to make brandy, with which to fortify the strong sherry and port wines.
>
> I have often wondered how the principal of the Stanford University could prohibit the use of uninjurious light table wines within three miles of the university and at the same time receive his salary from the grapes sold by the university at Vina, which are only fit for use in making intoxicating liquors and to fortify sherry and port wines. I see, however, that at last the vines at Vina are finally being

pulled up and the land used for other industries, which can be
readily done in this case, having the facilities for irrigation, but which
could never be done on hillside lands which grow the fine grapes
to make the choice quality of light non-intoxicating wines.

Whether or not it was justifiable, Sbarboro's pique was understandable. It was Stanford who had poured hundred of thousands of dollars into planting vines on his 3,825-acre ranch twenty miles south of
Red Bluff, California,[54] causing great distress for grape growers
throughout the state. A link could be made between the enormously
wealthy Stanford and the demise of the Icaria-Speranza colony next
door to Asti. The Icarians, the ISAC and Leland Stanford had each
gone into the grape business in 1881. By 1886, the Icarians had cleared
land, built homes and planted grains and fruit orchards for their consumption. Their cash crop was to be wine grapes and eventually
wine. Within the first five years of their moving onto the eight hundred acres immediately adjacent to Asti on the north, the Icarians had
about 100 acres planted to grapes.

ISAC, with considerably more land suitable for vineyard, and a
goal devoted to planting and operating vineyards, had about 700
acres planted by 1886, a little more than one half producing a commercial crop.

Stanford, on the other hand, spent $300,000 in 1882 to prepare the
land and plant vines. By the summer of that year, 1,200 acres were
planted. The next year, 1,500 more acres were planted to wine grapes.
By 1884, while the Icarians struggled to make their dreams a reality
and the Italians continued to plant vineyards at Asti, Stanford harvested 1,200 tons of fruit. It was, of course, no contest. The Icarians
folded in 1886 and Sbarboro, close to despair at the falling grape
prices, went back to his directors, got more money and built a winery. At Vina, they built a winery in 1885 but it was never capable of
processing all of the grapes from nearly four thousand acres, and
Stanford remained in the grape business.

Sbarboro's reference to the university is interesting. Leland Stanford
and his wife, Jane, had established Stanford University at Palo Alto in

1885 in memory of their son, who had died a year earlier. The Vina property was turned over to the university as a source of income for the new college. Ironically, Mrs. Stanford and the university administration were sympathetic to the drys. In 1890 the entire crop went to the distillery and Vina was the world's largest distiller of grape brandy, which accounted for Sbarboro's remarks.

Still, there is some question of just how much of university president David Jordan's salary came from Vina. Jordan complained that Vina was costing the university five hundred dollars a day. By 1919, economics and pressure from prohibitionists caused the University to sell Vina for $2 million, a sum considerably less than Stanford had invested in the property.

Sbarboro helped defeat the Littlefield Bill. but he could only slow the momentum of a divided nation headed for Prohibition. America went dry in stages. In 1907 Georgia became the first state to ban the manufacture, sale or use of alcoholic beverages. By 1915, six more states, all in the South, had enacted similar legislation. On December 18, 1917, Congress passed the Eighteenth Amendment. Under compromises worked out in Congress, the States would have seven years to ratify and, in a concession to the "wet" congressmen, the liquor industry would have one year to close down from the date of ratification. It took the states only thirteen months to ratify the amendment, and on January 16, 1919, the Eighteenth Amendment became law. For a while, government "by the people" was turned on its head. It was one of those unique times in a democracy when the minority ruled the majority.

On October 10, 1919, Congress passed the Volstead Act, which made provisions for enforcing the Eighteenth Amendment. On January 16, 1920, one year after the amendment was ratified, the American people were forbidden to manufacture, sell or transport any intoxicating liquor. The lights no longer burned in America's wineries. The wineries remained dark until December 5, 1933, a period of almost fourteen years.

13

A Winery in Every Basement

We must be hopeful, you and I.
Light always follows the rain,
Only once in life is the dark forever,
even then we can look to
eternal sunshine.

—Anon

WITH PROHIBITION A REALITY, Edoardo Seghesio now bore the added burden of a crushing debt. He had mortgaged the ranch, borrowed from family members, and somehow raised the down payment to acquire Asti. Now he had to raise $52,500 in a little less than one year. There would be only one harvest during that time and Edoardo wasn't even sure if he could sell the grapes. But son-in-law Prati, seeing a challenge where others saw ruin, took charge and that fall the Seghesio-Prati team sent thousands of gallons of grape concentrate from the 1919 crush to New York. Prati had planned to be first on the Prohibition market, but he was too early. There was still wine enough in family cellars, as consumers had stocked up. Not a drop of the perishable juice was sold. Pete Seghesio, Edoardo's son, estimates the family lost close to $100,000 (he cannot account for the source of funds or how much involved cash)—and they had owned Asti less than six months.

The mood at Asti after the harvest of 1919 was close to despair. Edoardo was 59 years old. A fifth child had been born earlier that year, adding to the responsibilities of Edoardo and Angela. There were three older children still at home, ranging in age from 14 to 23. At least they could help with the work in the vineyard. Things were not that easy for Prati either. He and Ida had a young family: daughter Josephine was five and son Edward was just two years old.

Seghesio and Prati owned nearly 1500 acres of grapes. Their first foray into the alcohol-less wine market was a failure. Money was tight, indeed, bordering on nonexistent. Christmas of 1919 would not have been a good time, nor Asti a good place, for a meeting of the Women's Christian Temperance Union. But it was Asti itself that saved the Seghesio family. The golden land of vines riding rolling hills to the edge of tree-covered mountains continued to issue her siren call, and the Rossi twins were no match for her seductiveness. It was a perilous investment that dark winter of 1919–1920, but the Rossi twins wanted in, and the prayers of the desperate Seghesio were answered.

By the end of February, which probably seemed like the longest month, rather than the shortest, to Seghesio, a deal was struck. Although the twins would not come up with their money for a few more months, the four shook hands and the deal was done. Edoardo Seghesio, Enrico Prati, Robert Rossi and Edmund Rossi would each own a one-quarter share of a new company, the Asti Grape Products (AGP) Company.

Asti Grape Products would acquire the Asti vineyards from Seghesio for $200,000.[55] Seghesio and Prati didn't have to put up any cash and the Rossi twins would each pay $50,000 for their one-quarter interest. Seghesio would pay off the outstanding mortgage of $52,500 owed to the California Wine Association and together with his son-in-law would still have cash to raise their share of the operating money for the new partnership. In less than one year, Seghesio had acquired Asti for $127,500 and would sell it for $200,000. After a miserable winter, spring came early to the Seghesio family in 1920.

The four partners agreed to put up $10,000 each to give the new company $40,000 working capital. Once again Edoardo could sleep at night and enjoy life among his vines.

Edmund Rossi would be president and Robert was made secretary and vice-president. Anxious to have everything in order, Ed Rossi had Seghesio's deed from the CWA purchase recorded in the County of Sonoma on March 2. The following month, on April 12, 1920, Robert purchased the Cloverdale Wine Company from the CWA. The Cloverdale Wine Company had specialized in making wooden picking tubs and other boxes. They would make the lugs for shipping grapes. On April 15, just three days later, Seghesio sold a one-half interest in his Asti holdings to Robert Rossi. The reason for this transaction is unknown. Present Seghesio family members were not even aware of the transaction.

We can only speculate as to why brother Edmund didn't participate in either of the two purchases. Possibly Seghesio needed money to pay property taxes that were due April 10 and the April 15 deal was an aborted attempt to get money to Seghesio in time to pay the taxes. Perhaps Ed Rossi was unwilling or unable to come up with his $60,000 during that late winter/early spring, but on May 1, 1920, Edmund produced his share and the Asti Grape Products company formally acquired Asti. Another deal was also struck that winter. On February 10, 1920, Bob Rossi, fresh out of the Army, married Nellie Mahony. Bob's pretty Irish bride must have wondered what she had gotten into. But Rossi, after two years in the Army, was making up for lost time. The four partners and their families turned to face an uncertain future.

At the start of Prohibiton, the growers of premium wine grapes such as those grown at Asti were in a precarious position. They could not turn to the raisin market—that market was already oversupplied. Besides, the cool, sometimes wet climate of the northern California counties made Asti a precarious location for producing raisins. The table grape market was also out. Just as a horse bred for racing cannot be used before the plow, the wine grape is a different fruit from its cousin, the table grape. Table grapes have been developed for their large berries and few seeds. Indeed, the most popular table grapes are seedless.

The wine grape is, for the most part, quite the opposite. The classic examples are the royalty of the wine world, the Cabernet Sauvignon and Chardonnay grapes. These grapes owe their highly desirable varietal character to their small size. Research has demonstrated that the flavoroids in the grape berry are located exclusively in the skin. The finest palates in the world could not differentiate between the white Chardonnay and red Cabernet grape if all they could sample was the grape pulp. It is a short exercise by mathematicians to demonstrate that the smaller the berry the greater the concentration of flavoroids in the berry and, of course, the opposite proves true.

Two other attributes keep wine grapes out of the table-grape market in spite of their enhanced flavor. First, the wine grape is filled with seeds. The second, more subtle, lies at the heart and soul of the wine grape. It is the presence of natural fruit acids that separates wine grapes from table grapes. If one were to blind taste a table grape and a wine grape, both equally ripe, the table grape would taste notably sweeter even though it might contain only ten percent sugar compared to the wine grape's twenty percent. This apparent anomaly is due to the presence of malic and tartaric acid in the wine grape which mask the sensation of sweetness on the tongue. The acid components are therefore a detriment to grapes intended to be eaten as fresh fruit. On the other hand, fruit acids in the wine grape are responsible for many of the most desirable characteristics in wine.

There is one more significant difference between grapes grown in the cooler north-coast regions of California and those grown in California's great Central Valley. The Central Valley is blessed with deep soils and seemingly endless blue skies and sunshine. When water for irrigation is added to the mix, the valley becomes a cornucopia of fruits and vegetables. Under these conditions, the grapevine thrives, producing prodigious crops. In the cooler, more barren soils of Asti, however, the vine struggles to produce a crop half that of the vine luxuriating in the warmer climate of the Central Valley.

Consequently the Asti vineyardists, faced with comparably low yields, could not compete with the growers from Fresno and other Central Valley areas.[N-11]

Edmund moved back to San Francisco to join brother Bob in setting up an office at 12 Geary Street. Enrico Prati would stay at Asti, where he would serve as vice-president in charge of production. Thus Enrico would be where he had been since coming to the United States: Asti, California. Within a year they would fill another spot on the team with the hiring of Bartolomeo Coppo. Coppo had joined ISC in 1919 and in a brief period had impressed the Rossis with his exceptional palate. After Repeal, he would become cellar master at Asti, in charge of making the blends.

The partnership had a more-than-ample supply of grapes and they were adequately financed. Outlets for their product were established in San Francisco and the major cities in the East. Most importantly, their product would enter the market with a reputation for quality established over thirty years.

The next question, one shared by all growers in California, was what to sell. A household was allowed to have two hundred gallons of wine on their premises, but the family had to make the wine themselves. The situation was a marketing executive's nightmare. There was neither time available to do test marketing nor experience upon which to devise a realistic marketing strategy. A perishable crop was already appearing on the vines. The attempt to market juice had been a nightmare. Robert thought that the idea of shipping grapes by rail to the Eastern markets was absurd. He didn't believe that millions of people would become winemakers in their own homes. But if the messy part of the operation was done by professionals in proper equipment, Rossi felt that the consumer could handle the fermentation. Besides, shipping juice or juice concentrate was easier and safer than shipping highly perishable grapes.

With Prati's 1919 experience still fresh in their minds, the company leaned toward offering concentrate, even though that meant a vacuum-pan operation that none of them had ever done before. Ultimately they offered all three products, juice, concentrate and, by far their most successful product, grapes. The three businessmen entered the crush of 1920 with considerable uncertainty.

As it turned out they, along with their fellow growers across the state, failed to account for that part of man's nature nurtured over five thousand years to change grapes into wine. In fact, Asti Grape Products found itself facing a bonanza. With foreign competition eliminated and the vicarious excitement of furtive fermentations exerting itself in dark basements, wine grapes were soon in great demand. During the next six years, the price of grapes would rise to astounding heights. The nation might be dry, but the wine-grape business was better than ever. Growers found it easy to relate to this parody of a popular song printed in the *New York World*.[56]

> Mother makes brandy from cherries
> Pop distills whisky and gin
> Sister sells wine from the grapes on our vine—
> Good grief, how the money rolls in!

San Francisco was a strong market for AGP. They would ship grapes to the city in boxcars. Customers went to the freight yard where boxcars from many areas would be sitting on sidings. The fruit was sold directly out of the cars. Asti grapes commanded a premium and the buyers learned to look for the Northwestern Pacific cars that carried AGP fruit. Many buyers would take their fruit to the AGP Company crushing plant. The plant was situated in a corrugated steel building at Davis and Broadway. Here the grapes went through a stemmer-crusher and the resultant juice was taken home in fifteen to twenty-gallon barrels.

Alternatively, the home winemaker could purchase grape bricks. The bricks consisted of compressed grape pomace saturated with grape concentrate which, when reconstituted with water, made grape juice with pomace. These bricks were kept in cold storage or under refrigeration for sale all year around. As part of the packaging and labeling of either juice or bricks, instructions were given how *not* to make wine. One was told that if the vial of yeast which was supplied with the grape juice should by chance come into contact with the juice, the grape juice would ferment, resulting in the production of wine. Of course, this process would be accelerated if the juice were kept in a warm place, like proximity to the kitchen stove.

After a sale, a service contract was entered into between the buyer and AGP salesman Mr. Leo Fazzi. Mr. Fazzi would supervise the fermentation process, aging and subsequent clarifying, filtering and bottling of the wine. In keeping with AGP's "arms length" distance from manufacturing alcohol, the contract was between Fazzi and the buyer; AGP was not involved. Sales brochures described Colony grape juice as a product to be used in preparing a beverage reminiscent of the "good old days."

Fermentation by nonprofessionals, done in their garages or basements, was an uncertain thing. Home winemakers often found it difficult to get the deep red colors they were accustomed to in professionally made wine. Since this was important to most home winemakers, a new grape variety became important in the marketplace. Alicante Bouchet, one of the few wine grapes to have red juice (most red grapes have colorless pulp), became popular with the Eastern market. The grape also traveled well. It did not suffer berry breaking and bruising during the three-thousand-mile trip to the East Coast in a rail boxcar.

A whole generation of grower children learned to pack Alicante Bouchet grapes carefully in their new wooden boxes, since the colored grape juice, if spilled from a broken grape, ruined the appearance of the box. But the grape made wine without character or merit, and it is to their credit that AGP never planted the varietal or shipped any in an effort to cater to the consuming public. Indeed, no new varietals were planted to satisfy what the Rossis felt was an interim market. They continued to grow premium wine grapes and ship them to the eastern markets just as they always had.

The Asti partners maintained consistency by using their established distributor in New York, Gambarelli and Davitto. Over the years G&D had worked in close cooperation and harmony with Italian Swiss Colony. The Colony used to ship on an open account to G&D, meaning the Colony would get paid when G&D had the money. Now

G&D got the opportunity to do ISC a favor in return. The grape harvest in the northern California growing regions typically takes place over a six-week period starting September 1. Tens of thousands of tons are picked during that brief period. While other growers would be forced to sell their fruit during the fall maelstrom, G&D would place AGP's fruit in barrels and freeze them. The fruit could then be defrosted and sold at a more advantageous time, possibly two or three years after the grapes had been harvested. The freezing and added sulfur dioxide kept the fruit sound.

In 1924 the Asti Grape Products Company acquired the Italian Swiss Colony name from the California Wine Association and AGP was able to fully capitalize on the old brand name. However, CWA wouldn't release the valuable trade names Golden State or Asti Rouge, although both of these names were directly attributable to the Rossi family. By the end of 1924, ISC ads for Asti products began appearing.

Also appearing for the first time in 1924 was Ed and Beatrice's (Brandt) first child, Ed Rossi, Jr. Twin brother and partner Bob and his wife, Nellie (Mahony), had presented Bob Junior to the world in 1921. Both of the cousins would follow the course set by their grandfather and fathers into the wine business. The two little ones would eventually carry the ISC flag nearly into the 21st century. It is a nostalgic coincidence that their births bracketed the passing of the two men most responsible for creating that flag in the first place. Marco Fontana, the Colony's first president and the financial bedrock upon which the Colony survived the misfortunes of the 19th century, died in 1922. Andrea Sbarboro, whose passion created ISC, passed away on February 28, 1923.

As the twenties rolled by, the demand for grapes increased, leaving growers to ponder the inexplicable—a thriving wine industry with no wineries. The grower reaction was as swift as it was predictable. New planting began almost immediately after the start of Prohibition. By the late twenties, wine-grape acreage had doubled. But a moment's reflection and the 20/20 vision afforded by hindsight would have suggested an uncertain future. Every basement in every house and apartment in "Little Italys" across the country was producing at

Celebrating Repeal, November 24, 1933. Courtesy of Beringer archives, Asti, California.

least two hundred gallons of wine each year. Whereas a family might readily consume one or two gallons a week, they could never handle the four gallons that it would have taken to equal their legal production quota.

Inventories began to build. Wives and mothers grew tired of corks popping in the night and the aroma from foaming barrels in the basement or garage, not to mention the flies. The mood of the country was changing. Formation of the Association Against the Prohibition Amendment in 1927 served notice of changing public sentiment. By 1929 several state legislatures had repealed state prohibition laws. The crash of 1929 resulted in an emerging concern for jobs. Postmaster James Farley announced that Prohibition was costing the country one billion dollars per year in lost jobs and tax revenue.

Perhaps the Italian ladies saw Repeal coming, for starting in 1927 grape demand dropped precipitously and over the next five years growers suffered the same crushing economic conditions that were sweeping the rest of the nation. By the beginning of 1933, America was openly thirsting for Repeal. During the 1932 political conventions, both parties declared in favor of Repeal. In February 1933, Congress voted to send the 21st Amendment to the Constitution to the states for ratification, thereby repealing the Eighteenth Amendment. The process of the individual state ratifications proceeded throughout the year. While the state total had not reached the required 36 by harvest, it was clear that repeal was certain, the only question being when. That year, the Asti Grape Product Company, once again named Italian Swiss Colony, made wine. It was the first time in fourteen years that the fermentation tanks at Asti were put into service.

Did the Colony produce any illegal wine during Prohibition? Some say they did, but there is no confirming evidence to support these allegations. Given its size and broad public image, it would have been difficult, but not impossible, for ISC to have produced a little bootleg wine.

The Rossis had waited fourteen years for this moment and they wanted to be the first to reintroduce wine to the country. They knew, of course, of the publicity that would attend the first wines released after Repeal. But the 1933 vintage, particularly the red wine, would not be ready for sale if Repeal came close to harvest. The Rossis solved this problem by purchasing wine that had been made in 1919. In fact, the twins were anticipating Repeal. In March 1933, they purchased 150,000 gallons of wine made in 1919 from the Peter & Caroline Holst Winery in Dry Creek Valley.[57] The wine was a blend of Zinfandel, Petit Sirah and smaller amounts of Alicante Bouchet and Grenache. They paid the princely sum of five and a half cents per gallon for the wine.

Like almost all wine stored during Prohibition, the Holst wine, after fourteen years in an oak tank, had likely suffered bacterial attack which would have resulted in an unsatisfactorily high level of volatile acidity (acetic acid). More than likely, the wine was suitable only for blending. It was the end of the Holst winery, which had been founded one year before Sbarboro founded Asti. (Holst was the second winery formed in Dry Creek Valley.) The plan at the Colony was to have wine on hand for immediate shipment when Repeal came. The Holst wine was used to blend with the Colony's wine so that the young wines could be smoothed out with the 1919 vintage. The young wine would serve to dilute the vinegary character of the older wine. On December 5, 1933, the state of Utah joined 35 other states in approving the 21st Amendment. Repeal was official. Sanity had returned to the nation.

ISC was ready. On Labor Day (three months before Repeal), the winery had begun accepting grapes for the '33 crush. Over two hundred thousand gallons of wine were made, both white and red. On the 24th of November, a gala celebration took place at Asti. The Bureau of Alcohol, Tobacco and Firearms was on holiday that day, for they failed to notice, probably by looking the other way, that wine was served openly and in copious amounts. Anne Matteoli, a student at Cloverdale High School in 1933, recalled the day in vivid detail.[58]

> November 24, 1933, while I was attending Cloverdale High School,
> all of the students were asked to go to the Italian Swiss Colony to

take part in the celebration of the repeal of the Eighteenth Amendment and the first shipment of wine from their winery. All of us girls were given Italian Swiss costumes to wear—red, white and green. We were photographed by many newspapers and Pathe newsreel. Tables of wine were set up and there were banners on the buildings. I was one of the two girls to roll the first barrel of wine into the waiting "boxcar." Mrs. Ida Prati, the Superintendent's wife, broke a bottle of champagne on the railroad steam engine that had banners on it too—while the steam whistles were blowing and cheers from the crowd added to the merriment. It was a very exciting day. We had all been hoping for Repeal to pass. At school in my locker, I showed a license plate type of advertising of the Repeal, which I still have. I remember a group of us going to Healdsburg to the movie so we could see ourselves on the Pathe newsreel. We felt very important.

Forty-five thousand gallons of wine were shipped that day from the 1933 crush. But Joe Vercelli, who assisted cellar master Bart Coppo, doubts if any of the 1933 vintage was ready for shipment that soon. More than likely the wine that was purchased from Holst, freshened up with 3.2 percent wine made at the Colony the year before, was shipped out that day. While drinking wine was still against the law, the winery was permitted to make and ship wine prior to Repeal. They were not, however, permitted to sell wine before December 5, 1933.

While toasts were drunk with eyes facing the future, one man all but ignored in the joyous celebration could only relive the forgotten past. Edoardo Seghesio was now 73 years old and in failing health. How much pain would his life have been spared if the Women's Christian Temperance Union had been named the "Tolerance Union"? He had started work for the Colony 47 years earlier, only five years after Andrea Sbarboro had decided that Asti was to be the place for his noble idea. Seghesio had planted Colony vines, met his future wife, Angela, through the Colony, had sold grapes to the Colony, and eventually owned the place. His oldest daughter, Ida, was married to Enrico Prati, a man who would help lead the winery into the now so promising future.

But at this time of celebration Edoardo was just an onlooker. His family had sold their quarter interest one month earlier to Adrian J. Merele. The Merele family, of the Simmons Mattress Company, was related to the Rossi family; P. C. Rossi and Adrian's father were cousins. Fontana and Sbarboro were gone and Seghesio would soon join them. The baton had been passed.

14

A People at Peace

Who is rich? He that is content.
—*Benjamin Franklin*

O NCE AGAIN IN THE WINE BUSINESS, the Colony families began planting new roots in the Asti soil. Starting in the late 1920's, the Rossi sisters, P. C.'s daughters, began to reinvest in the Colony. During the 1930's the Sbarboro family, which still owned Villa Pompeii, began to acquire shares in the AGP Company. The twins and Prati were diluting their share of ownership but they needed money to modernize and expand. Pee Wee Sbarboro, as the diminutive Alfredo, eldest son of Andrea Sbarboro, was called when out of earshot, became more involved. Alfredo, a senior vice-president at the Bank of America, served as a financial consultant and eventually took charge of special projects, generally involving new winery or vineyard purchases.

Life at Asti renewed its special rhythms as the winery itself came to life. Wages were tiny but they were equal to the little asked by the Colony families. Their wants satisfied, the people of Asti were content and at peace. The company built six new homes directly across the street from Bartolomeo's house and along the little creek that ran south of the Colony House. Each house had three bedrooms, a living room, kitchen with a pantry, one bathroom and a laundry porch. Each family planted grape arbors in their backyards to shade the outdoor dining table. Each house had a large vegetable garden and there was much friendly competition to see who could grow the largest specimens. Many had chicken coops and rabbit hutches. The cookhouse was only one hundred yards away, and on summer evenings smoke from the outdoor kitchens mingled with the aromas drifting from the cookhouse to fill the village air with the fragrance of dinner. Barelli bread and Colony wine graced every table. The bread, baked behind the cookhouse, was delivered to Cloverdale and Geyserville, and the locals figured it was better than the Colony's wines. After dinner the cookhouse became a social center. Occasionally the neighbors put on plays. The olive trees along the now-paved Redwood Highway and the orange trees in front of the superintendent's house completed a scene that could have been a small village in Italy.

Two miles south, in Chianti, Angela Seghesio spent afternoons on her front porch sewing new clothes and repairing old ones. The porch was shady, escaping the afternoon sun which sank in the western sky behind the house. The Sangiovese vines planted by her husband before the turn of the century grew up close to the house. They stretched away from the porch toward the highway a few hundred yards to the east. Beyond the road another fifty yards, the Northwestern Pacific railroad paralleled the highway. The afternoon train, now up to speed since leaving Geyserville a few minutes earlier, would charge across the landscape, momentarily shattering the quiet world in front of Angela. The train was never on time, but it was close enough to give Angela a sense that dinnertime would soon be upon her household.

Occasionally, the train would rumble to a stop at the tiny Chianti station and Angela would watch to see who was coming. If the passenger was wearing a tie and jacket, he was coming from the city, and if he started toward the Seghesio home, Angela knew it was a buyer looking to purchase wine.[N-12] Businesswoman Angela Seghesio would call to one of the kids within hearing distance to quickly kill a chicken. There's going to be company for dinner! Over chicken cacciatore and ample Sangiovese wine, a deal would be struck. The sated wine buyer was happy to sleep off the feast on the evening train back to San Francisco.

The kids continued to attend school at the little Washington School. The school itself was situated not more than thirty yards west of the tracks. The one-room schoolhouse had been built in 1872, the year the railroad reached Cloverdale. It was a sturdy, wooden building with a raised wooden floor, pitched roof, windows on all sides and a homey porch stretching across the front wall. In the beginning it had one large room with the teacher's desk about one third of the way down the sixty-foot building. A wood stove sat in the middle of the room several feet behind the teacher. A door at the back of the room led to the playground and, on a rise some fifty feet further back, the outhouse. The outhouse was used throughout the life of the schoolhouse although it was later refurbished with flush toilets.

The school had been sparsely attended during the 1870's, but the coming of the Colony in 1881 changed that. By 1920, it was essentially a school for the children of Colony employees. There were typically about fifty students, all of them Italian. The teacher was a classic old-maid schoolmarm who came from Petaluma but lived during the school week in Colony housing at Asti. She never owned a car. Like her students, she walked to school along the railroad tracks. Her name was Kate Geohegan and she was Irish, not Italian. But that was okay with the Italians. Miss Geohegan was a strong Catholic and she took her faith most seriously. Above all, she could be counted on to give the kids a good education.

Even though she went home to Petaluma on weekends, Miss Geohegan seemed to know if any of the children missed Sunday Mass. Monday morning thus became a day of reckoning. If you didn't go to church Sunday, "Why not?" That your parents didn't go was no excuse. If a student could walk to school each day, surely he or she could have walked to El Carmelo, the little church close to the Colony House—never mind that the church was three miles distant from the

Washington School, circa 1945. Built in 1872, the one-room elementary school operated close to one hundred years before closing in 1966. Eucalyptus trees (partially visibile to the right), whose branches once helped start the school's wood stove, still stand before the now-vacant site. Credit: Beringer archives, Asti, California.

homes in Chianti. There was no worry about kids of other faiths being left out when Miss Geohegan led the entire student body across the vineyards and past the winery on the afternoons when she taught catechism in the church; the entire school was Catholic.

Miss Geohegan was more feared than loved, but she devoted her life to the children of Asti. Her goal was to be respected, not loved, and if a little bit of fear crept in, that was part of her job. She saw her responsibility to teach this community of uneducated immigrants and their children and she poured her heart and soul into that obligation. Not only did she attend to the children's education and religious needs, but she taught the adults English and prepared them for citizenship as well. It is unlikely that this single Irish lady had any social life living in Asti five days a week and Petaluma two days. Her high ideals and notion of setting a "proper example" at Asti necessarily kept her an outsider to the warm and friendly Italians. She would surely have been accepted in the Asti community if she could have let her hair down, but she had her dignity to maintain and she simply could not fraternize with the families of her students.

In 1922, the now overcrowded schoolroom was divided in two. A young woman fresh out of college was hired to assist Miss Geohegan. Her name was Edna Cuneo and she came from Healdsburg. Edna, just 21, moved in with Miss Geohegan. Like Kate Geohegan, Edna would go home for weekends. But she was years apart, both literally and figuratively, from Miss Geohegan, and she could not stand living the Spartan life at Asti. One weekend Edna confided her unhappiness to her mother. Edna's mother laid it out for her young daughter. Edna had two choices, her mother explained: either you find another job or you buy a car. In 1922 buying a car, particularly for a young woman, was a big step. But Edna had spunk. Faced with the reality laid out by her mother, Edna bought a car and learned to drive it. Driving to Asti each day, she became one of the first commuters on what would seventy years later become the widely traveled 101 freeway.

But Kate Geohegan, beneath her stern professional demeanor, was as human as her students. Servant to her pride, she had for years worn an ill-fitting red wig. Having grown accustomed to the manner of Geohegan, Edna, like the children, was not prepared for the surprise the rigid Miss Kate laid on them one morning before class. Although Geohegan did not drive, she got a ride to and from Petaluma every weekend. One weekend her auto was in an accident and Miss Geohegan was injured and shaken up. She did not return to school for almost two weeks.

The morning she returned, Miss Cuneo and a few students were there to greet her. The group was shocked silent when Miss Geohegan walked to her desk and removed her wig to reveal a head of very gray hair. Kate Geohegan, the woman who had strived for perfection all her life, still couldn't let go of the lie she had been telling herself for years. As if no one realized that she had long worn a wig, she announced to the incredulous Miss Cuneo and the students that her hair had turned white as a result of the accident and she now wore a wig. Cuneo swallowed a grin and the kids snickered. The only one fooled was Kate Geohegan.

By the mid-1920's, the national Great Depression had finally reached Asti. AGP began to cut back and the population at Asti began to drop. Edna Cuneo left the little school in 1925 for a teaching career in a suburb south of San Francisco. Kate Geohegan retired in 1928 after teaching two generations of Asti schoolchildren the three Rs and their parents the rudiments of being American. The two-room schoolhouse once again became a one-room schoolhouse. Gone was the potbellied stove. No longer did the eighth graders have to gather dried eucalyptus leaves to start the kindling to start the oak logs in a mostly futile attempt to get the room warm by the start of class on cold winter mornings. Now an oil stove sat beneath the flue, but it had an even more difficult time keeping the schoolroom warm on cold days. Miss Geohegan was replaced by Miss Pacheco, who was followed after just one year by Miss Shear, and the record fades after Miss Shear. The class of 1966 was the last to close the door to the old schoolhouse. The abandoned building stood for eight years before burning to the ground, the smoke carrying everything away except the memories.

Alexis Carrey, fresh out of school, joined the Colony on September 10, 1935.[59] He was paid twenty cents per hour for a 48-hour work week, and was thankful for the job. These were the 1930's, the tough depression years. ISC was, of course, in the middle of crush when young Carrey came on board. The crush has always been a time of hard work and long hours. Even today it is not unusual for the winemaker to set up a couch or some kind of bed in a remote corner of the winery for the many nights when he will not get home.

At Asti during the thirties, the crush went on 24 hours a day. Carrey's workday was supposed to begin at 4:00 A.M., when he would begin weighing in grapes being delivered to the winery, and end at noon, completing an eight-hour day. This schedule lasted a few days before he found himself staying over to 2:00 P.M., then 4:00 P.M., then to 5:00 P.M. Often he was called back in to work from 7:00 P.M. to 10:00 P.M. At the end of the month, Carrey's paycheck was greater than that of either of the co-office managers, who were paid by the month, and who during crush worked 7:00 A.M. to 2:00 A.M.

Mr. Prati, the plant superintendent, came to Carrey and Alexis remembers well what happened next. "I remember Mr. Prati patting me on the back and saying: 'Alex, you are a fine boy. You don't smoke, you don't drink and you don't chase women.'" Carrey remembers thinking, "I don't know how I could have done those things... I had no time." Alex thanked Mr. Prati for the compliments but not for the new arrangement: Carrey was put on the monthly payroll at $75 per month. Alex knew what had happened. From then on, he would be working sixteen to eighteen hours a day and get paid for eight. Carrey deeply respected Enrico Prati nevertheless. "He did not ask you to do something that he himself would not do. I would be at work at 4:00 A.M. Enrico Prati would already be there. When the co-office managers left at 2:00 A.M. the following day, Mr. Prati was still there. When did he sleep?"

The post office, under postmaster Enrico Prati, was once again active. Prati was the fourth postmaster since the post office opened on March 24, 1888, under postmaster Ciacomo Gaggers. Andrea Sbarboro and Edmund Rossi had each had their turn in the years before Prati, who eventually held the post for 29 years. Just north of the cookhouse, on the highway, was the blacksmith shop. Diego Petruzzi, the blacksmith, was kept busy shoeing horses and repairing farm equipment.

Across the street and just north of the superintendent's house was the barn, built in 1894. In its day it was a beauty. The barn housed 32 two-team horses and several cows. Up until the late 1930's, the vineyards were run with horse-drawn equipment. By 1940 the horses were gone, replaced by tractors. Petruzzi's father, no longer needed around the blacksmith's shop, took care of the fifteen dairy cows which provided milk for the cookhouse. Extra milk was sold to the families living at Asti.

In 1917, Rose and Paul Pellegrini, both employed by ISC, got caught in the layoffs as CWA prepared for Prohibition. Rather than leave Asti, they approached Dr. de Vecchi, who owned the empty house across the highway, close to the Rossi villa. The wealthy de Vecchi had retired and moved to New York. The Pellegrinis had no money, but with the optimism typical of the residents at Asti, they proposed to move in and open a grocery store, and in a few years they would be able to pay de Vecchi for the property.

The doctor no longer used the house at Asti and he was willing to help the young couple. They started a grocery store in what had been de Vecchi's tank house. Shortly afterward, Rose's brother Henry (Hank) Del Sarto came up from San Francisco to help out. They later merged, and by 1933 Hank drove an old truck that delivered goods to the houses in Asti and kids to the schoolhouse. By the 1960's, Paul's youngest son, Carlo, was running the store. The Asti families merely had to dial "TWinbrook 4-5487" to have grocery items delivered to their homes. The Asti grocery store became a neighborhood hub. The Pellegrinis later added a machine shop, a pool table, and eventually a service station.

And, of course, there was the little church, Madonna Del Carmine, sitting next door to Coppo's house. The church stood roughly at the center of things, which was fitting, for it was the center of religious and social life at Asti. Everything was within walking distance of the church, except the Rossi house, which was three quarters of a mile distant, and the Lucca ranch houses, which were about a mile and a half across the rolling hills to the distant southwest corner of the Asti property. Sbarboro, had he lived, would have been happy for his people.

The thirties were terrible times across the depression-stricken country. But the people at Asti were eating apples, not selling them. The men living at the cookhouse paid ninety cents per day for room and board. They were earning twenty to twenty-five cents an hour and working a forty-eight hour week, so that their weekly salary was typically ten dollars, and room and board totaled six dollars and thirty cents.

Anyone working at the Colony but not living at the cookhouse could order lunch from the cookhouse kitchen. The meals were delivered in ten-inch oval aluminum canisters which measured about eight inches high. A soup, nearly always some version of minestrone, filled the lower half of the canister. An oval sleeve with a bottom plate slipped into the upper part of the canister above the hot soup. The sleeve contained a steak, potatoes and a second vegetable. A cover fit over the top. The soup served to keep the meal hot. The cost for this meal, delivered to the shop or office, was 25 cents.

Although there was some flow of goods to and from Asti by truck, the Colony, its residents and the winery, depended upon the Northwestern Pacific Railroad. Railway Express had an office at the winery operated by Colony employees. Lou Pellegrini, the office manager, and Alexis Carrey shared this duty. Mail and Railway Express packages arrived twice daily, about 6:00 A.M. on the northbound train and around 3:30 P.M. on the train headed south. If there were no incoming packages, the mail pouch would be simply thrown from the train, which would not stop.

Outgoing mail was a little tricky. The mail pouch would be hung on the "flycatcher" alongside the track. With the train traveling at full speed, the postal worker on the train would reach out with a V-shaped device and snatch the bag from the flycatcher. If there were packages to ship, Carrey or possibly the company watchman would go out to the middle of the tracks and flag the train to a stop. They could do this only during daylight hours, so packages typically went out on the afternoon train. The mail car and a separate Railway Express car were attached at the rear of the passenger cars. When passenger service ended in 1955, postal and express service came by truck.

If the nation suffered through the Great Depression, ISC was experiencing prodigious success. In 1937, ISC enjoyed the distinction of being the largest producer of dry wines in the United States. ISC would soon reach a capacity of eight and one-half million gallons, "larger than any winery, dry or sweet, in the United States."[60]

15

The Cavaliere

You'll have no scandal while you dine,
But honest talk and wholesome wine.
—Alfred Lord Tennyson

ASTI WAS THE CREATION of Andrea Sbarboro. He was a complex man, a man who dared to march to music of his own choosing. He was an elitist who demanded respect for his position in society but he would, from his own pocket, pay the immigration fees for many of his unnamed employees at Asti. Sbarboro the banker had a socialist streak and he read avidly the leading labor reformers of the day. But he was also an ardent Republican and a Taft elector in the defeat suffered by the GOP in 1912. He was a Catholic who became a Freemason.

Sbarboro paid Mrs. Coppo, wife of the cellar master, to go to the church every Saturday evening when the family was at Asti and dust the two front left pews for his family to use the following morning. He built an elaborate concrete structure for the exclusive use of his family while waiting for the train. Roughly one hundred feet distant stood a simple, but adequate, structure that served as the waiting room for everyone else. He once chastised a local farmer for driving

A dignified Andrea Sbarboro, about seventy years of age. Photo by Alfreda Cullinan (Sbarboro's granddaughter), courtesy of San Francisco Historical Society.

a battered wagon with a frowzy horse to church. Sbarboro's own carriage was drawn by an immaculately groomed horse whose mane and tail were carefully coiffured. The neighbor, who didn't work for the Colony, took exception to Sbarboro's comments. Leaving Mass early from the rear of the church, the offended farmer cut the tail and the mane off Sbarboro's horse.

Once Sbarboro was hosting a small group of San Franciscans who were not Italian.[61] "When we sat down at table, I looked at the four women, a mother and three daughters. None of them was particularly prepossessing, and so I selected the least ugly to sit at my right. She was extremely witty and from her bright conversation, I soon realized that she was very well educated. Presently she asked me what was the name of the flower with which the center of the table was ornamented. My answer was "Bella Donna," which in Italian means "pretty woman." I followed this up by saying, "L'unica bella donna a questa tavola" (the only pretty woman at this table). Without changing the expression on her face, the young lady turned to me and in the most beautiful Italian said, "Credevo oho si ohiamasse Oleander" (I thought it was called the Oleander). And with the tact of a refined young lady, she immediately changed the subject and went on with a pleasant conversation."

Andrea Sbarboro was born in Acero, Italy, on November 26, 1839. With his mother and four siblings he immigrated to America to join his father and two older brothers in 1844. They located in New York City. Andrea was not allowed to attend school, since his mother did not approve of the secular education offered in New York City public schools and the family couldn't afford a parochial school. Instead of going to school, young Sbarboro had to peddle toys on the streets of New York and on the ferryboats that plied the East River between New York and Brooklyn. Andrea was forced to pick up English as best he could.

Sbarboro never forgot the problems he faced learning English. In his autobiography, he recalled how on occasion he stole into the public school on Elm Street opposite the Tombs to get his first inkling of a formal education. He remembered his arrest, when, along with two friends, he pulled a boyhood prank in a building on Mulberry Street. When the boys, embarrassed and fearing a whipping at home, refused to give police their real names, they were sent to the House of Refuge on 23rd Street.

"It (living in the House of Refuge) was really very fortunate for me, a blessing in disguise," Sbarboro recalled, for when he wasn't making razor straps he was allowed to attend school. Ten years later he wrote his own English text so that he could teach English in his home to the children of San Francisco immigrants. After eight years in New York, Andrea's parents returned to Europe to live out their days in beloved Italy. Teenager Andrea, accompanied by a family friend, set out on the grand adventure of travel to San Francisco by way of Panama.

The youngster flourished, his personal frontiers falling before his drive in the setting of a frontier city. Within six years of his arrival in San Francisco, Andrea was a full partner in his brother's grocery business. In 1861, he visited New York City and while attending church met Maria Dondero. They were married in April 1861 before returning to San Francisco. The childless couple had been married seven years when Maria, who had been ill for some time, passed away.

Three years later Sbarboro traveled to Italy where he met and married Romilda Botto. Romilda shared Andrea's love for Italy and its long history. In keeping with custom, they named their first son, Alfredo, for Romilda's father, but they named their next two sons Romolo and Remo after the legendary founders of Rome. The Sbarboros had two daughters, Aida and Romilda, the latter named after her mother.

Sbarboro liked to say that his first daughter was named six years before she was born. During his trip to Italy in 1871, Sbarboro attended the La Scala opera house in Milan. The performance that night was the first of countless performances around the world of Verdi's *Aida*. Sbarboro was so impressed that he vowed, if ever he had a daughter, he would name her Aida.

None of his boys fathered sons and Andrea's surname closed out with his children's generation. Two of Sbarboro's granddaughters were alive close to the turn of the 21st century but neither, including Alfredo's daughter, Alfreda (Sbarboro) Cullinan, had children. Romilda (Sbarboro) Musto's daughter gave Andrea and Romilda great-grand-children whose identities are lost through the caprice of time and generations.

If Sbarboro had been asked, he would probably have said that his greatest contribution to the success of ISC was financial leadership. But the passage of time would suggest a second contribution, the tradition of hospitality. The gregarious Sbarboro loved people and he loved to entertain. Over the years he invited people by the train-load to share the bounty and the beauty of Asti. How much of his entertaining was motivated by business we'll never know, but enter-tain he did. During the early years before the Villa Pompeii was built, Sbarboro entertained his San Francisco friends and business clients at the superintendent's house, commonly call the Colony House.

Entertaining in those days was made difficult, but not impossible, by the Sunday train schedule, which saw only one train arriving from the city at noon and departing Asti for San Francisco shortly before 4:00 P.M. However, there was ample room for visitors to stay over-night. They could be accommodated in one of the nine bedrooms in the great house. Each bedroom had its own fireplace with an ample supply of firewood to ward off the chill of frosty nights. In spite of the inconvenient train schedules, there were visitors at the Colony House nearly every weekend. Throughout the summer Sbarboro was in his element, hosting luncheons on the terrace with its olive trees and oranges growing amid the immense oaks that surrounded the big house.

In 1902, Sbarboro's villa was built. Entertainment at Asti rose to new heights. Sbarboro solved the inconvenient train schedule by hir-ing private trains—not just a passenger car, but an entire train. The trip, including a thirty-minute ferry ride to Tiburon, took about three hours. The train would park on the siding in front of the winery and wait until the guests were ready to return in the late afternoon.

Sbarboro was a leading banker in San Francisco at the turn of the century. He had been in the banking business since the 1870's, and

HOUSE OF REPRESENTATIVES
WASHINGTON

HON. ANDREA SBARBORO,   January 17, 1907.
ITALIAN-SWISS COLONY,
   SAN FRANCISCO, CAL.

MY DEAR MR. SBARBORO:

I have just returned from a trip to Panama, where I went on a little tour of investigation with Senator Flint and a few Congressmen. While in Panama, I attended a Dinner given by the American Minister, Mr. Squires, who was the Secretary of the American Legation at the time of the "Boxer" uprising in Peking, and I was so fortunate as to be placed alongside of him at dinner. In the course of conversation, the subject of Wine was brought up for discussion and Mr. Squires remarked to me: "You make splendid Wines in your part of the State, Mr. McKinlay," and then he related to me a little incident.

During the time of the "Boxer Rebellion," when the Allied Forces had established themselves in Peking, he had given a dinner at which a number of the Foreign Officers were present and amongst these was Count Waldersee, leader of the German Contingent, and nominal Commander of the Allied Forces. Mr. Squires said that, owing to the trouble and chaos existing in the Country, his stock of Wines had run low and the European Brands were exhausted, but he happened to have a few cases of "Tipo" and "Sauternes" from Asti, California. He supplied these to the guests and the dinner seemed to pass off pleasantly.

Shortly after, Count Waldersee visited him again and remained to dinner. By that time, Mr. Squires had replenished his stock of European Wines, which were served to the Count. He drank a little of the European Brand, and then, turning to Mr. Squires, said: "Mr. Squires, I wish you would give me some of that fine wine you served me on my last visit to you," and Mr. Squires said he was compelled to put aside the European Brands and send to his cellar for Tipo Chianti.

I meant to tell you this story when I returned to California, as it is the same as related to me by the American Minister, while on my last visit to the City of Panama.

Yours very truly,
D. E. McKINLAY.

in 1899 he founded the Italian-American Bank. His friends Pietro Rossi and Marco Fontana were on the board and another friend, J. J. Crocker, was vice-president. When A. P. Giannini, looking for a name in 1904 for his new bank, picked a name similar to Sbarboro's bank, Andrea objected. Giannini deferred to the senior Italian banker,[62] settling on the name Bank of Italy, which eventually became Bank of America. Sbarboro's oldest son, Alfredo, ultimately sold the family bank to Giannini. The younger Sbarboro went with the bank and became one of Giannini's senior vice-presidents and a close confidant.

Sbarboro had a large circle of friends in San Francisco. To this group the affable consigliere would add important politicians and San Francisco businessmen as his guests at Asti. Visiting elite, particularly Italian royalty, could count on a trip to Asti as part of their visit to San Francisco. Prince Ferdinand of Savoy led a list of Italian dukes and counts who visited Asti during the ten years that bracketed 1900. Politicians of every stripe and from every level spent time at the Villa. Luther Burbank, who lived in Santa Rosa, visited the Villa and later sent Sbarboro some of his prized hybrid fruit trees. One of these, a plum tree, was planted alongside the Villa by the Italian ambassador to the United States, Edmund Mayor des Planches, when he visited Asti in 1903.

In recognition for the regard in which Sbarboro was held in Italy, he was knighted on July 7, 1904, by King Victor Emmanuel III with "La Croce della Carona D'Italia." At the exposition held in Milan in 1906, Sbarboro was presented with a gold medal by the Italian government for the services he had rendered his native countrymen who had immigrated to America.

If the train brought first-time visitors, their day at Asti would begin with a tour of the winery. But the attention of the visitors would invariably be drawn to the vistas in all directions. From the winery, looking to the west, the foothills seemed only a few hundred yards away. The winery stood on the only flat land at Asti and the visitors could see vineyards to the northern and southern horizons. To the east the Villa Pompeii stood out in stark contrast to all the rest. Behind the Villa a row of trees lined the bank of the hidden Russian

River. Beyond the trees the Mayacamas Mountains served to frame the picture.

Early-morning visitors would be treated to the sun rising above the shoulders of Mount St. Helena in Napa County. By late morning visitors would see an Asti awash with the bright white light of the California sun. And everywhere, grapevines. A grapevine standing alone is a nondescript thing. But aligned with thousands of others, covering the land in marching rows of green, it assumes a compelling beauty. Vineyards the world over exude an unfathomable lure that invites men to walk their rows. There are no attractive blossoms or heady fragrance, only the brown earth between the rows which, like all country roads, reach out for company.

Certainly the setting at Asti made Sbarbaro's job easier, but his personality and talent with people helped. Sbarboro started what has become a nearly universal custom of wineries everywhere, the practice of winery hospitality. He took hospitality and public relations to heights most wineries can only envy. Not only did he do it first, he did it better than most of those who have followed him. Partly as a consequence of Sbarboro's flag waving, Colony wines were being shipped to all corners of the world and the Colony label was known in all of the principal cities of Europe.

Colony wines were distributed throughout the United States. Their wines could be found in all the leading restaurants, hotels, and clubs across the country. Dining cars of transcontinental railroads and passenger steamers departing San Francisco served ISC wines. Colony wines were distributed in South America, China and Japan, the Philippine Islands, Alaska and British Columbia. In Europe, Colony wines were available in England, Germany, Holland, Belgium and Switzerland. One year, owing to the failure of the vintage in Europe, ISC shipped 250 barrels of wine to France.

By the 1950's Asti ranked as one of California's leading tourist attractions north of San Francisco. The Northwestern Pacific was replaced by the auto. Along the Old Redwood Highway billboards marked the distance to Asti. All of this attention, started by Sbarboro, was encouraged through the years by an effective hospitality program.

When the winery started up in 1933, after Repeal, they opened a small sampling and sales room in a wooden building whose primary purpose was to house the winery office, post office and laboratory. The building was outgrown in just four years and in 1937, the present office building with hospitality room specially designed for visitors was built. By the end of the 1930's organized wine tours were offered. Soon ten thousand visitors a year were sampling Colony wines in the hospitality room.

Although slowed by the war, the number of visitors to Asti continued to increase. By the mid-1950's, one hundred thousand people per year were driving the Old Redwood Highway north through Marin and Sonoma Counties to reach Asti. By the end of the fifties, Asti rivaled Yosemite and the giant redwoods as a tourist attraction in California. As prosperity grew, so did attendance at Asti. The tasting room was enlarged to double its original size. A gift shop and delicatessen were added to meet the needs of the hoards who came. Ultimately, over one third of a million people would visit the tasting room each year before a cost-cutting move by R. J. Reynolds closed it in 1982, almost fifty years after Enrico Prati began greeting visitors to the winery.

Entertainment at the Sbarboro Villa ended when Sbarboro passed away in 1923. The Villa stayed in family hands until 1942, when the property was sold to National Distillers along with the rest of ISC. But the days of lavish entertaining at the Villa were not ended forever. The Villa would rest for twenty years until the late fifties, when it would return to its days of glory.

Andrea Sbarboro accomplished much in his long life. He was father of the building-and-loan associations in the Bay Area. He was a banker who influenced the early days of the Bank of America. Sbarboro was a founding partner in the Sanitary Reduction Works (garbage collectors) for San Francisco. It was during those days that horse manure, gleaned from the streets of San Francisco, was shipped to Asti to fertilize the vineyards. Sbarboro served on the Relief and Reconstruction Committee after the 1906 earthquake. He served on the committee that framed the new charter of San Francisco in 1908. It was in this function that Sbarboro fought for, and won, the right of grocery stores to sell wine and beer. He served as chairman of the San Francisco County committee of the California Promotion Committee. As president of the Manufacturers and Producers Association of California, he advocated pure food and drug laws.

In 1908 Sbarboro added his personal touch to grape grower history. In the spring of that year, he was invited to Healdsburg to address the town folks in support of their fight against a proposal to make Healdsburg dry. The initiative was narrowly defeated and the alerted grape growers began to form groups across the state to fight the increasing threat of Prohibition. Sbarboro saw the need to organize these groups to enhance their effectiveness. Through the Manufacturers and Producers Association of California he called for the growers to meet in San Francisco.

On July 22, 1908, the Grape Growers of California was formed. Sbarboro was elected president. He was honored but expressed his misgivings. "I could only accept on condition that an efficient and able secretary was furnished to co-operate in the great work that was before us." A friend recommended Mr. Horatio F. Stoll. Sbarboro recalled,[63] "I sent for him and found him quite enthusiastic about accepting a position whereby he could be of service to a great industry and the State." Sbarboro found Stoll "… not only a brilliant writer, but he proved to be an equally good speaker…" Stoll signed on as secretary of the new organization, joining Sbarboro and a group of industry leaders in the effort to stave off Prohibition.

The first officers of the Grape Growers of California were:

Andrea Sbarboro	President
Clarence J. Wetmore	First Vice-President
E. C. Priber	Second Vice-President
J. P. Overton	Treasurer
Horatio F. Stoll	Secretary

The board of directors included Carl Wente, Theodore Gier, M. F. Tarpey, C. L. La Rue, F. T. Swett, W. C. Chisholm, A. E. Burnham and John Kerwin. Stoll went on to become publicist for ISC. The battle to save the nation from Prohibition was all but lost when Stoll found a new way to express his and the industry's voice. In December 1919, Stoll released the first issue of his new magazine, the *California Grape Grower.* One month later the country went dry. Fourteen years later, Prohibition behind them, Stoll changed the name of his magazine. The new name was *Wines and Vines.*

Sbarboro's battle for national sanity peaked in 1908–1909. In 1910 he wrote his memoir. In it, Sbarboro describes his battles with the prohibitionists, but he presents no asides, no new appeals for temperance. Following the appearance of his memoir in January 1911, we hear little more of Sbarboro's public voice. Clearly, his enemies were gaining strength even as he was losing his. The passionate Sbarboro who had spent much of his life fighting causes lost his last great battle, the fight for temperance, not abstinence.

Years earlier, at a time when banks had little interest in working people, Sbarboro had started his building-and-loan companies for just those poor people. Later he had attempted to provide work and financial security for the unemployed by founding the Italian Swiss Agricultural Colony. In both cases Sbarboro also stood to gain, and critics were free to question the existence of altruism in these endeavors. But there was little self-serving interest in his war against Prohibition.

It was Sbarboro who had the dream, and the drive to make the dream a reality. It was Sbarboro who created the paternalistic setting in the vineyards of Alexander Valley that resulted in the thriving village of Asti and, in large measure, the town of Geyserville. It is fitting that Sbarboro should leave his initials cast in stone on the Asti bank of the Russian River. No more appropriate stone could have been cast to a man's memory than the Villa Pompeii, where food and good fellowship continued under Sbarboro's arbor for over fifty years after his death.

Sbarboro, by 1910, was no longer a young man. He turned 71 that year and was easing into retirement. In one of his appearances before Congress, Sbarboro had said that if his crusade succeeded, he could die happy and have engraved on his tombstone the epitaph, "Here lie the bones of Andrea Sbarboro, who first sowed the seeds in the halls of Congress which caused the removal of drunkenness from the United States." Unfortunately it was not to be. Cavaliere Sbarboro died February 28, 1923, of influenza. He had enjoyed a full 83 years.

16

Beginning of the End

So fleet the works of men
Back to their earth again
Ancient and holy things
Fade like a dream.
—*Charles Kingsley*

WITH REPEAL, AMERICANS WERE ONCE AGAIN permitted to purchase wine. But for the winemakers it was a dramatically different wine market from the one they had known. In the early twenties the nation, based upon wine-grape tonnages shipped, was consuming around one hundred million gallons of wine a year. The wineries didn't know it yet in 1933, but over the next three years the market would average only 46 million gallons a year. It would be twenty more years before California's wine shipments would reach the level of the early twenties.

Not only did the market shrink following Prohibition, but the type of wines demanded by the marketplace had changed dramatically. The dry, light wines of Sbarboro's day were a thing of the past. Perhaps as a consequence of Prohibition, Americans wanted high-alcohol wines. And they had to be sweet. Such wines, typically eighteen to twenty percent alcohol, could be made by adding brandy to wines whose fermentation had been stopped before the grape sugars had been fermented to zero. Inexpensive, lower quality grapes worked fine for producing the wines now in favor with the consumer. The Rossis would soon recognize the disadvantage that Asti would have competing in such a market. Neither inexpensive grapes nor the proper equipment to make brandy in volume were available at Asti.

In order to be competitive, the Colony found itself buying large quantities of grapes from Kern County grower Joseph DiGiorgio. What started in 1932 as a supply of grapes that would lower the average cost of grapes used at Asti ultimately became a case of the tiger consuming its rider. The need to acquire ever larger quantities of grapes led to a serious negative cash flow for ISC that continued through the thirties. Originally the deal between the Colony and DiGiorgio was good for both parties. The Colony got inexpensive Central Valley grapes yet no cash changed hands, since DiGiorgio agreed to take payment in shares of ISC stock. In 1941, ISC purchased the seven-million-gallon LaPaloma winery at Clovis, near Fresno. Now DiGiorgio could deliver his grapes to the Fresno facility and save the cost of shipping to Asti. Unfortunately, the LaPaloma owners needed to be paid cash and ISC had to borrow heavily from the Bank of America to acquire the winery.

By 1941, ISC had fully extended itself. The cherished days after Repeal had turned sour for the Rossis and Prati. Stripped of their Central Valley wineries by the CWA sell-offs prior to Prohibition, Asti was no longer where the action was. Major co-ops were formed in the Fresno-Lodi area and giants such as Roma and California Fruit Industries began to dominate the business. The latter was led by ex-employee Antonio Perelli-Minetti. Old friend Sophus Federspiel, second in command to P. C. Rossi and a Colony employee for close to thirty years, joined with a partner to operate the Colonial Grape Products Corporation. These Central Valley giants used a small quantity of north-coast premium grapes to adjust the quality of their wines while keeping them competitive. The Colony, on the other hand, needed to "import" large quantities of Valley grapes to blend with a small

Robert Dominic Rossi, twin brother of Ed Rossi. Courtesy of Beringer archives, Asti, California.

Edmund Arthur Rossi, the other twin. As the boys grew older their appearance changed, but the two remained close all their lives. Courtesy of Beringer archives, Asti, California.

amount of Asti grapes if they were to remain competitive in the fortified sweet wine business. The Rossi twins and partner Enrico Prati found themselves holding the wrong end of the tiger and it proved fatal.

The Rossi and Sbarboro families remained supportive until the very end, with both extended families buying shares during the thirties. But it was too little, too late. In 1942 National Distillers Corporation came to San Francisco and announced they were looking to buy a winery. DiGiorgio, after ten years of trading grapes and wine for shares in the Colony, had accumulated 37 percent of the company. Now he wanted to cash out. The Rossis and Prati, whose combined holdings had shrunk from 75 percent to about 37 percent, didn't need too much encouragement from the Bank of America, which was getting concerned about its own large stake in the company. The twins recognized that without an infusion of still more capital, capital they could no longer raise, they had little choice but to sell out. Ed Rossi, Sr., and Alfredo Sbarboro went back east to negotiate the sale to National Distillers. The price was reported to be $3,673,000. The Rossi brothers and Prati were kept on, Ed as president, Robert as vice-president. Prati was named vice-president in charge of production. With the exception of the brief Edoardo Seghesio period, this was the first time since Andrea Sbarboro had organized ISC 61 years earlier that there was not a single Rossi or Sbarboro owner of the once grand venture.

The twins were offered five-year contracts to stay on and run ISC.[64] They refused, feeling that if they got along with the National Distiller people, they would stay the five years without a contract. If they didn't get along, they could leave if and when they pleased. The new owners offered Ed Rossi, as president, a salary higher than his brother or Prati since the latter two would be vice-presidents. Ed Rossi insisted that as partners they had all received the same income, and it must stay that way now. There is no record of whether Ed Rossi's salary was lowered or the other two increased. More than likely, a compromise was reached.

ISC wasn't the only California winery to be acquired by a big distillery during the days of World War II. By 1943, Schenley, Seagram and Hiram-Walker had all made major purchases as they sought additional alcohol capacity to meet wartime demand. Wine also offered the spirits companies a product to make up for decreased production of whiskey during the war years. A Schenley representative expressed the attitude of the large whiskey companies when he announced that Schenley was going to produce "the wine of the people," a euphemism for screw-top bottled wine. And so the Colony found itself still mired in an uncertain miasma, part high-quality table wine and part Central Valley "wine of the people." This was the mix that nearly destroyed them in the thirties and would take them, unchanged, into the next decade.

In 1939, National Distillers made their first foray into the California wine industry when they purchased the four-million-gallon Shewan-Jones winery located at Lodi, California, from its owner, Lee Jones. The winery produced fine wines, but with a Central Valley character. Although National Distillers used the ISC label for their premium wines and Asti as their flagship winery, new brands involving Shewan-Jones were now offered at the tasting room at Asti. There was the Chateau Lejon (a contraction of Lee Jones) label offering a Chateau Lejon white, Chateau Lejon red, a Lejon brandy and sweet and dry Lejon vermouths. They were good wines, but one day these Central Valley brands would contribute to the doom of ISC.* During the fifties and sixties, ISC and its tasting room at Asti defined the wine industry in northern Sonoma County. But with the seventies came the rebirth of the premium wine industry in the north coast and especially in Sonoma County. The market was changing swiftly, and those wineries who had remained devoted to the high-quality wines of

---

* Once Jones found himself with wine left over; wine that was essentially lees. Lees are the sediment of yeast pulp and tartrates that settle in aging tanks. Normally the bottoms from the tanks would be pressed out and the high-tannin wine recovered to blend back in with the first-quality wine. But this year, Jones decided to distill the lees and make brandy. The Bureau of Alcohol, Tobacco and Firearms directed that the notation "lees" appear on the label. Shewan-Jones had no trouble with that and the brandy was proudly labeled "Lees Brandy." This became the subject of much insider humor, since Mr. Jones's first name was Lee.

Sonoma County, such as Simi Winery, now could reap the rewards of their long-term business strategy.

The Colony, on the other hand, saddled with Lejon, Petri and other brands suggesting the Central Valley, found itself out of step, out of place, and eventually out of sight.

The war ended in the summer of 1945 and, adding to the celebration, Mother Nature had produced a large crop. For a short while wine prices fell, reflecting the crop size. But as 1946 went on the price for 1945 wine almost tripled, to $1.40 per gallon. The trade and the distillers saw a huge, pent-up demand on the horizon. This was a chance to finally achieve the profits that heretofore had been denied them in the wine business. This foresight was no doubt encouraged by the lifting of wartime price controls that summer. As the 1946 harvest approached, the distillers practically salivated. One of the distillers, bent on capitalizing on the situation, contracted with independent wineries to produce wine for it on a "cost-plus" basis.

The harvest of 1946 was a circus. The contracted wineries were not concerned about the cost of grapes. They had cost-plus contracts, and the more wine they made, at any cost, the more profit they would earn. The average price for grapes in Sonoma County reached $124 per ton, up 73 percent from $72 per ton the year before. The demand for grapes reached such a height that buyers would stop grape-laden trucks on the road and offer incentives to the driver to take the grapes to the buyer's winery. But the anticipated demand didn't materialize, and by 1947, wines produced under contract stayed at the winery as the speculators walked away from their deposits. The average price for grapes dropped to $35 per ton and would not exceed $100 per ton for the next fourteen years. By the early 1950's, the distillers had mostly left the California wine industry, taking with them only bad memories to add to their losses. The distillers were never interested in the mystique of the wine business and the bean counters wouldn't accept the capital-intensive nature of the business. Furthermore, the wine business operated to strings pulled by Mother Nature, not by executive committees. CEOs, with polish on their nails, not dirt under them, were never comfortable explaining to stockholders that the success of company business plans was dependent upon the weather in California.

The Rossi twins completed their five-year stint in late 1946. They were losing interest in working for National Distillers and with the war over, National Distillers began to think that a fresh management team should run their wine interests. As a result, General John Deane was sent to San Francisco as president, and the twins agreed to stay on an extra year to assist Deane. On September 15, 1947, the Rossi twins, now 62 years of age, left the company. They had worked 38 years, the first 32 in what amounted to a family-owned business, the last six as employees.

National Distillers closed Shewan-Jones in 1949. They held ISC a few more years, but by early 1952, their intention to sell was public knowledge. They offered their properties to E & J Gallo, who paid National Distillers $25,000 (the same price Sbarboro paid for Asti in 1881) for the right to examine ISC's books over sixty days. Gallo did not grow to become the largest vintner in the world by being less than thorough. They pored over ISC's books. The Gallo people measured and evaluated the wine inventory. They looked at the staff and considered ISC's management systems. They did not like what they found.

Charles Crawford, Gallo vice-president, participated in the review. His conclusion: "… We learned that Italian Swiss Colony was in trouble. National Distillers didn't understand the wine business… there were many problems. We found warehouses full of unusable merchandise and tanks of unsalable wine."[65] Although industry observers thought it was a done deal, Gallo opted not to buy. Sensing the great disappointment at National, Louis Petri, then forty years old and president of the Petri Wine Company, as well as the Wine Institute, stepped in, and on April 15, 1953, he came away the fifth owner of ISC. Petri brought with him his executive vice-president in charge of sales, B. C. Solari. This was the same Solari who, along with General Deane, had been fired from ISC by National Distillers just a year earlier. Title to the company went to Petri's wholly-owned company, United Vintners. Petri, with a total storage capacity of over 45 million gallons, was now California's largest wine producer.

For approximately $16 million, Petri acquired three wineries with a total storage capacity of close to 26 million gallons. The purchase included Italian Swiss Colony and all of its subsidiaries.

> Italian Swiss Colony—10,000,000 gallon storage
> LaPaloma at Clovis—13,500,000 gallon storage
> Lodi—2,500,000 gallon storage
> Gambarelli & Davitto, Inc. of New York
> Bottling plants in Chicago and Fairview, New Jersey
> Over 2000 acres of vineyards, including 300 acres of the Stelling Ranch in Napa Valley

Adolph Heck, who had replaced General Deane, stayed on as president.

Italian Swiss Colony was once more in the hands of California vintners. The Colony was the flagship brand for United Vintners, owing to its worldwide premium reputation. But the Colony winery at Asti represented only twenty percent of United Vintners' production capacity. United Vintners was essentially a Central Valley wine producer with major wineries at Madera (the Mission Bell Winery built by P. C. Rossi 56 years earlier)[N-13] and the original Petri family winery at Escalon, California. These two facilities had a total capacity over twenty million gallons. With its other Central Valley wineries at Clovis and Lodi producing sixteen million gallons annually, United Vintners was in a good position to produce the sweet or fortified wines demanded by the marketplace.

No one seemed to notice, particularly the folks working and living at Asti, that the Colony, with its high-cost, premium vineyards in the north coast, did not fit in.

At the urging of Petri in 1951, his growers had organized what would become the largest grower co-op in the world, Allied Grape Growers (AGG).[66] For the first few years the growers (AGG) were paid a price for their grapes that reflected United Vintners' profits. This arrangement proved too complex, so Petri solved the problem by selling his wineries to the growers (AGG). The growers were to pay off the acquisition by 1960. Under the agreement, Petri's United Vintners would be the exclusive sales agent for AGG wines.

By 1959, AGG had paid off its contract to acquire the wineries, and on September 1, 1959, the growers acquired United Vintners itself. Petri agreed to stay on as president of United Vintners for seven years. By 1962, Allied Grape Growers had grown from 240 members in 1951 to 1,539. Expansion of their wineries and the acquisition of John Cella's Napa Wine Company in Oakville and his Reedley plant brought AGG capacity to over fifty million gallons. As the growers expanded, Asti's importance diminished.

In 1964, two more blows were suffered along the banks of the Russian River. The first was the acquisition of Inglenook by AGG. To capitalize on the name of this grand old dame of Napa Valley, AGG created an inexpensive brand of Inglenook generic wines. The brand created a home for the members' Central Valley fruit, since few or no Napa grapes were used in the brand. Inglenook thus competed, in house, with ISC. ISC lost the competition.

The second blow, more immediate to the families at Asti, was the move of the bottling plant from Asti to Madera. The bottling plant had been the envy of the industry and the pride of Asti. Asti had been National Distillers' only bottling plant. After crushing and fermenting at the LaPaloma winery, the wines were shipped to Asti for final blending and bottling. By the time AGG started relocating it, the bottling plant had ten bottling lines. Each line was a complete unit wherein bottles were cleaned, filled, sealed and packaged. Each line filled a bottle of different size or shape. The "A" line was the largest. It filled 86,400 fifths (750 ml) bottles—7200 cases—during an eight-hour shift. Other lines filled tenths, quarts, gallons, half-gallons, Tipo bottles, even two-ounce salt-and-pepper wine sets.

One line was used exclusively for premium label wine with a cork finish. The total capacity of the bottling plant, exclusive of the champagne and brandy bottling lines, was 25,000 cases per day. These lines maintained an average storage level in the warehouse of 300,000 cases. Roughly 20,000 to 25,000 cases were shipped out daily. This number could double during peak holiday seasons. There were over nine hundred different items being bottled, cased and shipped from Asti. These included 74 different kinds of wine bottled under different labels, in different sized and different shaped bottles. The most popular label was Italian Swiss Colony, with Tipo, Asti, Lejon and Hartley labels in broad use.

Even as he was creating the industry's cutting-edge bottling plant, the innovative Petri addressed another problem. During the early fifties Petri was engaged in an ongoing battle with the railroads over their wine tariffs. Petri thought they should be lower, but the railroads protested that they were as low as possible. Petri decided to go around the railroads. He set about converting a WWII liberty ship into a wine tanker.[67] A new bow section was constructed and then welded to the stern. The wine tanker was 530 feet long, with a displacement of 21,800 tons. It cruised at fifteen knots. Named the S.S. *Angelo Petri,* after Louis's father, the ship carried 2,383,840 gallons of bulk wine in 26 stainless steel tanks. Its home port was Stockton, California, from which the vessel would make seven rounds each year to Houston, Texas, and Port Newark, New Jersey.

Along with the ship, Petri built two special barges to haul wine from Houston to New Orleans and then by river to his franchise bottler in Chicago. The cost of the three vessels, together with special terminals, was between ten and eleven million dollars. The vessel carried only red wines, and most of those were dessert wines. The financial viability of sailing a tanker of this size demands a back haul. In Petri's case, the back-haul product couldn't contaminate the wine tanks. The answer was food-grade corn syrup and aqueous solutions of soda ash. Neither would contaminate the tanks. In fact, the soda ash, a component in many soaps, facilitated cleaning of the tanks before refilling them with wine.

The S.S. *Angelo Petri* made its maiden voyage in 1959. The railroads then did "the impossible" when they lowered their wine tariffs. Within ten years, wine tariffs were less than half of what they were when the *Angelo Petri* first sailed, its holds filled with wine.

The ocean-going wine tanker once made San Francisco columnist Herb Caen's column. The vessel had barely cleared the Golden Gate Bridge in stormy seas when disaster nearly struck. The vessel lost its engines and floated aimlessly in the rough water until it could be towed away from the rocky shoreline. There was considerable concern at the winery over the possibility that salt water might have gotten into the wine-filled holds. Those worries proved groundless, but Caen could find humor in the event—the next day his column announced the name of the new "in drink" in San Francisco, Petri on the Rocks.

The *Angelo Petri* was taken out of service in 1975. Its usefulness became marginalized with the market's rising interest in white wines. The quality of white wines could better be preserved if the wines were bottled at the winery. The seventies were also the time when franchise bottlers began to leave the industry.

17

Brandy

Claret, sir, is for the boys, port for men
But he who aspires to be a hero
Must drink brandy.

—Samuel Johnson

F OR OVER TWENTY YEARS, a small group of men met twice a
month in a Cloverdale hall. It was an exclusive group, not by
design but by circumstance. Outsiders seldom sought admission for the simple reason that few new people moved into Cloverdale
or Geyserville. Most of the men were born in the shadows of ISC or
would spend their lives working there. Several were farmers, and
their crop was wine grapes. Wine had always been a part of their
daily lives.

The minutes would be read, the mail reviewed and new business
quickly dispensed with. With the formal meeting closed, it was time
for a half-hour "social period." For six months of the year, the leading subject was grapes. Were the fields dry enough in early spring to
get in a tractor? Is pruning finished? Having trouble getting a crew (of
field workers)? There would always be talk of the peach crop and
probably tomatoes. And of course hunting outings were of major

interest during the hunting season. These men, some brothers, some related through marriage, had known each other all their lives. They enjoyed easy, comfortable relationships.

They did not suffer that narrow-mindedness that so often inflicts isolated people bound by common ideas or heritage. Strangers were welcomed to their group. In a sense they seemed untouched by the social evils that pervade other societies. Perhaps it was living in the idyllic confines of Asti, Cloverdale or Geyserville. Or perhaps their lifestyle was a reflection of another part of their twice-monthly gatherings. Sure as January rain in California, the twenty-year ritual was played out. At the close of the business meeting, glasses were taken from the cabinet and a bottle produced. Its contents, ISC brandy.

Brandy is produced by the distillation of wine. Brandy has been produced since at least the Middle Ages. Today its production serves three principal purposes:

1. Production of beverage brandy.
2. Production of a high-alcohol grape product used to fortify sweet wines.
3. To recover a valuable byproduct (alcohol) that would otherwise be lost to waste.

The Colony began producing beverage brandy before the turn of the 20th century. Like all major Central Valley wineries after repeal, ISC produced brandy in significant quantities during the forties through the sixties. Much of the brandy was produced to fortify the popular sweet wines of the day. When the juice of freshly crushed grapes enters the fermenters, it contains roughly twenty percent natural grape sugars. Fermentation is the process by which yeast converts these sugars to alcohol. If the yeast is left alone, it will convert all of the sugar to alcohol, with the latter settling at about twelve percent. The result is a dry (sugarless) table wine.

However, the winemaker can add alcohol to the fermenting wine and stop the process at will, since yeast ceases to function at about seventeen percent alcohol. Typically, a little bit extra is added "to be sure," and the wine is thus stabilized at eighteen to twenty percent alcohol. Were it not for the added alcohol, the wine would continue to ferment in the winery, or worse, in the bottle. (It should be noted that modern winemakers have the technology and facilities to produce wines containing residual sugar without introducing brandy.)

The production of brandy is made all the more interesting by the involvement of the federal government. Beverage alcohol (ethanol) has long been a favorite source of income to the U.S. Treasury. By the end of the fifties, the Treasury Department's unit, the Bureau of Alcohol, Tobacco and Firearms (BATF) had a busy sort of joint venture at Asti. So great was the brandy activity at Asti that a federal inspector was assigned full time to the ISC premises. As the brandy went through production the winery would pay the inspector the tax due at the various steps in the process. Prepurchased stamps were used for these transactions. The BATF also required color-coded paper strips be used as seals over the bottle caps, blue for brandy to be exported, red for regular brandy, and green for 100-proof brandy. These strips were placed across the caps immediately after bottling under the watchful eye of the federal inspector.

Experts generally agree that the quality of brandy does not stem from the quality of the grapes used. Rather, the quality of the finished brandy is a product of the care exercised in distillation and aging of the product. Since grape quality was not an important issue, California brandies were always produced from inexpensive Central Valley grapes, including the widely adaptable Thompson Seedless. In 1942 National Distillers transferred all brandy production from Asti to its Central Valley winery, LaPaloma. For the next thirteen years, brandy was produced exclusively at their two valley wineries, Shewan-Jones and LaPaloma. In 1955, the processes of aging and bottling brandy were returned to Asti so that brandy shipments could be coordinated with wine deliveries.

Some brandy was shipped from LaPaloma to Asti already in oak barrels. Most, however, was shipped immediately after distillation in stainless-steel tank trucks or tank cars. The alcohol level was a little under 116 proof (58%), and since the tax had yet to be paid, the tanks arrived under government seal. Until the tax was paid, all handling and transfers of the brandy had to be done in the presence of the BATF inspector. After the inspector broke the tank-car seal, the brandy was "barreled down," a process whereby the brandy was put into fifty-gallon oak barrels for aging. Under the watchful eye of the BATF inspector, the barrels were weighed and checked for leaks. After agreement as to count by the ISC staff and the inspector, the barrels were placed under government lock and key in a storage area specifically approved by the government for this purpose.

The door to the storage room from then on could only be opened by the BATF inspector. At Asti, they would barrel down about twenty thousand gallons, or four hundred barrels, per day. There were four approved buildings for the storing and aging of brandy, with a total capacity in excess of twenty thousand barrels. Since the federal tax was $21 per proof gallon (a proof gallon is one gallon of pure alcohol), the one million gallons of brandy in the full warehouses represented about eleven and a half million dollars to the U.S. Treasury. Unfortunately for U.S. taxpayers, by the time the barrels were emptied, as much as twenty percent of the brandy was lost to evaporation and leakage, costing the government almost $2.5 million.

The brandy would remain in barrels for at least two years, which was the minimum aging length established by BATF. Some brandy was aged for as long as four years, sometimes longer. When ready for bottling, the brandy was transferred to the gauging room, generally in one-hundred-barrel increments. The barrels were emptied into the gauging tank, which held 5,220 gallons. Just as the brandy was weighed before going into the aging room, it was now weighed again. The entire tank sat on a scale so that the contents could be weighed.

The final alcohol content would be measured in the presence of the gauger (the BATF inspector), and before the brandy left the gauging tank, the winery would hand to the gauger the proper number of prepaid internal revenue stamps. For the first time since the wine was charged into the still, the brandy belonged to ISC, although BATF continued to watch carefully to be certain that all government regulations regarding purification and rectification were strictly followed. Rectification was any treatment of the brandy in a manner not specifically approved in the regulations. In this case another tax was due. Since the Colony added sherry to the brandy to adjust the alcohol content and flavor the product, they paid an additional 37 cents tax per proof gallon with blue rectification stamps.

Most of the brandy was bottled at eighty proof. A small market existed for hundred-proof brandy. This brandy was handled separately, always under close government scrutiny. After bottling at one hundred proof, the brandy was returned to a secured bonded storage area. The federal tax was paid as the bottled goods were removed from the warehouse.

The tax code was completely revised in 1979. The new code did away with the gauger or inspector. Henceforth, taxes were paid by check based on accounting practices to determine the tax due.

18

Heritage Lost

Unrest of spirit is a mark of life;
one problem after another presents
itself and in the solving of them
we can find greatest pleasures.
                    —*Karl Menninger*

A LTHOUGH NOT OWNERS, the third generation of Rossis, Robert
Jr. and Edmund Jr., were in the fold. Robert, who had joined in
the spring of 1946 after being discharged from the Army, worked
in operations at the LaPaloma winery near Fresno. Edmund, after
graduation from U.C. Davis in 1949, started in the laboratory in San
Francisco. They were, of course, cousins. Bob was never assigned to
Asti. His job at LaPaloma lasted ten years. In 1956, United Vintners
transferred him to San Francisco as assistant production manager. By
1962 Bob was vice-president of production and grape management.
The production people at Asti affectionately called Bob "cowboy,"
because he would come to Asti to "ride" the staff.

Of the three Rossi generations, Bob was the only one not formally
trained as an enologist or viticulturalist. Yet he spent his life in both
fields. Ironically, one of Bob Rossi's last assignments was to advise

Robert Dominic Rossi, Jr. Like his father, Bob spent his life working for various divisions of the Colony, but he was never assigned to Asti. Courtesy of Beringer archives, Asti, California.

Heublein as to the disposition of the decaying vineyards around Asti, the very vineyards planted by his grandfather. Rossi was equal to the integrity passed to him by his grandfather. Bob's recommendation: Take them out. With the grapes gone, Heublein could rent out the fields for cattle grazing.

With the acquisition of ISC by United Vintners in 1953, Ed Rossi, Jr., was moved to Asti as chief winemaker. It was a job he would love, but the assignment lasted only four years. In 1957 Gallo introduced Thunderbird, a flavored wine containing twenty percent alcohol. It was a major success and United Vintners needed to develop a competing brand. Rossi was asked to develop a competing product within six weeks. The assignment became permanent and Rossi was given a new title, director of research and development. Over the next eleven years, Rossi developed numerous "special natural" or "pop" wines, the mention of which brings back college-day memories to many present-day Chardonnay drinkers. Rossi's contributions included Silver Satin (in direct response to Thunderbird), Golden Spur, Swiss Up, Aruba, Rhythm Hombre, Red Showboat, Vin Kafe, Collins, Zombie and Cuba Libre. The last three were clearly losers, but the rest had their day in the market sun. Lower-alcohol wines introduced by ISC included Bali Hai, Gypsy Rose and Satin Rose.

Ed Rossi and his staff were dealing with products and public acceptance parameters for which they had no training. Experience was accumulated "on the fly," but they had expert help.[68] Asti's tasting room was enormously popular during those years and Rossi turned to the tasting room visitor. The staff would spend weekdays in the lab blending fruit juices and wine in various proportions. The more favorable concoctions were delivered to the tasting room, where two young ladies would invite visitors to participate in a research project. Most patrons readily agreed. They were given a score sheet and asked to evaluate on a scale of one to ten the various potions put before them. On a good weekend, between three hundred and five hundred people would participate. Rossi and his staff would evaluate the results on Monday. The results would steer "research" the rest of the week.

The preoccupation with flavored wines continued past 1969 and into the Heublein era. Continuing the trend toward lower-alcohol wines, by 1970 the flavored wines were at nine to ten percent alcohol. Developed at Asti were Key Largo, Sangrole, Zapple and Waikiki Duck (a sparkling wine). These were followed by the famous, or infamous if one prefers, line of Annie Greensprings. Developed in direct competition with Gallo's Boone Farms, the A.G. line included A.G. Chevvy, A.G. Berry Frost, A.G. Peach Creek, A.G. Plum Hollow and A.G. Apricot Splash. Was P.C. Rossi watching? These ten-percent-alcohol, flavored wines led to the "wine coolers," which were under seven percent alcohol and weren't really wines at all. By 1974, Americans were drinking fifty million gallons annually of special natural wines.

In more quiet moments Ed thought of his dad, Ed Senior, now in his eighties and in failing health. Ed Rossi, Sr., became winemaker in 1909 and moved to Asti at that time. After his father Pietro's death in 1911, Ed became plant superintendent, while twin brother Bob ran the San Francisco operation. Ed presided over the shutting down of the winery at Prohibition. In 1920, Rossi became president of Asti Grape Products. He moved from Asti after eleven years to establish offices in San Francisco. It wasn't so much that Edmund didn't like Asti, but in 1920 he had turned 32 and the social life for a young, eligible bachelor would be significantly improved in San Francisco.

In October 1932, Ed joined half a dozen other industry leaders to form the Grape Growers League of California. Their goal was primarily to convince Congress to modify the laws of Prohibition to allow production of table wine. Table wine, they reasoned, was less alcoholic than fortified wine, and the production of twelve-percent-alcohol wines should be allowed. The group shortly became the Western Wine Producers Association which, in 1934, became the Wine Institute. Edmund Rossi was a director of the Wine Institute from its inception until 1947, the year he and brother Bob resigned from National Distillers. In 1938, the Wine Advisory Board (WAB), made possible by a State marketing order, was formed. The job of the Wine Advisory Board was to educate the public to the joys of California wine. Ed became manager of the Wine Advisory Board on January 1, 1948. He managed the WAB until July 1, 1960, when he retired.

Rossi was then 72 years old. By his own words, he was tired. He had been a leader among leaders. He had grown up in the wine industry. Thanks to his father, Edmund had been a university-trained enologist at a time when American winemaking was a craft learned on the job, in the wine cellar. Ed and brother Bob had enjoyed less than two years working under their father but they were fruitful years.

Above all, Edmund remained a quiet, principled man of unquestioned integrity. These were qualities passed to his son. The seed of P. C. Rossi flourished in both his sons and remains evident in the Rossis to this day. Ed's love for wine was passed to his son Ed Junior, who spent his life working for the Colony. And the genes didn't stop there. Daughter Yvonne, Ed Junior's younger sister, married an Irishman, Paul Dolan. Their son, Paul Dolan, Jr., is president of one of California's most dynamic wineries, Fetzer. Edmund Senior died on September 24, 1974. He was 86 years old.

Ed Rossi, Jr., had devoted over twenty years of his professional life to developing "pop" wines. It was not a total loss. Americans, except those from Mediterranean cultures, were not attracted to wine. But they loved cold, sweet drinks and if wine could be offered in that way, Americans could possibly be tempted to try wine. Ed could thus take comfort, knowing that the special naturals led some consumers to what would become a lifelong attraction to fine wine.

Rossi had been trained as a winemaker and the years devoted to flavored wines of the month were not happy ones. But Rossi was a loyal soldier. Like his father and grandparents, he was highly principled and deeply religious. Unlike the Sbarboros, the Rossis seemed uncomfortable with wealth and the status wealth brought. Whereas the Sbarboros kept to themselves during visits to Asti, the Rossi cousins swam with the local boys in the Russian River. Whereas the Sbarboros drove Pierce Arrows and big Packards, Ed Rossi, Jr. drove the same Buick for years. Rossi and his wife, Gerry, owned just two homes together. The first was a modest home in Healdsburg where they lived for 24 years, and the second was in Madera, where they lived for almost twenty years before Ed's death in 1996.

If Ed Rossi was content with his material possessions, other parts of his life were less satisfying. Grandfather Pietro had suffered alone through the devastating moments in his life and now Ed silently fought his personal battles. He had spent much of his life in the center of a colossal battle with another winery. He would rather have spent that time finding better ways to make fine wine. His feelings about his days since leaving the laboratory in San Francisco were probably embodied in the story he would tell, over and over, at meeting after meeting, for thirty years.

From 1953 to 1983 he had worked for just two masters, United Vintners and Heublein, the latter eventually owned by R. J. Reynolds. He had been an integral part of company management for all those years, although mostly in a staff position rather than a direct part of the chain of command. There is no record of his ever being offered an officer's position where he might influence company policy. Instead he remained at a distance from the sources of power, in charge of special projects.

And so Ed would tell his staff the chocolate chip story. He would tell the story of a mythical company that produced a highly successful cookie containing thirty chocolate chips. Then somebody in accounting suggested that no one would notice if they took one chip out of the cookie, and thousands of dollars would be saved. So the chip was removed. The cookie was still widely successful so a second bean counter suggested they could take out a single chocolate chip and no one would know the difference. Thousands more dollars were saved. And so it went until people did notice, and now the successful cookie was no longer making money. A final bean counter, anxious to make his mark as had his predecessors, suggested that production of the unprofitable chocolate chip cookie be discontinued. Elimination of the unprofitable chocolate chip cookie would save thousands of dollars.

Rossi's chocolate chip story bore a remarkably close resemblance to Heublein's treatment of the decades-old premium Tipo line of his father's day. Tipo Red and Tipo White were the premium Colony wines but the brand did not fit in Heublein's product lineup. Shortly after acquiring ISC in 1969, Heublein canceled the Tipo marketing budget. When sales began to fall, Heublein dropped the Tipo brands. It is possible that the Tipo story inspired the cookie story. But bitterness never showed in Ed's voice. Those who worked for Ed liked and respected him. Those feelings turned to love, the more closely people worked with the quiet, reserved Ed Rossi.

Rossi's problems continued. In 1983, Allied Grape Growers reacquired the Colony. Ed Rossi came with the deal and AGG gave him the job of upgrading ISC wines. By 1986 it was clear that AGG, with its grower-tilted management, should never have acquired ISC. What was left of the bottling line was put to work doing custom bottling. Safeway was a big customer. The winery took on custom crush

Edmund Arthur Rossi, Jr. Ed's only employer throughout his career was the Colony or its various owners. Courtesy of Christine Rossi.

contracts including one for making kosher wine. Kosher wines were sweet wines. They did not meet Rossi's goal of turning Asti into a producer of award-winning dry table wines such as the market was now demanding. The kosher wines required special provisions which made a rabbi part of the winemaking process. It was a fine product but not one for Asti. Rossi apologized to the winery crew, some of whom Ed had brought to Asti to help him make super-premium table wines, for their assignment.

In the spring of 1987, Ed's wife, Gerry, passed away. With the children out of the house and his wife gone, Ed moved to the Rossi villa at Asti. Alone in a ten-bedroom house, his friends two hundred miles away in Madera, life was lonely. Things were not going well at the winery either. On July 29, 1987, ERLY Industries took over from Allied. But the decline continued. Finally, in the spring of 1988, almost to the date of losing his wife, Ed had to tell the staff that Asti was closing. The winery that his father and grandfather had spent their lives building into the largest winery in the world was about to shut down. There was an especially heavy weight on Ed's shoulders that afternoon. The winery closed its doors on the last Friday of May 1988. It was 102 years since the winery's first crush and the end of 101 consecutive years of the Rossi family's involvement with the winery at Asti.

Ed kept busy. He continued to consult for Lancers (a Heublein subsidiary) and occasional European wineries that wanted assistance in preparing wine blends for the United States market. His assignment for Lancers ended in 1991 but Ed was financially secure. On December 17, 1993, he turned 69. Within a few days Rossi suffered a serious stroke. His son Brandt, visiting for the holidays, rushed his father to a hospital in Santa Rosa where Ed began a lengthy period of rehabilitation. One year later, a severe stroke sent Rossi to Sisters of Mercy Hospital in the hills above Oakland. Here he could get good care and, most importantly, be close to his only sister, Yvonne Dolan. He lived a little more than another year. Ed Rossi died in March 1996.

19

The Spiral Tightens

Not a day passes over this earth
but men and women of no note
do great deeds, speak great words,
and suffer great sorrows
                    —*Charles Reed*

THE ROSSI TWINS guided ISC from the days following Repeal until they retired in 1947. It was Enrico Prati, however, the third man in the managing triumvirate, who made the most lasting mark on Asti.

The Prati family lived in Rimini, Italy, a village on the Adriatic Sea. Family members were beginning to emigrate to Argentina when Olinto Prati headed for California. He arrived at Asti about 1895, and went to work in the vineyards. Over the next ten years, Olinto worked hard and his skill with the grapes was noted by his bosses. Olinto became vineyard foreman, and letters home became increasingly enthusiastic about life in America, particularly Asti. In 1909, Olinto's brother, twenty-year-old Enrico, arrived at Asti. It was September 1, the same day the twins joined Italian Swiss Colony.

Prati left Rimini with one goal, to reach his brother at Asti without delay. Traveling with others who also spoke no English, Prati's exposure to America and Americans was through the window of a train. When he reached Asti, Prati found himself in an Italian-speaking world, not unlike that which he had left in Rimini. Tireless and unafraid of work, he immersed himself in the labor of the Colony vineyards. Although uneducated, Enrico was bright and filled with ideas. For a while he worked alongside Olinto, but then, for reasons no one remembers, Olinto left Asti to join family members in Argentina. Enrico remained at Asti, where he would spend the rest of his life. Two years after arriving at Asti, Prati married Ida Seghesio, Edoardo's oldest daughter. Their first child, Josephine, was born in 1914. A second child, Edward Victor, was born in 1917. Prati, like his father-in-law, worked harder than the others and the company rewarded his efforts with constant promotions through the ranks. By the time of Prohibition in 1919, Prati was the Asti plant manager.

Prati had spent his life at hard work, under demanding bosses. Unlike some men who recoil from hard labor and responsibility, Prati drove himself harder under the pressure of the job. Like so many self-made men, Prati expected those who worked for him to match his own ambition and dedication. This was an unrealistic expectation, as few could rise to his level of drive and performance. Prati's response to those who didn't measure up was to drive them harder. His professed managerial credo was to "put the fear of God into them."

Prati was literally and figuratively from the old school. The only system Enrico knew was the padrone (paternalistic) system, and he was made for it. The system prevailed at Asti for sixty years. Andrea Sbarboro had created and nurtured the paternalistic environment at Asti. Indeed it was to take care of less fortunate paesani that the Colony had been founded in the first place. Prati developed a unique form of dress and a tyrannical managerial style. Dressed in a manner to command respect, he wore a white shirt with a starched collar and a neatly fashioned tie, even in the informal surroundings of Asti. He wore a fully buttoned vest under a light, waist-length jacket during the cool season.

The most unique feature of his outfit were the pants. During his days as vineyard manager, Prati would ride a horse to keep track of his crews working the 1,500-acre ranch. Every day he came to work in khaki breeches, similar to those worn by Army cavalry units. As in the cavalry, Prati wore leather puttees. He was well groomed, clean shaven, with wavy black hair. At slightly over six feet, he was an imposing figure.

But Prati was not simply tyrannical. He was a leader. Those who worked for him respected Enrico, even if they didn't love him. Nello Baiocchi, who worked for Prati for almost eleven years, remembers Enrico as "the fairest man I've ever worked for." He never asked others to do what he wouldn't do or hadn't already done countless times in the past. He didn't hesitate to punish those who incurred his wrath. Typically, he would withhold a worker's pay for a few days, thereby extending the poor man's misery to recriminations at home. But no one was ever docked, and most significantly, in all his years running Asti, only one worker was ever fired at the hands of Enrico Prati. The unfortunate fellow was Mike Buti, who had the temerity one day to question Prati's judgment. The next morning, at the regular work assignment meeting, Prati called the men by name and gave each his work assignment for the day. When he called out Buti, there was no work assignment, only the announcement that Buti could go home, he was through.

By 1917, Prati viewed the coming of Prohibition as an opportunity. With the optimism of youth, Prati pestered his boss Edmund Rossi constantly about the opportunity to acquire Asti from the California Wine Association. Prati, lacking business experience, looked to Rossi for guidance in putting a deal together with the CWA. Enrico knew that the CWA, facing shutdown at the hands of Prohibition, would sell Asti for a bargain price. Prati had very little money, but his in-laws, the Seghesios, could probably raise the money. He found an ally in his mother-in-law, who shared Enrico's drive and penchant for business. Together they convinced Edoardo Seghesio that this was an opportunity they must not let pass. Seghesio somehow raised the money to acquire Asti when the CWA offered the property for sale.

Prati had always been able to take on any challenge and prevail, but Prohibition was another matter. After a nearly disastrous first harvest, Prati and Seghesio were rescued by the Rossi twins, who still loved Asti and wanted back in. Edoardo was overjoyed to sell three quarters of the Asti property to his new partners, Prati and the Rossi twins. When asked why they had taken Enrico Prati as a partner in the Asti Grape Products Company, one of the twins joked "because we'd rather have him working for us than against us." In truth, Prati was innovative and hard working. In just ten years he had risen from field hand to plant superintendent. He knew Asti and the workers and he was a proven leader. There could be no one more qualified than Enrico Prati to serve as vice-president in charge of production. Prati ruled Asti from 1919 until 1947. During those 28 years, Enrico and his family lived in the Colony House provided the superintendent by ISC.

In 1939, Prati's son Ed graduated from the University of California at Berkeley. After a stint in the Army, Ed Prati received a medical discharge stemming from an ankle injury sustained in an automobile accident, and he joined his father at Asti. Ed Prati began to assume an important role under his father.

The serene, isolated life at Asti was blown apart by the winds of war in 1941. In 1942, ISC was sold to National Distillers Company. While the twins ran the company from San Francisco, Prati continued as vice-president of production at Asti. In 1946, with the war over, National Distillers revamped management at ISC. General John R. Deane was sent to San Francisco to take charge. There was room for one Rossi but not two. As always, the twins acted together, and they both quit. Enrico stayed on but he was transferred to San Francisco in September 1947.

Enrico made son Ed the new superintendent, so a Prati continued in charge at Asti. For a while Enrico would leave Asti each morning about four o'clock for his drive into San Francisco. Prati had lived and worked at Asti for 38 years. Asti was the only home he had known since coming to America in 1909. He was now in his middle fifties and for the first time would not be working for or with a Rossi.

Prati took an apartment in San Francisco when the commute from

Asti became unbearable. In 1949, National Distillers closed the old Shewan-Jones winery in Lodi. Probably as a result of Prati's management style, the staff at Lodi received no advance notice of the pending closure. On the day the plant closed, Prati went into the young chemist Myron Nightingale's lab and told him to report to Asti the next morning. The plants were approximately 150 miles apart. Paul Heck, plant manager at Shewan-Jones, was also transferred to Asti.

By the fall of 1949, the separation from Asti and life in an apartment in San Francisco were wearing at Prati. On October 6, 1949, he turned sixty years old. Like so many men before and since, he probably muttered the ageless expression, "I'm getting too old for this." The job was no longer fun. His friends the Rossis were gone and Enrico was no longer an insider; the insiders now were National Distillers people. It was time to rethink the future.

On November 7, 1949, one month and a day after his sixtieth birthday, Prati acquired the Colony House from National Distillers. It was the only house he would ever own. It was a beautiful house with nine bedrooms, seven of them on the second floor. Each of the bedrooms had its own fireplace. There was no central heating. A full basement provided Ida with a large, cool storage cellar. The parlor had a great picture window that looked toward the gardens in front of the house and the orchards across the street. The patio and gardens off the dining room were on the east side of the house and provided a beautiful place beneath the orange and olive trees for outdoor dining. He had lived in the house for over thirty years, and now he and Ida owned the beautiful house that was built 39 years earlier, almost to the same date.

Alone in his San Francisco apartment each night, Prati had a lot of time to think. His thoughts reached back nearly forty years, to the summer of 1910. He had been at Asti less than a year when he and other immigrants were set to work building the new cookhouse. How hard they worked in the broiling sun. The fun they had. A small upturn at the edges of his mouth betrayed an inner smile. The earthy stories, the obvious bragging, tales of girls back home—they don't have times like that anymore, Enrico mused. While they built the

The Colony House, circa 1900, built about 1870 by Isaac Bluxome, Jr. The building served as ISAC headquarters at ISC until it was destroyed by fire in 1910. The land rising to the left of the house is the hill often portrayed in this text as the view hill of Sbarboro et al. Ed Prati would build his house on top of the hill in 1951.
Courtesy of Beringer winery, ISC Archives.

cookhouse, Prati recalled stealing glances at the construction across the street where the new superintendent's house was being built. Enrico had trouble envisioning the house before it was completed. It was huge. Only in America could such a house be built. And of wood, no less. They wouldn't believe it back home.

With a vision that comes only to a man of sixty, Enrico could see the days shortening. Sitting in his lonely apartment, he thought about his children. Daughter Josephine was now 35 years old. The beautiful Chi Chi was a willowy brunette who had left many broken hearts over the landscape at Asti when she announced her plans to marry. She had married Fred Rolandi, whose father had built the Stockton Street tunnel in San Francisco. Josephine was a schoolteacher, loved by her students. Enrico had no worries about Josephine. It was son Ed who caused a little concern.

Ed was 32 years old, the same age Enrico was that first year of the Asti Grape Products Company. The "problem," Enrico thought, was his son's personality. Ed could never manage men as Enrico had. Ed lacked fire. Whereas the men might respect Enrico, they would love Ed. Enrico felt respect was the better of the two, but Ed was a Prati, he would do well. If only he liked working for the Colony half as much as he loved hunting. Ed had a good job and a beautiful family. He had married Billie Rowland, a girl from Texas, in 1943. Their daughter, Joan, was growing up. She was already past five and would soon be starting school. He'd have to talk to Ed, maybe get him to buy his own place.

On August 16, 1950, Ed and Billie acquired the hill alongside the Colony House. This was the hill of Andrea Sbarboro in 1881, of Pietro Rossi in 1900, and now it would stay safely in Prati hands. For the moment, all was right with the world. The moment didn't last. General Deane had brought with him the management style taught in university business schools. Deane, in evaluating the staff at ISC, decided he had three young men with promising talent. Edmund Rossi, Jr., was working in the lab in San Francisco and seemed on track for a technical career.

The other two, Ed Prati and Paul Heck, were numbers one and

The Colony House. Built in 1910 on the same spot and closely imitating the original, this house served as ISC headquarters until 1949, when it was acquired by Enrico and Ida Prati.

two respectively at Asti. Deane decided to give Prati an exposure to sales, a common stop on the path to top management, and to give Heck, recently transferred from Lodi, the experience of managing Asti. In January 1951, Ed Prati and his family moved to frigid Chicago and Paul Heck took over as superintendent at Asti. Ed's training program took him to the New York office after just three months in Chicago.

While Ed Prati and his family sampled life in two of America's biggest eastern cities, life at Asti began to move in a way it had never moved before, particularly for the Prati family. On a personal level, Enrico was not happy to see his son transferred back east. Things no longer felt right. For the first time since brother Olinto had come to Asti before the turn of the century, there were no Pratis working at Asti. Enrico didn't feel good about the changes in San Francisco either, and when Elmo Martini came to him with an idea, Prati listened.

At the time, Martini was working at the Sebastopol winery founded by his grandfather years earlier. The winery had been sold to Hiram-Walker at the outbreak of World War II and Elmo knew he could now get it back. But the deal would take money, more money than Martini could raise. Besides, Elmo had very little business experience. Martini figured Enrico had both and he asked Prati if he would go in with him to buy the Martini family winery.

Events over the past few years had steadily deteriorated Prati's relationship with ISC. Prati could see a "changing of the guard" taking place. He was no longer on the inside track. It hurt professionally, but now he was also concerned for personal reasons. With Enrico in the city and Ed and his family back east, Ida was now alone at Asti all week. Prati was ready for change. He jumped at the opportunity, and his name would grace the Martini & Prati Winery long after people had forgotten Italian Swiss Colony.

Ed Prati was also ready for change. Neither he nor Billie liked Chicago or New York, and Ed didn't like sales. In short, they missed Asti. Letters from home spoke of his father's growing frustration with ISC and a growing interest in a new winery venture with Elmo Martini. Ed could feel the stirrings grow. He was, after all, the son of two adventurous families. It wasn't long before the pull of Asti and new adventure overcame any concern about leaving a well-paying job for no job at all. Like the Rossi twins before him, Ed returned. Enrico and Ida welcomed their son and his family back to Asti late that summer of 1951.

On September 2, 1951, Enrico and Elmo acquired the winery, now named Martini & Prati. It was not an easy time. It was just two years since Enrico had acquired the Colony House. That had taken much of Prati's savings, and young Ed had spent much of his savings when he and Billie acquired the hill just twelve months earlier. Enrico knew his days at ISC were numbered, and young Ed was now out of a job. On top of everything else, Ed and Billie were determined to begin construction of their new home. In fact, they had hired the building contractor shortly after returning to Asti. In a cautious mood, Prati and Martini leased the winery from Hiram Walker with an option to buy. They put up very little cash. Elmo Martini and Enrico Prati would make lease payments for seven years before acquiring title to the winery on September 2, 1958.

Meanwhile Ed busied himself building his house. He played no visible role in the first days of Martini and Prati. Enrico Prati was almost twenty years Martini's senior. The Martinis lived at the winery and business was conducted in the Martini kitchen. Enrico sat at the head of the table with Elmo and his wife, Harriet, looking to Prati for leadership. Elmo and Harriet became very close to Prati that winter of 1951–52 as they began their own great adventure. Prati's involvement with the new winery did not go unnoticed by an unhappy General Deane. The rift that had started a few years earlier spread rapidly, and early in 1952 Enrico left ISC. It marked the end of the second generation of ISC leaders.

Prati moved back to his beloved Colony House at Asti. In his early sixties, Enrico was not an old man. He had suffered from high blood pressure for years, but otherwise was in good health. The man who had "raised the fear of God" in his men didn't show it, but events of the last few years were taking their toll. The new winery venture was not without worry. Without a salary, neither he nor his partner,

Martini, could bring the much-needed money to help the new venture in its first few critical years. And money was tight. In fact, they would need to borrow money for operations. On April 7, 1952, they were forced to arrange a crop loan whereby they mortgaged the harvest of 1952. If the harvest failed, what would they do? Now Enrico knew how Edoardo Seghesio felt in 1919.

Prati had another problem. There was no man who deserved more than he to live at the Colony House. Yet there was no man who would suffer more than Prati by living in the big white house. He had devoted 43 years of his life to the vineyards, wines and men of Asti and he had loved every minute of it. Asti was his life. The cookhouse, bakery, barn, workers' houses, the church, all surrounded the Colony House. From nearly every window, Prati could see the men, his men, going about their daily jobs. Only now Prati wasn't included. He was no longer needed. There would be an emptiness for Enrico living out his remaining days in the Colony House. Not even his new venture with the Martinis could fill that void.

It was about 7:30 A.M. on May 25, 1952. From his window Enrico could see the vineyard crew gathered around foreman Andy Vasconi. He could see Andy gesturing with his hands and heads bobbing in understanding. Prati knew that Vasconi was giving the men their instructions for the day. Prati hurried over before the men broke up. He needed some dirt moved and asked Andy if he could use the Colony dump truck later that morning. Vasconi wasn't sure if Mr. Heck would approve, but Mr. Prati would always be boss at Asti. He answered "sure." Enrico turned and started back to the house. He got halfway and collapsed. He was dead when Andy reached him.

The trauma and pressure-packed events of the past few years had exacted the ultimate price. Pietro Rossi had died in the Colony House in 1911 and now, 41 years later, Enrico Prati would die just a few yards away. Unlike Rossi, Prati left a grown family. Both Josephine and Ed were in their thirties, and Ida would continue to live in the Colony House for another 23 years, until she died in 1975. Today her grandson and his family occupy the Colony House, grateful for Enrico's foresight when he purchased the house almost half a century earlier.

Change continued at the front office. Before the year was over, General Deane was replaced by Adolph Heck, Jr. Adolph Heck, Sr., had owned a winery in Sandusky, Ohio, that he sold to National Distillers before the war. His sons, Adolph and Paul, joined National at that time. Adolph Junior's final assignment for National Distillers was to serve as president of ISC, and his primary job was to sell the company. E & J Gallo paid National Distillers $25,000 for a thorough look at ISC's books. When Gallo passed, Louis Petri moved in and acquired the Colony in 1953. The following year the Heck brothers acquired the Korbel Winery and left ISC.

Myron Nightingale was not amused by the rapid changes and un-certainty at the Colony. The young enologist left the Colony after less than four years at Asti and joined the Cresta Blanca winery in Livermore as winemaker. Nightingale, a pioneer U.C. Davis enologist, went on to an illustrious career at Cresta Blanca and finally at Beringer.

20

God's People

... asking his blessings and his help,
but knowing that here on earth God's
work must be our own.
—*John F. Kennedy*

FOR ALL THE TUMULT AT THE TOP, life at Asti remained pretty much as it always had. Sharing lives with their neighbors from Geyserville and Cloverdale, the same families continued to live and work for ISC at Asti. The tasting room was the envy of the industry and thousands of visitors continued to take photos of the church "built from a wine barrel" to show the folks back home. Remarkably, no tourist-driven restaurants opened in Geyserville and no tacky souvenir shops operated along Cloverdale Avenue as the highway went through the little towns.

Oblivious to the stream of visitors, the Seghesios, Del Sartos, Domenichellis, Pastoris, Trusendis, Mazzonis, Giampaolis and Matteolis continued as their parents had, living their pastoral lives and worshiping at El Carmelo. While the families remained strong and vigorous, their little church, converted from Ginocchio's greenhouse fifty years earlier, was showing its age. Major repairs in the fifties failed to stop leaks in the now porous roof.

The pastor at St. Peter's Church in Cloverdale since 1954 was Francis Reali. Father Reali was born in Canton Ticino, Switzerland, just north of the Italian border. He was from the northwestern part of Italy/ Switzerland from which most of the inhabitants of Asti had immigrated. In a word, he was a paesano. Father Reali was a devout priest and lived his priestly vows. But Father Reali was also a character. His sermons were short during hunting season so that he, as well as the men of his congregation, could hunt on their days off. Father Reali drove the local fish-and-game warden to distraction by his custom of shooting birds on the church lawn, the birds used to lend flavor to his evening pasta. But by far, Father Reali was a man who got things done. By 1959, he realized that his pastory involved one church, St. Peter's in Cloverdale, that was too small for a growing congregation, and one church that was beginning to fall down, El Carmelo at Asti. The most sensible and obvious solution was to close the mission church at Asti and build a new, larger church in Cloverdale.

But the obvious solution was not an option for Father Reali. He faced a divided parish. The parishioners at Asti numbered about one hundred, most living in Geyserville. The Cloverdale congregation was more than twice that of Asti, but they were no match for the tightly grouped Catholics from Geyserville. The Asti church and the parishioners living in Chianti and Geyserville were no ordinary team. There were still family members living in 1960 who had helped to remove the glass panes of the old nursery over fifty years earlier. Together, their roots entwined and grew deep in the Asti soil. El Carmelo was family. She was old and tired, but no way would they leave her. They fully realized the need for a new church, but there was no way they would give up Asti for Cloverdale. The more El Carmelo caved in, the more they were drawn to it. Building two churches at the same time was something that the small congregations would never have considered but for Father Reali.

Faced with a dug-in congregation, Pastor Reali went to Louis Petri, president of United Vintners, and explained his dilemma. The two were, after all, paesani, and over a few glasses of red wine a deal was struck. The old winemaker's house, just a few yards away from the little chapel, was now old and in disrepair. It and the two houses alongside would be torn down and the site given to the diocese. On top of that, United Vintners would provide the wood from some large redwood tanks that had been in service for many years for construction of a new church. Finally, Petri agreed to contribute $35,000 to help with the building costs of the new Asti church.

Asti and Our Lady of Mount Carmel had worked their magic. A large, for-profit corporation gave the land, money and materials without which a new church could not have been built at Asti. Petri deeded the land to the diocese and he took back the 0.3 acre that El Carmelo sat on. Whether or not Petri came up with all of the money is questioned by some parishioners, but in 1960 Father Reali went ahead with construction of the new church for Asti. This church was truly built from old wine casks. The tanks had held 650,000 gallons of wine in the winery's "redwood forest" and now they provided over 50,000 board feet of redwood for the new church. The redwood staves were cleaned and sanded by members of St. Peter's Knights of Columbus. The beautifully arched ceiling required over 46,000 board feet of redwood. There is not a single knot or knothole in the entire church structure. The wood, however, did carry with it a little of its past. Alex Carrey remembers that when the church was first built, after an hour at Mass you knew the building was made from old wine tanks because of the vinous odors that only time could remove from the staves.

Is there some divine ordinance that sets some redwood trees apart from the rest? The redwood tree stands alone in beauty and size among its forest peers. But most of the beautiful wood is, in the end, trod underfoot in decks and walkways of California houses and office buildings. But not all. Somehow out of the forest a few trees spent half a century fashioning man's most revered beverage and then, in a second life, shielding men and women from the sun and rain as they knelt in prayer.

Father Reali barely paused after construction of the new church at

Asti was completed. He proceeded immediately to build the new St. Peter's Church in Cloverdale. The church was completed in 1962. Between the two churches, there was seating capacity for about six hundred persons, about twice what was needed.

The power of Asti had worked her magic but at a price. The two churches stood side by side, their similar shapes but different sizes suggesting a robust young son standing next to his aged mother. Only a small, gravel parking lot separated the two churches. Worshipers turned their backs to El Carmelo as they entered Our Lady of Mount Carmel, but they had to face her as they left church and walked to the parking lot. The Old Lady wasn't done yet. Her invisible arms reached out to the old families each Sunday, although each week they grew a little more feeble.

It took sixteen years, but in 1976 some of the folks gave in to the feelings stirring within their souls. It was time to save El Carmelo. On August 19, 1976, the Sonoma County Planning Commission, at the urging of ISC and the people of Asti, passed Resolution #7749 recommending that county supervisors designate the "Chapel of Our Lady of Mount Carmel at Asti" as a county historic landmark. The little church was now a county as well as state historic landmark.

On October 13, 1976, El Carmelo Corporation, a California nonprofit corporation, filed articles of incorporation. The first directors were: Robert Bogner, Frank Domenichelli, Alan Trusendi, Thomas Naughton and the Reverend Jerald N. Thomas. Father Thomas was now pastor of St. Peter's Church in Cloverdale, as well as the mission church at Asti. Optimism was everywhere. The following year, ISC once again reached out to help that which it has fostered for nearly 85 years. On November 4, 1977, ISC, now 82% owned by Heublein, recorded a Gift Deed to El Carmelo Corporation for the 13,150 square feet of land upon which the chapel sat. The deed required that "the chapel shall be repaired and restored in a good and workman-like manner and in a manner befitting the historic and religious significance of the chapel."

Today, 36 years later, Mass is still celebrated at 8:30 A.M. at Asti just as it was at the little church over ninety years ago, and in the one-room schoolhouse one hundred and five years earlier. Our Lady of Mount Carmel is nearly filled now on Sunday mornings, but the old families are thinning out. Herewood (Hey) and Edith Peterson sit in the front right pew just as they have since the church opened 39 years ago. But there are fewer Trusendis, Baiocchis and Mazzonis than there used to be. Buddies all their lives, longtime ushers Frank Domenichelli and Allie Trusendi are now buddies in heaven.

Eugene (Pete) Seghesio and his wife, Rachel Ann, still attend the 8:30 A.M. Mass. Pete and his father, Edoardo, span an amazing 140 years. Pete and Rachel Ann still live in the house that Edoardo acquired in 1894 and expanded one room at a time as the children came. It is still beautiful and if they choose, they can sit on the front porch and look over the Sangiovese vineyards that stretch down to the river. The train no longer goes by or brings wine buyers from San Francisco, and there is a freeway where the Old Redwood Highway used to be, but otherwise it's exactly the view that Angela Seghesio surveyed from the same porch a century earlier.

21

The Good Times

Man is a history-making creature
who can neither repeat his past
nor leave it behind.
—*W. H. Auden*

ALMOST FROM THE MOMENT that Andrea Sbarboro selected it as the site for the Colony, Asti was a mecca for tourists. During the closing decades of the 19th century, Asti hosted European royalty. By the turn of the century, Sbarboro was bringing private rail cars to Asti filled with American dignitaries and captains of industry. Politicians, including James Gillette, governor of California, visited Asti to be a part of the scene.

Shortly after Repeal, the Colony opened a tasting room adjacent to the lab. We cannot be certain if it was the area's first tasting room, since Simi Winery also opened a tasting room around the same time. The Colony's tasting room was used primarily by those in the industry—brokers, distributors and others. By 1936 the level of business and the number of visitors required a new office and a formal tasting bar. Before the thirties had ended, as many as ten thousand people were visiting the tasting room each year. The war years slowed the stream of visitors, but by the mid-fifties, the tasting room was hosting one hundred thousand people each year. As the hospitality center grew, it offered more than wine, brandy and champagnes. Now it was a deli offering picnic foods and a fine gift shop.

Statistics for tasting room activity are difficult to believe, particularly with the passage of forty years. Consider the following:

1958—200,000 visitors consume over 4,000 gallons of wine.

1959—Fifteen people work the tasting room on weekends.

August 16, 1959—1,461 men, women and children tour winery.

August 1959—33,000 people take tours which last 30 to 45 minutes.

1961—Hospitality room doubled, two cash registers needed to handle sales.

Prompted by the widely successful television character, the Little Old Winemaker, the Colony had become a tourist destination in itself. By 1960 ISC had become one of the major businesses in Sonoma County. The winery had roughly two hundred employees and an annual payroll exceeding $1,000,000. The Colony paid over $40,000* each working day in taxes. Over $1,500,000 was paid annually to local grape growers. ISC was the largest dinner-wine producer in the world. One out of every three gallons of table wine consumed by the American public was produced at Asti.

In a move to create a strong television image, ISC had turned to their San Francisco ad agency, Honig, Cooper and Harrington, in the late fifties.[69] Creative Director Bob Haumeser was joined by Norm Solari** and Chuck Lawrence to develop a new commercial. Their first idea was to create an animated character whom they would call "the lovable winemaker." Nobody liked it. Haumeser decided to try a real person for the winery's image and Chuck Lawrence knew just the man to fill the role, Ludwig Stassel.

Stassel was an experienced actor. He had played Lou Gehrig's father in the film *Pride of the Yankees*. Stassel had a natural German accent and Lawrence felt he looked the part. They agreed that Stassel

---

* Fully 90% of this amount was the tax on brandy production.
** B. C. Solari's son.

Tasting room, circa 1960. Italian Swiss Colony photo.

was right for the part, and a courtyard was created on the Columbia Ranch in Burbank to shoot the commercials. This became the same courtyard used to shoot the "Flying Nun" television series.

As rehearsals got underway, the three advertising men were still not satisfied. Something was wrong. Finally they agreed, it was Stassel's accent. But what was the correct accent for an Italian living near the Swiss border? They never answered that question, and Stassel couldn't have imitated it if they had. The decision was made to drop the accent entirely and go instead for a good TV voice. As a result, Jim Backus of Mr. Magoo fame and a leading "voice" in Hollywood, got the job doing the voice-over for Stassel's part. Stassel was furious, and he never got over his pique at being forced to act to Jim Backus's voice. It was Jim Backus who coined the famous line: "Who is responsible for the quality of the wines?... The Little Old Winemaker, me!" Music for the commercials was provided by Vince Degan. At the time Degan was also providing the music for Gallo commercials.

By 1960 they were ready to start shooting. Filming was done both in Burbank and at Asti. Much filming was done in the "redwood forest," among the massive redwood tanks in the storage cellars at the winery. Occasionally, the troupe would go out into the vineyards and locate on a knoll now under freeway concrete. Typically, the cast consisted of Stassel, an attractive model and a donkey. The donkey was a professional who would come up from Hollywood for the shooting. The cast was rounded out by the donkey's mascot, a small mongrel dog. It generally took a week to shoot each twenty-second commercial.

Stassel was a short man with the rounded belly of a man in his sixties. He dressed in an alpine hat, a short-sleeved white shirt and green suspenders that held up leather shorts over his prominent paunch. His outfit was completed with knee-high hosiery, a feather in his cap and steel-rimmed eyeglasses on his nose. The Little Old Winemaker danced around the wine barrels and into the homes and hearts of millions of television viewers. Playing in prime-time commercials across the country, the Little Old Winemaker became one of America's most beloved characters. Joe Frediani and several other ISC employees would play the part of the Little Old Winemaker around the tasting room and at special winery events, leading to the conception that several people played the lovable character on TV. But only Stassel, aided by Jim Backus's voice, played the part on television.

Stassel and the donkey could make shooting the commercials memorable events in themselves. Stassel loved cigars, slivovitz and beautiful women, in no particular order. Ron Berman, just starting his career with Honig, Cooper and Harrington, got the job of seeing to it that the cigars and slivovitz were always on the set. There wasn't much Berman could do about the women whose derrieres were the targets of Stassel's pinches. But who could get angry at the "cute antics" of the lovable, gray-haired guy in leather shorts? Besides, Stassel's wife, Laurel, was always on the set.

There was even less that Berman could do with the sometimes troublesome donkey, who on one memorable occasion ruined a day

The Little Old Winemaker gets kissed in the Colony tasting room. Italian Swiss Colony postcard.

of filming. The scene called for baskets of grapes (purchased from a grocery market) to hang over the shoulders on either side of the donkey's head. It was a pastoral scene of harvest shot in the vineyard above the winery. The donkey, oblivious to the seriousness of the situation, busied himself with liberal portions of the grapes so close at hand. The animal soon developed a severe case of diarrhea which made shooting impossible. The crew waited for nature to take its course and resumed filming.

But the donkey wasn't finished. Shooting became impossible when, inexplicably, the animal became sexually aroused and nothing could be done to restore matters to normalcy. There was no way they could shoot around the donkey's magnificent demonstration of his sexuality. Then there was the day when the crew spent hours chasing the donkey, who was chasing the dog through the endless rows of grapevines.

For two years the troupe entertained America as the number one commercial on TV. The commercials continued to run until 1967, but in the latter years Stassel's ever-increasing demands for more money slowed ISC's enthusiasm for the Little Old Winemaker. His demise became inevitable when the lovable character became more recognizable for himself and less and less for the Colony. Perhaps it was merely a coincidence, but both the Little Old Winemaker and Louis Petri left ISC the same year.

Whether or not the man in knee-high hosiery and leather shorts had reached the end of his time, the Little Old Winemaker had made Asti the toast of the wine world. For millions of Americans, ISC and their wine would be associated with the Little Old Winemaker. In 1968, Allied Grape Growers sold an 82% interest in the Colony to Heublein. Fifteen years later, when Allied Grape Growers returned to full ownership of the Colony, there was an immediate cry for return of the Little Old Winemaker. But it was not to be. Allied was planning a new image for the wines from Asti. It was an upgraded image, one consistent with the emerging market demand for premium-quality wine. Ludwig Stassel and the Little Old Winemaker would not return. They had done their job, perhaps too well for Stassel.

1962 was a record year for the tasting room. It wasn't just a big year, it was colossal. 1962 was the year of the Seattle World's Fair. It was the time just before jet travel became popular and vacation travel was still primarily by automobile. Situated in the northwest corner of the nation, Seattle was reached primarily by the highway that linked it to Portland and San Francisco. That road, as it crossed over the Golden Gate Bridge and headed north through Marin and Sonoma Counties, was the Redwood Highway. And the Redwood Highway passed within one hundred yards of ISC at Asti. Asti, about three hours north of San Francisco, became a convenient and enjoyable stopping-off place for travelers headed to Seattle. It was also the point where the squirming in the back seat became serious and the plea "Are we there yet?" began touching sensitive nerves.

The Redwood Highway generally followed the route that Sbarboro and his group took by rail in 1881. It was a pleasant drive through

Shooting a commercial in the vineyard with the often-troublesome donkey. The spot shown is now under the freeway. Courtesy of Beringer Archives, Asti, California.

the dairy country of Petaluma and into the thriving town of Santa Rosa, with its neon signs, bowling alleys, two-story motels and burger drive-ins. Leaving Santa Rosa, the two-lane highway traveled through the sparsely inhabited farmland of Windsor, the tiny village of Healdsburg and finally into the vineyards of Alexander Valley.

Progress north was marked by the ubiquitous billboards counting down the miles to Asti. No one counted the percentage of cars that turned in at the gardens of the Colony, but many succumbed to the inviting solicitations from the Little Old Winemaker, who looked down from the highway billboards. In 1962, the tasting room poured over five thousand gallons of wine, which is equivalent to well over two thousand cases. That year an estimated 400,000 people visited the tasting room. By actual count, 328,000 visitors went on winery tours.

Even today, with the tremendous interest in premium wine and the intense effort with which the wineries invite visitors to their tasting rooms, there is not a tasting room in the entire county that pours five thousand gallons of wine in a single year. The closest is probably Sebastiani Vineyards and they pour approximately three thousand gallons per year. Although the data is not available, it is likely that all of the tasting rooms in Alexander Valley combined do not pour as much wine in a year as did ISC in 1962.

During the summer months, visitors consumed one hundred pounds of free cookies each day. These were not token cookies, they were Danish cookies delivered daily from a bakery located in Redwood Valley, north of Ukiah. They cost the Colony 25 cents a pound, but the tasting room personnel felt they were worth it, except possibly when the bikers came by. Almost every weekend a group of 25 to 30 Hells Angels would pay the tasting room a visit. They stayed only thirty to forty minutes, about the time it took to clean out the cookie barrel.

Nello Baiocchi, a Colony employee since his graduation from high school 42 years earlier and chief tour guide, remembers the bikers' visits. As the fearsome-looking bikers in black leather jackets came in, the other visitors left, leaving the tasting room exclusively to the Angels. When the bikers left, the first group returned, resuming their places at the tasting bar. But the bikers were always model visitors. Only once was there a near problem when Baiocchi refused to serve a biker lady whom he believed was underage. When Nello wouldn't be dissuaded, the slender young lady decided to prove her age by undressing. She didn't get far before Baiocchi decided she must be at least 21 years old.

But young, developed lady bikers were not the only memorable visitors to the Asti tasting room. On January 24, 1951, a trucker parked his rig some fifty yards from the office/hospitality building. He was delivering wine bottles to the bottling room just a short distance from the office. It was a nasty winter day and there were few people

---

FIGURE 1

ISC WINERIES AND STORAGE DEPOTS

1919

WINERY	CAPACITY (GALLONS)
Asti	4,000,000
Madera	3,000,000[1]
Lemoore	1,000,000
Kingsburg (Fresno)	1,000,000[2]
Selma (Fresno)	750,000
Cloverdale	500,000
Fulton	500,000
Sebastopol	500,000
Mt. Diablo	400,000
San Francisco Depot	2,000,000
New York Depot	1,000,000
Total	**14,650,000**

1960

LaPaloma (Clovis)	11,940,000
Madera	11,400,000
Asti	8,940,000
Escalon (Petri Winery)	8,840,000
Lodi (Community Winery)	4,300,000
Depot Storage	9,549,000[3]
Total	**54,969,000**

---

[1] See Note 13, Chapter 16 for history
[2] Sold to L. Martini 1923
[3] Stockton, CA; Houston, TX

around. A sole visitor sipped wine in the tasting room. The driver parked his big rig, set his brakes and ran to the office to check in. The friendly banter in the office was silenced as the building shook and the sound of breaking glass shattered the ordinariness of the day. The truck driver, followed by the office clerk, ran outside to be greeted by the sight of a truck body sticking out from the tasting room wall. There was no cab—that was inside the building.

The tasting bar sat against the far wall, opposite a pair of tall double windows that looked up toward the highway. The attendant chatted with the tasting-room visitor as the gentle rain outside enclosed the nearly quiet room. In a shattering instant the double windows crashed open and behind the glass came the monster grill of a very large truck. It wasn't moving fast. There was no loud noise, only a full size truck cab rolling slowly but inexorably into the tasting room. The truck stopped in the middle of the room. It was as if a giant, unaware of his own bulk and strength, and not knowing about doors, had come in to taste wine. The wall was mostly unharmed. The truck had entered slowly, directly through the double windows. As if to proclaim its innocence and ignorance of the shattered glass around it, the truck's motor hummed, its wiper blades still wiping.

In 1962, twelve to sixteen people worked in the tasting room during the summer months. While two people ran the two cash registers, most of the staff poured wine and led winery tours. The tours went out almost continuously, through the gardens, past the statue of Bacchus and on to the winery. They could last as long as 45 minutes but on busy days the tours would be cut to an average of thirty minutes. The most popular wines in the tasting room during the fifties and sixties were Tipo White and Tipo Red. These Chianti-style wines were bottled in the traditional raffia-wrapped fiasco, or flask. Tipo Red was primarily Sangiovese. The used bottles would typically end up as vases on checkered tablecloths in Italian restaurants around the country.

Anticipating huge crowds in 1962, the Colony had six million postcards printed. There were always about six thousand postcards in the tasting room, offering five or six selections. Not only were the postcards free to visitors, the Colony also paid the postage when the cards were dropped in the wine-barrel mailbox in the tasting room. During the summer months, as many as three thousand postcards would be mailed each day. Visitors could mail other material as well, using the Asti post office, which was located in the tasting room.

Approximately five million people visited Asti between 1950 and 1969. By 1962 an estimated ten percent of the cars traveling the Old Redwood Highway turned into the winery. So great was the stream of visitors that when the freeway came through in 1963, off and on-ramps in each direction were included at Asti. Less than one mile north, the freeway provides for connections to Dutcher Creek Road and southern Cloverdale. At Asti, there are no connecting roads, and almost no houses. Other than the tourists, only the winery, the chapel and a few homes were served by the freeway. Thirty years later, with the tasting room closed, the ramps are virtually deserted.

While millions sampled wine in the tasting room and toured the winery, there were other visitors to Asti. Thousands more enjoyed private tasting and tours followed by lunch or dinner at the Villa Pompeii. Holding the door open to these visitors was Joe Vercelli. Joe had joined the Colony on August 22, 1933. He was 21 and had not quite finished his undergraduate studies at the University of California at Berkeley. Financial pressures of the depression forced him to leave school to take a job that paid twenty cents an hour. The work was ten hours a day, six days a week. Room and board were one dollar a day.

He lived in the "white house," a building that housed three other single men. They ate their meals at the cookhouse. Vercelli found that he didn't like the food served in the cookhouse and asked permission to have a hot plate in his room to cook his own meals. The hot plate was approved, but not Joe's request that he receive a food allowance. Asti offered simple pleasures in those early years of the Great Depression. On a summer evening, sitting by an open window, Joe could hear sounds of laughter filtering through the trees from the Rossi house. Across the road, a giant oak tree embraced the old de Vecchi place, now alive with the Pellegrini family. To the west, just over the sloping land before him, Joe could hear the sounds of parents coaxing little ones to bed now that the late sun had set and the air had begun to cool. Faint wisps from the cooking grills floated in the stirring air before him. As darkness enveloped Asti, Joe could hear the booming voice of Guido Musto singing opera to Andrea Sbarboro's descendants spending a weekend at the Villa.

🐛

In the deepening shadows two figures stole hand in hand up the hill. Only fifteen, she might already have married in her grandmother's day. But now romance was before her. Choir practice over, the two met outside of church. Shyly he took her hand as they climbed in silence to the empty crest above the village. The organist had stayed for a few more minutes of her own practice and the music followed the young lovers up the hill. At the top, surrounded by darkness, they gazed upward at the wonder of the heavens. Like countless others before them over the span of human experience, they discovered, that early evening, a universe belonging only to them. Above, with no streetlights or clouds to screen their view, the Milky Way formed a celestial tiara, and heaven's stars hung like blue diamonds over the young lovers and the people of Asti. Powerless to stop, he leaned over and tentatively kissed her. She would remember always the stars that night and her first kiss.

22

The Impresario

The night is filled with fragrance of silver spaghetti.
—*Clem McCarthy,*
a guest of Joe Vercelli
at the Villa, November 14, 1972

V ERCELLI WAS A NATURAL for the Colony. He was Italian, born and raised in the North Beach area of San Francisco. His father died when Joe was a baby. He was raised by his mother, a woman who brought a winemaking tradition with her from the old country. She made wine in the tub in which she bathed her sons. Upon joining the ISC, Vercelli became an apprentice chemist, learning the wine business under Enrico Prati and Edmund Rossi, Sr. In the lab, he listened and took notes as the two partners discussed blending strategies or evaluated wines in the cellars.

"You can never add too much tannin to sweet wines," Ed Rossi explained to young Vercelli during a tasting session in the lab. "Don't taste wine after eating cheese, nuts or celery. No matter how bad the wine is, it will always taste good. Use dry, heated bread to neutralize the palate when tasting wine. Taste only in the morning to do justice to the wine."

Fifty years before White Zinfandel became a huge success in the marketplace, the winemakers at Asti were making "white" wines from red grapes. According to Vercelli's lab notes, Pinot and Carignane grapes (red) made very favorable dry white wines. "These wines are, to my taste, superior to Malaga and Tokay wines in body, character and bouquet." But elsewhere in his notes, written in 1935, Joe notes that the white wine made from the Mission grape (the famed father of all California *vitis vinifera* grapes was red) was "nothing outstanding. Colorless Carignane was much better, probably make a good, smooth sauterne."

Joe Vercelli had worked at the Colony only three years when he left in 1936 to take over the ailing Scatena brothers' winery in Healdsburg.[N-14] The new job paid $200 per month, a $50-per-month increase. Joe immediately set about the business of cleaning up a cellar filled with poor wines and establishing procedures to make sound wines. On May 29, 1938, he married Livia Prigioni in St. Peter and Paul's Church in San Francisco. By 1942, six years after taking over at Scatena Brothers, Joe had sold off the inventory and resolved the winemaking problems. Now he was ready to go out on his own.

Together with his brother, Joe acquired the Costa Magna Winery from Dominic Ferraro. The winery was located about where the Foss Creek School is located on Healdsburg Avenue, north of town. For eighteen years Vercelli produced wine. In 1945 his Alpine label wine was served at the banquet celebrating the newly chartered United Nations. The end came in 1954. Vercelli owed $300,000 to the Pacific National Bank in Ukiah. Business was good enough to carry the loan and Joe was comfortable with his debt load. But the bank hired a new loan officer who wanted to tighten up the bank's loan portfolio, and one of his actions was to call Vercelli's loan. There was no way Vercelli could pay off the note. He tried to sell his inventory and was offered twelve cents a gallon for wine that cost him over one dollar a gallon to make. Joe faced ruin until friends in the industry helped him. Thanks to Jeff Peyser, the attorney for the Wine Institute, and Herman Wente and Harry Bacigalupi, Vercelli found buyers willing to pay market price for his inventory. Joe sold everything he had and

Joseph Vercelli. Picture taken in the Healdsburg Wine Library, 1998. Joe is in front of a "Vercelli Exhibit." A younger Joe, tasting wine, is pictured to the right. Courtesy of Anne Vercelli.

escaped bankruptcy. Vercelli describes his experience as an entrepreneur as a case of "riches to rags."

Broke and chastened, Vercelli returned to the Colony in 1954. No longer a junior chemist, Vercelli, now 42 years old with nineteen years of experience, was hired as plant manager. He was the sixth plant manager at Asti since the Colony was founded, a span of 73 years. The job opened when plant manager Paul Heck, along with his brother Adolph, quit to acquire the Korbel winery.

Vercelli was a product of the Great Depression, a man who had enjoyed success and faced down the terrors of a very competitive, cruel business world. In some ways, he was like his noted predecessor Enrico Prati, tough, hard working, loyal, honest and principled. But the year was 1954 and Vercelli was missing other character elements that he needed to manage people during the late fifties and through the sixties. Joe could not see past his own experiences in the thirties and early forties, when a man was thankful for a job that offered long hours and low wages. Vercelli never understood the now liberated worker's side and he never learned to work with the unionized work force he now faced at Asti.[N-15]

He found out the hard way that it was no longer simple for the boss to fire an employee who had failed in his obligation to the company. The union demanded proof of misdoing and Vercelli, blinded by a set of principles that he must remain faithful to, set out to do the right thing as he saw it. He took to carrying a camera so that, hidden behind a tank, he could photograph transgressing workers and thus acquire the proof that the union demanded. Or he carried a hidden tape recorder to record incriminating conversations. Like his predecessor Enrico Prati, Joe Vercelli didn't need his employees to love him, but he did want their respect. And yet he unwittingly went out of his way to destroy any respect his men might have had for him. If only they had understood each other...

Vercelli ran the Colony at Asti for seventeen years before senior management replaced him. In 1971, at 59 years of age, he was given a new job. His new title was Manager of Hospitality. It was a job, at last, that was perfectly suited to his talents. But Joe hated it. He worked primarily at the Inglenook Winery in Napa Valley. He reported to an ex-newspaperman with no wine experience who, worst of all, was twenty years Joe's junior.

Heublein could take his job at Asti away, but they could never take away the memories. Joe had worn two hats during his days at Asti. Not only did he run the plant, but for fifteen years he had served as host to the thousands of people who visited Asti for special tours, tastings and banquets. If he struggled with the former, there was no one on earth who could have done a better job at the latter.

Vercelli had shades of Enrico Prati in him on the one hand, but he was more like Andrea Sbarboro on the other. Sbarboro, had he ever been given the choice, would have unhesitatingly chosen Joe Vercelli as his successor at the Villa Pompeii. As if ordained by fate, Vercelli "met" Sbarboro when Joe was just five years old. It was an event that occurred some eighty years ago, but Vercelli remembers the day as if "it had happened yesterday."

Joe clutched tightly at his mother's hand as they prepared to enter Sbarboro's Italian American Bank on the corner of Sacramento and Montgomery Streets in San Francisco. Momma had briefed the five-year-old on the intricacies of the revolving door and explained how he would have to go through the door by himself, since there wasn't much room in the moving space. And now they faced the door. Little Joe, heart pumping, entered the great door alone. His senses on overload and pulse pounding, Joe followed the door as it moved before him. He turned to look over his shoulder for Momma's support and to be sure the door behind him wasn't catching up. Suddenly he was inside a big room. Directly in front of him stood a gigantic man who was greeting people as they entered the bank. It was Andrea Sbarboro. It is doubtful the great man even noticed the tiny boy who would one day entertain visitors at Sbarboro's cherished villa at Asti.

Within a few years of his return to Asti in 1954, Vercelli's bosses recognized his talent as a host and speechmaker. Slowly at first, but with increasing frequency, Joe was asked to "arrange something" for visiting VIPs. By early 1959 Joe had created the "Villa Activity File," which detailed every lunch, every dinner, every event that Joe would host over the next twelve years. In meticulous detail, each event was chronicled down to the type of serving ware, the kind and amount of meat served and the wines poured. Detailed cooking notes included such items as quantities of food used for parties of a given size, cooking times and seasonings used. Seating and serving arrangements were carefully recorded. The notes were written in pencil. After each event, Vercelli would write a critique, this time with notes written in red pencil.

Many of the events involved special winery tours. The tours were planned with military precision. Senior tasting-room people manned trams that would arrive at selected locations on a minute-by-minute schedule. Narratives at each spot were written and rehearsed in advance. Particular wines were made ready in the hospitality room.

Linens, silverware, flowers, all were carefully and meticulously planned.

Vercelli's file folders eventually filled two cartons. Over twelve years, Joe hosted approximately four hundred events, a prodigious sum that averaged not much less than one per week. Vercelli's notes would indicate that as many as ten thousand people enjoyed his hospitality during that twelve-year span. The visitors were an eclectic group. They included people in the wine trade and bank presidents. United Nations Day, January 6, 1963, saw thirty UN ambassadors and delegates visit Asti. Sebastiano Cardinal Baggio, prefect of the Congregation of Bishops in Rome and a potential candidate for the papacy, was a visitor for an evening dinner under the arbor. Radio personalities and politicians of every stripe visited Asti. Rudy Vallee, America's top male vocalist before Bing Crosby, was a signatory for Joe's guest book.

But success drifted to excess. Asti had reached such acclaim that groups with only a casual interest in wine began to pay for their events at Asti. Under Allied Grape Growers, the idea of promoting Colony wines began to fade and at times was forgotten. In 1968 Heublein acquired the winery. Heublein, the master at marketing, never understood the power of the tools they had in Joe Vercelli and the Villa Pompeii. Rather than focusing on Colony wines, Heublein events became pure entertainment functions. Beer, cocktails and particularly Smirnoff vodka were served as Heublein forfeited the opportunity to expose its guests, and particularly its sales force, to the pleasures of wine.

Vercelli retired from the Colony in 1978. He was Sonoma County's elder wine statesman. He was known and loved by people both in and outside the wine industry. As the 21st century approaches, Joe still lives in his house of 38 years in Healdsburg, California. His walls at home are filled with awards and mementos of a full career. His wife, Livia, and daughter, Anne, are still with him. While neither woman received the public accolades awarded Vercelli, Joe deeply appreciates the help the two ladies of his life afforded him. Livia suffers from Alzheimer's disease but Anne is there, lovingly caring for her mother and still active father. She teaches cooking at the Santa Rosa community college two nights a week. Joe, at 86, has slowed down but the sparkle in his eyes is as bright as it's ever been. Andrea Sbarboro would be proud.

Owners came and went. Millions of visitors came and went. But the people of Asti stayed. They alone enjoyed the pulsing seasons of Asti. Living to the rhythms and tempo given them by earlier generations the families enjoyed a life that the visiting luminaries might have envied if only they could have looked with seeing eyes. Life was complete at Asti. Babies were born, the elderly died. The young did what the young do everywhere, fell in love and got married.

🐦

The full church grew quiet in anticipation. What were they waiting for? She peeked past the bridesmaid into the waiting church. Inexplicably, her mind wandered to the last time she had processed down that aisle. That time, too, she had worn a white dress. She remembered it like it was yesterday, the slow march down the aisle, her hands folded piously, all eyes seemingly on her. She recalled worrying about what communion would taste like. How would it feel? What if she couldn't swallow it?

She remembered all those Sundays, sitting on the hard concrete ledge that supported the walls of the church. She thought of the days in spring and summer when her attention was distracted by the birds in the tree outside the window—she suppressed a smile as she recalled the days when she listened to the singing birds instead of Father's sermon.

She noticed Grandma in the front pew and a momentary sadness swept over her as she recalled holding tight to Grandpa's hand as he used to escort her down the aisle before Mass. The reverie was suddenly broken when Jo Del Sarto struck up the first notes of the Wedding March. With a nudge from Dad, they started toward the altar, gleaming white in its fresh coat of paint. The incoming light streamed through the golden chalice in the stained glass window above the altar.

Father Dillon and the man of her life stood there, solemnly look-ing straight at her. Friends and families she'd known all her life filled the little church and now all eyes were upon her. She took a breath and started down the aisle while a few giant tears made their way down her cheeks. It was over in a matter of minutes. She and her husband made their way back up the aisle. El Carmelo watched her leave, a married women, ready to play the next act in her role at Asti.

23

Circus at the Top

Man will err while yet he strives.
—*Johan Wolfgang von Goethe*

ON SEPTEMBER 1, 1959, Allied Grape Growers purchased United Vintners from Petri for $24 million.[70] There would be no down payment and the loan was to be paid off in ten years. Petri agreed to stay on as president of United Vintners for seven years. B. C. Solari continued to serve as executive vice-president in charge of sales. Petri, with an ailing heart, was clearly thinking of retirement but he knew only one way to run a business, aggressively. While he now reported to chairman of the board Bob McInturf, Petri did not slow down.

In 1961, Petri moved United Vintners into Napa Valley with the purchase of the Cella family wineries, including the Napa Wine Company in Oakville. In May 1964, United Vintners acquired the venerable Inglenook Winery from John Daniel, Jr. This put Allied Grape Growers in the super-premium wine business even though most of its grower members were growing base-quality fruit in the Central Valley. But as long as Petri was around, the quality image of Inglenook was maintained.

Petri's plan for Inglenook was described in the press by B. C. Solari:[71]

1. Continue Inglenook's estate bottling practice, i.e. United Vintners (AGG) would grow 100% of the grapes used for Inglenook wines.
2. UV would continue vintage dating of Inglenook wines.
3. UV would continue using the Napa Valley designation of origin.
4. UV would produce only varietal wines at Inglenook.

In 1966, less than three years after acquiring Inglenook, Allied Grape Growers completed their payments for United Vintners to Petri, who promptly retired. B. C. Solari now ran United Vintners, reporting to Bob McInturf. It wasn't long before Solari repudiated the policy established by Petri in 1964. In a move to increase sales volume, Solari created a line of Inglenook vintage-dated generic wines wherein inexpensive Central Valley grapes could be used to lower the price of what the public perceived as an Inglenook brand. As anticipated, case sales increased dramatically. Louis Petri's reaction: "... After I left, United Vintners did do certain things with Inglenook that I very much disagreed with. They went into generics, which they should never have done."[72]

At retirement, Petri could look back on a productive career. He had created United Vintners nearly twenty years earlier and was responsible for the formation of Allied Grape Growers in 1951. He was 55 years old and had been a dynamic leader of the California wine industry most of his adult life. In 1953 he brought his family winery with its Petri brand together with Italian Swiss Colony and its ISC brands. He maintained the ISC brand as the top label in his wine empire. Louis Petri was the last wine man to see the value in the ISC brand and in the marvelous wine center at Asti. But change was in the wind.

With the departure of Petri, Allied lost its wine leader and resident genius. It wasn't long before Allied missed Petri and his experience. When Heublein expressed an interest in acquiring the company, Allied Grape Growers jumped at the chance to join with this marketing-savvy company. In November of 1969, Allied sold 82% of its stock to Heublein, Inc. Heublein paid in shares of company stock, the value equivalent to over $33 million.[73]

With this acquisition, Heublein owned eight wineries with a total storage capacity over fifty million gallons (See Figure 1, page 240). That same year Heublein added the venerable Beaulieu Vineyards to its winery holdings. The wine people were enthusiastic about Heublein coming into their lives. Heublein was a master beverage marketeer, with a sales force in place in practically every city in America. Under Heublein, they reasoned, their problems with marketing wine would be over.

Heublein was a company of bean counters and salesmen and they did their work well. Heublein's major product was Smirnoff vodka. It was the world's number one vodka. Heublein had recently "invented" the cocktail in a bottle, a product that was enormously successful. The airlines were particularly keen customers for the premixed drink that saved work for busy cabin attendants.

A successful salesman must have a large ego. That ego is nourished by success. The success at Heublein led to a "know-it-all" staff, which led in turn to a company with a fully developed corporate ego. It is a maxim taught to every marketing and would-be salesperson in business schools everywhere that knowledge of the product is a major requirement for success. Not even a product as simple as a beverage is exempt from this fundamental requirement. Heublein knew spirits but it did not know wine. That should not have been a problem for Heublein. They had a successful team of beverage marketeers and salespeople; all they had to do was learn about wine and the tenets of its marketing. But Heublein's very success got in its way. Egos built on successful vodka sales now obscured vision. Heublein was unable to recognize their inadequacy when it came to marketing wine.

Heublein's plan for their California wine empire made sense at corporate headquarters in Connecticut. They had invested heavily in their California wine venture and they wanted a return on their investment. Under the plan, Heublein would continue to emphasize their Central Valley wine production, since those wineries produced wine for the major market. They would serve the premium end of the market with the Beaulieu Vineyards line.

But it was the Inglenook brand and its sales potential that drew special attention. Heublein wanted to capitalize on the special niche that B. C. Solari had created by expanding production of the Inglenook brand. Solari answered the call. He now created the Inglenook Navalle line of "popularly priced wines." The Navalle line started out using primarily north-coast grapes, but in the interest of lowering the bottle price, these expensive grapes were gradually replaced with Central Valley fruit. Eventually, there wasn't a single Napa Valley grape in the blend. Ironically, the name Navalle was a contraction of Napa Valley.

There can be no question as to Heublein's success with the Navalle line. When United Vintners acquired the winery in 1964, Inglenook's case sales totaled about 25,000 cases a year. By 1979, ten years after Heublein acquired United Vintners, case sales of Inglenook wines, based primarily on the Navalle brand, reached almost eight million cases per year. The strategy was a success. But there was a second result, one the decision makers didn't care about. That was the continued devastation of the once proud and venerable Inglenook brand.

Heublein tried to work the same magic with Beaulieu Vineyards. Here, however, Heublein had to contend with Leigh Knowles, president of BV. Knowles insisted that Heublein use standard marketing tools to test and evaluate their marketing strategy at Beaulieu Vineyards. When it became clear that a scheme to move more wine through the use of magnum bottles was lessening public esteem of the Beaulieu brand, Heublein was forced to back off and BV was saved the fate of Inglenook. It is interesting to note Louis Petri's views, expressed to Ruth Teiser in the fall of 1969. "What fools they (Heublein) would be if they bastardize or lessen the quality, or mass-merchandise something like Beaulieu."[74]

For its part, ISC was in no man's land. Years earlier, during the 1930's, the twins had placed ISC in the "screw-top" wine market segment. This made sense, since that was where the market was. That decision kept ISC alive, but it would destroy the Colony under Heublein. The Heublein wine empire included four giant wineries, with a combined capacity close to forty million gallons, which operated in

The tasting room in 1934. Behind the bar: Walter Del Tredici. Facing camera: Enrico Prati in customary tie and chaps. Man with back to camera is likely Lou Pellegrini. Italian Swiss Colony photo.

the jug-wine segment of the wine market. ISC had just nine million gallons capacity at Asti, and the grapes at Asti cost appreciably more than those in the Central Valley. Furthermore, ISC's market image was considerably closer to the Central Valley than it was to Napa Valley.

For Heublein's marketing experts, it was a no brainer. The marketing budget for ISC's world famous Tipo brand was eliminated. Sales of the brand went down and the product was consequently dropped. The bottling line at Asti, long the cutting-edge facility in the wine industry and the pride and joy of the workers at Asti, was now in the wrong place. Machine by machine, roller by roller, the lines were dismantled and sent to the Mission Bell winery at Madera. As if completing a self-fulfilling prophecy, Heublein ignored or cut back at Asti and ISC sales fell.

Asti was unlike most commercial localities. From its first day in 1881, Asti had been a somewhat isolated "company community." It was a place for which its people had given up their native country and had endured years of separation from wives and children. Asti embodied their lives' aspirations. This was an investment of their very lives, for all time, under whose glare the concept of short-term profits withered. By the time Heublein came into the picture, the people of Asti had worked there all their lives, as had their parents and grandparents. Asti was not an Appalachian mining town. There was no drive to escape the misery of the infamous mining towns. They worked as hard as ever, did what was asked of them, and still the fortunes of ISC fell. The decline was painful and unfathomable to the people of Asti and the surrounding towns, Cloverdale and Geyserville.

The tasting room was where Asti showed itself off to the general public. Its enormous success was in no small measure due to the genuine pride the employees had in ISC, and the joy they felt showing their company and its wines to visitors. For the bean counters three thousand miles away in the East, and light years away in mentality, however, the tasting room was anathema to the bottom line. And so the tasting room was nudged into a slow decline, and ultimately oblivion. First to go were the free cookies, then the free postage and finally the free postcards. It was a classic chocolate chip cookie case.

The public continued to support the tasting room, but with time the support diminished. In 1982, R. J. Reynolds acquired Heublein. Legend has it that shortly after the acquisition, a senior member of Reynolds went into the tasting room one winter morning in midweek and hung around to see firsthand the level of activity. After a morning that saw just a few bottles of wine sold, the Reynolds man had seen enough.

A few mornings later, Nello Baiocchi came into the tasting room to prepare for the day's tours. Baiocchi had been doing this for over forty years. This day however, was different, for Nello's boss greeted him with instructions to report to the production department the next day. The tasting room was closing. For the first time in almost fifty years, the tasting room went dark. An institution ended, an era was over.

Baiocchi will never forget that moment nor will the others who worked there. It seemed that most of Cloverdale was employed at Asti, and if you didn't work full time, you worked part time at the hospitality center. There was a pall over Cloverdale that evening, and from that pall would emerge bitterness and ultimately hatred. The people of Asti had never before experienced the ways of big business. Like unrequited lovers, they were angry and stunned to their very cores. There was one more dimension to the bewildering event. In addition to closing the tasting room, Reynolds transferred additional bottling responsibility to the winery at Madera, further reducing operations at Asti. Between the two cutbacks, thirty people lost their jobs. It was three weeks before Christmas.

The vineyards around the winery, having grown old under Heublein's neglect, had now become profit-stealing millstones, so they were bulldozed over. The shock waves of the events at Asti spread far beyond the tiny community. County newspaper stories reflected the dissolution and despair of the north-county communities. It would not be until 1988, when Wine World Estates acquired the property, that any steward of Asti would work to assuage the feelings at Asti and throughout Sonoma County.

Heublein's decision to downgrade ISC wines was commercially defensible. Their use of Asti as a party park, however, approached malfeasance. Inglenook clearly had the most beautiful winery in the Heublein family. Neither Inglenook nor Beaulieu Vineyards, however, had Asti, with its special ambiance. Neither did they have the Villa Pompeii, Andrea Sbarboro's gift to Asti. And Asti alone had Joe Vercelli, so well-suited to the unique stage provided by the Villa. It was the perfect prop and Joe the perfect actor to extol the beauty of one of nature's gifts to man, the fruit of the vine, the nectar of the gods.

Instead Heublein changed Asti into another kind of hospitality center. Heublein was a marketing company and they did a lot of entertaining. Now customers and employees visiting San Francisco or the Bay Area were invited to dine beneath Sbarboro's arbor. Sometimes there would first be the obligatory winery tour and wine tasting. But Heublein was downgrading Asti wines, so that enthusiasm for promoting the ISC brand was muted at best. The principal reason for visiting Asti was R & R, and high on the list of visitors were Heublein vodka salespeople and whiskey trade customers.

Guests would savor the stroll down the palm-tree-bordered road to the Villa and gather the fullness of the ambiance that is Asti. As they entered the shaded gardens beyond the Villa, they could feel the beauty and serenity of the place. There were tables set with white tablecloths, good silver and place settings. Wineglasses were carefully set at each place for the Italian banquet about to unfold. The staff of waiters greeted the guests and offered the featured beverage of the evening, Smirnoff vodka. If the affair was an afternoon luncheon, plenty of cold beer was available.

There is no record of the wineglasses that went unused at those affairs. It is easy to assume, however, that few if any guests remembered the ISC wines they were served that day. Perhaps it was just as well. In a squandering of resources, Asti had been reduced to producing such wines as Key Largo, a "taste of oranges sweet as wine," Bali Hai, an "exotic grape wine punch" and Vin Kafe, a "grape wine… with pure flavors of tantalizing… coffee and rich cocoa."

By summer of 1983, after only a year, Reynolds had completed its look at the wine business. It did not like what it saw. The business of growing grapes and making wine was highly capital intensive. Deciding they could find better ways to invest their capital and time, Reynolds looked for a buyer. They found Allied Grape Growers. On July 12, 1983, Allied Grape Growers signed an agreement to purchase ISC. Allied was optimistic about the future for ISC wines, but once again they were mostly interested in a home for their members' grapes. For $62 million, the Grape Growers acquired four wineries: Asti, Lodi (Community Winery, close by the now closed Shewan-Jones), the old Petri Winery at Escalon and the plant at Reedley. None of these wineries had bottling facilities, so AGG had to rely on Heublein to bottle for them at the Madera winery. This was, of course, the old Asti bottling plant, which Heublein had retained.

The wine labels involved were Italian Swiss Colony (dessert wines), Colony (table wines), Petri (table wines), Annie Greensprings, Lejon and the J. Bonet brand (champagne). The new company was named ISC Wines. Reynolds kept the cream, holding on to Inglenook and Beaulieu in addition to the Madera winery with its state-of-the-art bottling facility. Incredibly, the purchase did not include the heart of the Asti vineyards, approximately one thousand acres that stretched almost two miles from Dutcher Creek Road to the Lucca Ranch. Of course, these vineyards would have competed for winery space with those of Allied's members.

Allied Grape Growers put up $12 million and financed the rest, nearly $50 million. With so much on the line, Allied hired ERLY Industries to manage the company. ERLY also got an option to purchase the company. ERLY owned the Sierra Wine Company, with Central Valley wineries located at Tulare and Delano, but ERLY's principal business was bottled fruit juices. Allied was pleased. They owned four large wineries which would assure homes for their members' grapes, and they had marketing professionals (ERLY) to sell their wine.

The folks at Asti were overjoyed with their new owners. Once again there would be wine people, not vodka people, in charge. That fall, Asti was the site of still another major celebration. The faces had changed, but the crowd had a familiar look. Although the Sbarboros were gone, the Rossis were represented by Pietro Rossi's grandson and ISC winemaker Ed Rossi, Jr. Practically the entire Asti team of employees was there to welcome Allied back.

Many in the crowd had worked at the Colony for over forty years, and their parents had met working at Asti. Pete Seghesio was there. It was Pete's father, Edoardo, who had been at Asti almost from the beginning and who had probably saved Asti from subdivision at the dark days of Prohibition. Pete and Edoardo spanned 97 years of Colony history, all of that time within walking distance from the site of the party.

While the theme of the day was the future, there can be no future without a past. In 1983, one hundred and one years had passed since the *Cloverdale Reveille* reported on the first party at Asti on May 6, 1882. In 1882, 75 visitors came by train from San Francisco. A sizable contingent came from Geyserville and Healdsburg and a very large number of guests came from Cloverdale. They had a brass band, violins and a new dance floor. The *Reveille* reported that "the hospitality of the Colony was unbounded." The San Francisco guests stayed until the next afternoon and departed on the two o'clock train. For the revelers of 1882, there was little past, but an endless future. For the party-goers in 1983, there was a past. Years of frustration watching Asti being gradually dismantled could not be forgotten in an instant. There was a deeply felt element of skepticism that fall afternoon at Asti, but the folks hoped, rather than reasoned, that this would be the dawning of a new era.

The party in 1983 had tours of the winery. They didn't have brass instruments and violins, but they had a Ferris wheel. And to regale the guests and herald the reopening of the tasting room, the Little Old Winemaker was there. Missing was Edmund A. Rossi, Sr., who of all the Rossis had spent the most time at Asti.

Sentiment that day looked for return of the Little Old Winemaker, but it was not to be. ERLY decided that the Little Old Winemaker would not be consistent with the new image they planned to create for ISC Wines. New brands were established including Creekside Cellars, the North Coast Cellars brand which was acquired from Chateau Souverain, a winery located in nearby Geyscrville. The Creekside Cellars label would seem to provide a glimpse at the mindset of the ERLY people. It was not vintage dated and was generally sold in one-liter bottles. North Coast Cellars had been a successful second label for Souverain. Ed Rossi, Jr., once told Ruth Teiser,[75] "We upgraded the quality in that brand as part of the new product list [sic] North Coast Cellars."

ISC Wines was focused on "good price-to-value relationship" for its wine, a sure sign they were aiming for good but not necessarily outstanding wines. Clearly the ISC business plan was market driven, the only problem being it was the wrong market for Asti-based ISC Wines. Pietro Rossi had blended a small portion of Central Valley wines with Asti wines to make the generic dinner wines popular in his day, but the older Rossi operated at a different time, in a different market. P. C. Rossi sought to make the finest California wines possible. That heritage continued up until Prohibition but seems to have

262   Legacy of a Village

been lost after Repeal, when the domestic wine market called for
screw-top wines. ISC Wines was stuck with a Central Valley image
built over fifty years and ERLY did little to dispel that image.

Along with the four wineries, Heublein sent Ed Rossi to Allied,
although the vodka distributor reserved the right to continue using
Rossi one month each year in a deal worked out between Jack Power
of Heublein and Bob McInturf of Allied. Rossi would thus be free to
continue his consulting role at Lancers, Heublein's winery in Portugal. Rossi was assigned by Allied to Asti and given the job of producing award-winning dinner wines. But there was a catch. Allied had
gone heavily into debt in the Heublein deal, close to $50 million
worth. They needed to push wine to handle the debt load. There
would be little, if any, money available to upgrade the production
facilities or to acquire the grapes necessary to produce a premium
line of wines.

Asti's vineyards, which should have been Asti's most valued pos-
session, were now a detriment. Allied was, after all, a grape-grower
cooperative. They had acquired the winery at Asti as a home for their
grapes. Allied's owner/growers did not want to compete with the
grapes grown at Asti, so the vineyards, or what was left of them after
Heublein, were not rejuvenated. Nearly two hundred acres east of
the freeway, some in vines over one hundred years, were plowed
under or just ignored. In fairness to Allied, it must be noted that the
vineyards reflected the neglect given them by Heublein. Heublein
had shown little interest and made no investment in the vineyards.
Now in disrepair, planted to the wrong grapes for the market, the
vineyards were of little immediate value.

Allied, desperately short of cash, could never have made the investment necessary to upgrade the vines. Of course, Allied must have
known this prior to spending all their money on what they did get.
Unfortunately, precious old Zinfandel vines went out, along with
Chenin Blanc and other out-of-favor European varieties. The thousand acres that Heublein kept west of the freeway were now planted
to oat hay, and cattle roamed where once Truett's sheep had grazed.

In a bizarre twist, Ed Rossi, working for grape growers with excess grapes, had no fruit for his new line of super-premium wines. Rossi set about acquiring grapes from the top growers in Sonoma County, particularly Chardonnay and Sauvignon Blanc. He didn't need a lot of fruit; his budget would allow only for limited production of the new brand. Rossi wanted only Sonoma County grapes to go into the new, top-of-the-line label, Sbarboro. He completed arrangements with growers in time to supply grapes for the 1984 harvest. But Rossi had still another problem. By the 1980's, most premium white grapes were crushed by bladder-type presses. These presses subjected the fruit to a more gentle crushing than the old screw-type process, which crushed stems and seeds, lending a herbaceous, tannic element to the finished wine. But Allied did not own a bladder press and they refused to spend the roughly $20,000 it would have taken to purchase one.

Determined to set the highest possible standards for the new brand, Rossi sought the services of a small premium winery located just three miles west of Asti. The winery, owned by San Francisco businessman J. Fritz, had been in operation only a few years and owned the modern equipment necessary to make the high-quality wine that technology made possible in 1984. Rossi arranged to have his premium white grapes crushed and pressed at the J. Fritz Winery. The juice would then be shipped to the winery at Asti where it would be fermented, finished and bottled. Unfortunately, it was an exceptionally hot late summer and the grapes arrived at the winery overripe and beyond the perfection that Rossi sought. The fruit was deemed unsatisfactory for the Sbarboro label and Rossi had to wait another year before pursuing his life's dream.

In 1985 Rossi and Fritz repeated the process. Rossi was particularly excited about a small lot of Johannisburg Riesling. He had found the grapes at the highly acclaimed Belle Terre vineyard in Alexander Valley and Rossi was certain they would produce a wonderful late-harvest wine. There was a problem, however. The lot was far too small to process at Asti. But Fritz, with its small tanks, was perfect. In an arrangement that has always been widespread in the industry, Rossi asked Fritz to do a custom crush.[N-16] Under the custom crush arrangement, Rossi would supply the grapes which Fritz would make into wine under Rossi's specific instructions. The winemaker at Fritz, as quiet and self-effacing as he was brilliant, was David Hastings. Dave had no problem producing Rossi's wine from Rossi's detailed written instructions. Hastings remembers Rossi as a high-strung, nervous wreck worrying over the wine as it went through production. It became a winery joke that if Rossi continued to sample the wines, there wouldn't be enough left to bottle.

Rossi and his team dumped the grapes, as they arrived at the winery, on trays for close inspection. This was a step unheard-of in the production of jug wines. If there was rot on any cluster, the cluster was discarded. Only grapes in perfect condition went into the press. Rossi was all over the winery, directing and watching every step made by Hastings and his staff. At last the wine was bottled and set to rest on the cork. Rossi was thrilled with the quality of the wine. Finally released in September 1986, it would eventually win four awards.

But for Rossi, the long sought-after achievement would be tarnished. Shortly after its release, the wine was sampled by the widely syndicated wine columnist, Dan Berger. Berger tasted the wine and loved it. He found the wine to be "excellent, better than any Colony wine I had ever tasted." Berger's eyes were drawn to the "mandatories," that information printed at the bottom of the label as required by the Bureau of Alcohol, Tobacco and Firearms. He saw the words: "BW 5018, Cloverdale, CA." Berger knew that the Colony was located in Asti and not Cloverdale. It was a simple matter to identify BW 5018. It was Fritz Cellars. He called the winery. Afraid that Hastings might be reluctant to discuss the matter, Berger carefully constructed his questions so as to draw Hastings out. And Hastings did not sense the nature of Berger's call, which was to find out who in fact had produced the wonderful wine. He answered the questions put to him, including those about his own winemaking career. For Hastings, that was the end of it.

Berger's column[76] appeared in the *Santa Rosa Press Democrat*. It was a straightforward, factual description of events as Berger had found them, but the column headline hinted at an underlying story. The headline read: "Despite label, Colony wine excellent." For Ed Rossi, it was devastating. Clearly Berger didn't believe the Colony was capable of producing such a fine wine. When he learned that Hastings had trained in Germany, Berger felt his notions about ISC were confirmed. In his column Berger stated, "Hastings, who studied how to make Riesling at Geisenheim, Germany for eighteen months during 1981 and 1982 said that experience helped him make this exceptional wine."

The years of frustration finally boiled over for Ed Rossi. He blew his top, his anger directed at Hastings, who Rossi felt had tried to steal credit for the wine. It is probably true that Hastings' experience and skill as a winemaker contributed to the exceptional quality of the Colony Riesling. Could Rossi have produced such a fine wine with the right equipment on his own? It is likely that he could have. Berger quoted Hastings as saying, "The Colony should get the credit for picking the grapes. They came in in perfect condition." Eleven years later, Hastings remembered events of that autumn. He will never be certain that he convinced Rossi that he (Hastings) wasn't trying to take credit that belonged to Rossi or ISC Wines. The record unfortunately suggests that Hastings never did make amends with Rossi. Starting in 1986, Rossi went elsewhere to have his premium white grapes crushed in a bladder press. There is one final note to this story. Rossi never got his bladder press, although it was one of the first pieces of equipment installed by Wine World Estates after they acquired the winery in 1989.

In 1987, after three years of managing the Colony, ERLY exercised its option and purchased ISC Wines. To operate their new wineries, ERLY created a new entity, the Beverage Source. In a move to stop the losses that ISC had suffered until then, the Beverage Source closed down the Community Winery at Lodi, and the Petri winery at Escalon was sold to Heublein. ERLY Industries, which had owned the Sierra Wine Company wineries at Tulare and Delano, closed the Delano facility, but the Tulare plant continued in operation. But outside of a new name on company letterhead, nothing changed at Asti. On a path to oblivion, the new owners struggled to forestall the inevitable. This was not the case with ERLY's principal competitor, E & J Gallo.

Ernest and Julio Gallo founded and operated the most successful winery the world has ever known. Success is often ascribed to being in the right place at the right time. It can be argued that the Gallos took the maxim one step further. They seized the moment following World War II when many of their competitors were still owned by the distilling companies. While the distillers looked for ways to get out of the wine business, Gallo mounted a major advertising campaign to promote their brand.

The giants of the day, Roma (Schenley) and Italian Swiss Colony (National Distillers) saw their massive market share shrink. By the late fifties, a span of less than ten years, Gallo had drawn even. Gallo and the Colony fought head to head during the sixties and seventies, Gallo from its home offices in Livingston and ISC from Asti. They competed for the same market, but in many ways they were the antithesis of each other. Gallo was located in the heart of the San Joaquin Valley and its supply of less costly grapes. Gallo blended a small proportion of wine from Sonoma and Napa Counties to enhance their wines. The Colony did the opposite. They "imported" large quantities of fruit from the San Joaquin Valley to add to their own small portion of premium grapes grown in Sonoma County.

Gallo was managed continuously by the same team located at the winery. Top management at ISC never operated from the winery. Furthermore, entrance to the ISC executive suite seemed to be through a rapidly turning revolving door, while the Gallo family has run their winery for over sixty years. The Gallo brothers were masters of their craft. One can only wonder about the fireworks had the two the opportunity to enjoin Pietro Rossi and Andrea Sbarboro or Louis Petri in battle.

Gallo always kept an eye on Asti. In 1952 they paid for the privilege of a thorough examination of the Colony books. Gallo decided not to buy. Thirty-seven years later, Ernest and Julio, still leading the family business, made their move. In 1989 they acquired the one thousand acres of Asti vineyards west of the freeway and still owned by Heublein. Heublein had let the land go fallow, but now, six years after selling the wincry to Allied Grape Growers, Heublein received an estimated $13 million for the heart of old Asti. This was the same vineyard that Antonio Perelli-Minetti had termed "a lemon." This was the land the Colony had treated with trainloads of horse manure collected from the streets of San Francisco.

But in 1990, E & J Gallo had the vision of its owners and sixty years of vineyard technology working for them. A horde of massive bulldozers and graders moved onto the land. The vineyard workers of the 19th century could never have pictured the work of these giant machines late in the 20th century. The beautiful contours of the land were maintained, if not improved. The low yields of Perelli-Minetti's time were solved with the latest techniques in soil improvement.

Drip irrigation, unknown in the early Colony days, brought increased life and vigor to the vines. Its days long gone, what was left of the Lucca Ranch was pushed aside and grapes planted. Local senior citizens agree that the beauty has returned to the Asti vineyards. In her eighties, Bernice (Baiocchi) Trusendi says the walk to school from her old house in Chianti would look the same today as it did when she was seven years old.

By the mid-eighties, Gallo, showing why it was the number-one winery in the world, recognized the market shift to premium wines produced from the premium vineyards of Sonoma and Napa Counties. Gallo rapidly expanded their operations in Sonoma County, even as AGG and ERLY were shrinking theirs. Not only did Gallo acquire most of Asti, they expanded their winery in Dry Creek Valley and purchased new vineyards in Dry Creek, because Gallo recognized the liquid rubies that were Dry Creek's red wines.

But the Central Valley mentality continued to plague Colony owners and in early 1988 ERLY, unable to see what Gallo clearly perceived, decided to get out of Asti. That spring they found a buyer, Nestlé, the European food giant. Nestlé was not interested in the Italian Swiss Colony brand name or the product line. They wanted only the production facility and vineyards at Asti. For the grand Italian Swiss Colony venture, nearly 107 years old, it was over.

Nestlé also didn't want the Teamsters union at Asti. The union contract would be rendered null and void if Asti shut down so that no teamster worked at the winery for a thirty-day period. On the last Friday of May 1988, ERLY shut down the winery at Asti. The entire work force was laid off, including many who had worked for over forty years at Asti. A little more than thirty days later, ERLY reopened the winery in preparation for the 1988 crush. Many of the old employees were hired back and most of them at better wages than they had been earning before.

But it was not really ERLY who prepared for the 1988 crush, it was Wine World Estates, the American wine arm of Nestlé. The sale to Wine World Estates was finalized on December 20, 1988 when the production facilities at Asti were acquired by the European food giant for six million dollars. The purchase included 540 acres of now unplanted vineyard land. Asti, (but not Italian Swiss Colony, which no longer existed) became a part of Wine World, Inc., a consortium of wineries consisting of Beringer, Chateau Souverain, Chateau St. Jean, Maison Deutz and Meridian Vineyards.

Wine World, to their enormous credit, proved sensitive to the sentiments of the local inhabitants of Cloverdale and Geyserville. They read the widely circulated *Santa Rosa Press Democrat,* with its consistently negative stories about recent stewardship of the once great Asti facility. Guy Kay and Bill Knox, the latter Community Affairs Specialist for Beringer, took charge. Knox worked closely with the people who had spent their lives working at Asti.

Anne Matteoli led a small group who went into every nook and cranny of the old facility and carefully stored and cataloged literally thousands of items, many of which would be treasured pieces in a museum. Joe Vercelli, Alex Carrey and "Peli" Pelanconi helped catalog the enormous collection. Thousand of bottles of wine were recovered from throughout the plant, including Golden State champagne, a case of over 100-year-old Mouton Rothschild and a wide variety of European wines, as well as Colony products. Hundreds of photos chronicled the ages at Asti. Statues and paintings added to the extensive collection.

The grounds around the plant were refurbished. The visitors' parking lot, although no longer used, was cleaned up and maintained. The Villa had been rented for weddings and receptions, so those grounds had been kept up. Wine World closed down the catering business but continued to tend the landscaping for the benefit of no one but the past.

On January 1, 1996, Nestlé got out of the California wine business. Its California wineries were sold to a Texas investment group. Walter Klenz, president of Wine World Estates, stayed on as president of the new company, Beringer Wine Estates. The legacy of Andrea Sbarboro and Pietro Rossi now rests with Mr. Klenz.

Little has changed at Asti. The winery is still there, including several new buildings built in the last few years. But several of the buildings built during the glory days over one hundred years ago are there also. The love tunnel is there, exactly as it was the day San Francisco society walked through its curving passageway from the pompone building to the floor of the giant wine tank. There is no need for it now, and black widow spiders have taken up residence in the dark labyrinth of the tunnel. The tasting room is closed, but a pervasive aura of the past envelops the room. The occasional visitor today is at once transported to the last time he visited these rooms, no matter how many years may have passed since that last visit. Little has changed. The serving bar is dusty and the empty shelves behind the bar reveal a room that is not in use but could be back in service after a little dusting. Beringer's unprecedented sensitivity to the past glories of the place is evident.

While Beringer Wine Estates is in no way related to the old ISC wine company, it has gone to exceptional efforts to preserve Asti. Grapes are still brought to the same scale where Alex Carrey toiled for twenty years, and wine is still made at Asti today. The only discordant note on the knolls at Asti is the brand name of the wine being produced there, Napa Ridge. But they are good wines, produced from carefully selected grapes and made with the finest equipment under the direction of outstanding winemakers. Andrea Sbarboro and P. C. Rossi would once again be proud of Asti's stewards.

Why not Asti Ridge? Alas, it's an imperfect world.

24

Footpaths to Highways

Go joyously for there is great beauty
around the bend.

—Anon

J UST AS EYES ARE the windows to the soul, roads are paths to the
past. The road between Geyserville and neighboring Asti to the
north gives a vivid reflection of life as it existed through the centuries in this tiny portion of northern California.

Today the six-mile distance between Geyserville and Asti is an all
but invisible segment of the nearly 800-mile-long California 101 freeway. Whereas an automobile takes about six minutes to make the
trip, a millennium ago the trip would take a determined traveler on
foot close to three hours. A family could easily spend the better part
of a day picking their way around hills and negotiating steep ravines
or rocky streambeds.

Two hundred years ago, the area was pristine Indian country, as
yet undisturbed by Mexican encroachment. For the Indian traveling
north toward Asti on the west side of the Russian River, the way
north was blocked by two hills about two miles north of town. Through
untold generations, the Indians turned toward the west about where

the Seghesio house is situated to avoid the hills, each of which rose almost three hundred feet above the valley floor. The route made a gentle arc, passing over what would become the Baiocchi place and the neighboring Fretteche house before reaching the hills that rose steeply along the western edge of the valley. The path then headed north, following the foot of the hills before turning eastward, and reached what would one day be the Old Redwood Highway north of the Prati house. Most of the route, as time approaches the 21st century, is a Gallo vineyard. The Baiocchi place, now over ninety years old and recently refurbished, and the Fretteche house, owned by financial advisor Kenny Kahn and his wife, Dr. Cheryl Kahn, are still served by a dirt road, portions of which follow the creek that likely defined the trail used for centuries by the Indians.

In 1859 American settlers, traveling on horseback or pulling wagons, changed the route. Instead of traveling west around the twin hills, they rode up the grade between them. This new path would one day become Chianti Road, then the Old Redwood Highway and finally the 101 freeway. Once past Asti Hill on the right, the road immediately turned east toward the Russian River. This section of the path was later named Viola Avenue (see maps page 274 and inside back cover). It is now a private driveway leading to the Hidden Springs vineyards. The road turned north at the river, crossing what is now Washington School Road, before looping back below and just north of the Rossi villa to the present highway.

In 1865, Truett decided that the hilly terrain over the western portion of his holdings was good only for sheep grazing. He hired Calvin Bosworth to tend the sheep and built Bosworth a house roughly in the middle of the ranch. There was a good spring and even a little flat land for a garden. It was a perfect location for the sheepherder's house. When the Italians came in 1881 they would name the place the Lucca Ranch, after the town in Italy. The only problem for Bosworth was that the roadway turned toward the river before reaching his house. So Truett changed the road once again. Now, instead of turning east behind Asti Hill, the roadway continued north to Bosworth's house, then made its way north along the most convenient hilltops

CABLE ADDRESS - ASTICOLONY - CODES USED A B C CODE 4ᵀᴴ EDITION AND W U TELEGRAPHIC CODE AND CABLE DIRECTORY

P. C. ROSSI, President
A. SBARBORO, Secretary

TEL. MAIN III,

NᴱW YORK BRANCH 20 AND 22 DESBROSS. ST., COR. GREENWICH ST.

ITALIAN SWISS COLONY

TRADE ✚ MARK

WINERIES
ASTI & FULTON
SONOMA CO CAL
MADERA,
MADERA CO. CAL

PRODUCERS OF

FINE WINES ᴬᴺᴰ BRANDIES

SALESROOMS AND VAULTS:
717 719 721 BATTERY STREET,
SECRETARY'S OFFICE. 516 MONTGOMERY ST

GOLD MEDALS AWARDED FOR OUR WINES AND BRANDIES IN
GENOVA ITALY 1892 CHICAGO U S A 1893
DUBLIN IRELAND 1892 SAN FRANCISCO U S A 1894
BORDEAUX FRANCE 1895 ASTI & TURIN ITALY 1898
PARIS 1900 Grand Diploma of Honor

San Francisco, Cal. July 7, 1903

To the Honorable Board of Supervisors,

of Sonoma County,

Santa Rosa, Calif.

Gentlemen:—

The undersigned respectfully and
most urgently request your Honorable Board to have the
county road sprinkled from the northern end of
the Geyserville district to the northern end of the
Washington district on the road to Cloverdale.

Many tourists and visitors are now driving over
this road, some of them are new comers and might be
induced to settle in this locality, but they can hardly
form a good opinion of the county when they can only
see it by driving through a cloud of dust.

Furthermore it will be economy to sprinkle the road
as it will keep it in good condition and not be cut up
by the heavy teams which will soon be hauling grapes
over the road. The saving of a few dollars in omitting
to do this work is certainly false economy.

Hopping that you will give this matter your
favorable consideration, we remain,

Respectfully yours,

Italian-Swiss Colony,

Secretary.

LARGEST PRODUCERS OF FINE DRY AND SWEET WINES IN THE UNITED STATES.

Letter signed by Andrea Sbarboro reflecting an early 20th-century road problem.

until it reached the river about where the Washington School would be built. The road then followed the path of the old road to the north.

In 1872, the railroad came through, hugging the Russian River. Truett, figuring on the boom that was to come to the area, deeded a small piece of land, alongside the road where it met the railroad right of way, for a school. A few years later Truett prepared to divide the flat land that would eventually become the site of the Italian Swiss Colony winery from the hilly sheep land. He extended a line from the schoolhouse in a southwesterly direction a little more than 0.3 miles to a giant live oak tree. The ancient tree, an obvious landmark, had developed two main trunks that grew into parts looking remarkably like each other. The tree was dubbed the "Siamese Twins." A line from the tree headed north, where it reached the neighboring Turner property at a point roughly where the freeway off-ramps would one day be located. The tree itself lies squarely beneath today's freeway, not far from the Rossi villa.

To facilitate the subdivision that produced the two parcels, Truett made the final changes to the roadway, which established the route followed by the Old Redwood Highway today. Truett created Washington School Road along the line separating the two parcels. The road connected the schoolhouse to the new county road a few yards short of the Siamese Twins. Situated on the old 1859 roadway, the Washington School was now about one third of a mile off the main road. For the kids, this meant the walk home included a climb up a hill, as Washington School Road went straight up the incline from the river to the county road. In 1878, the flat piece was sold to English land investor Henry Hutchinson. Two years later, Hutchinson acquired the sheep ranch.

For today's freeway builders, hills and ravines are not an issue. Following behind giant earth movers, the freeway goes where it wants to go. Fortunately, only a few houses were lost to the ravenous freeway right of way, but a lot of history was lost. The six-minute trip in a speeding car barely gives time to consider the Indian family making its way over half a day a few hundred yards to the west to make the same journey.

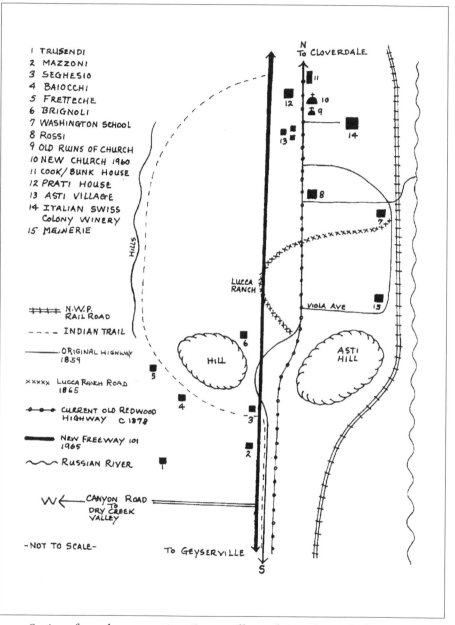

1 TRUSENDI
2 MAZZONI
3 SEGHESIO
4 BAIOCCHI
5 FRETTECHE
6 BRIGNOLI
7 WASHINGTON SCHOOL
8 ROSSI
9 OLD RUINS OF CHURCH
10 NEW CHURCH 1960
11 COOK/BUNK HOUSE
12 PRATI HOUSE
13 ASTI VILLAGE
14 ITALIAN SWISS
   COLONY WINERY
15 MEINERIE

N
TO CLOVERDALE

HILLS

┼┼┼┼ N.W.P.
      RAIL ROAD

------- INDIAN TRAIL

———— ORIGINAL HIGHWAY
      1859

xxxxx LUCCA RANCH ROAD
      1865

•—•—• CURRENT OLD REDWOOD
      HIGHWAY C 1878

▬▬▬ NEW FREEWAY 101
      1965

∿∿∿ RUSSIAN RIVER

W ⟵ CANYON ROAD
      TO
      DRY CREEK
      VALLEY

-NOT TO SCALE-

LUCCA
RANCH

VIOLA AVE

HILL

ASTI
HILL

TO GEYSERVILLE

S

Series of roads connecting Geyserville and Asti through the years.

And flying over smooth concrete at a mile a minute does not give one time to reflect on a dog being chased by a donkey being chased by production hands while a man in an alpine hat and shorts waits to resume filming a television commercial. That spot too lies below the very concrete beneath the speeding auto. Today fifteen thousand drivers pass through Asti every day. How many of them even blink as they speed under the sign announcing the now empty Asti off-ramps which once accommodated nearly half a million visitors each year?

25

The I's Have It

... man will not merely endure, he will prevail. He is
immortal, not because he, alone among creatures, has
an inexhaustible voice, but because he has a soul, spirit
capable of compassion and sacrifice and endurance.
                                    —*William Faulkner*

I F THE SAND OF THE HOURGLASS poured quickly for the winery
at Asti, its flow, while impossible to stop, has moved more slowly
for the people at Chianti. The prewar depression of the 1930's
barely touched Asti and Geyserville and the postwar boom of the
fifties missed the little enclave. While an army of Americans rushed
to a new life in southern California, they missed the garden of paradise just ninety miles north of San Francisco. It wasn't that visitors
ignored Sonoma County and the beautiful lands north of Santa Rosa.
Over two million people visited Asti during the two decades that
followed World War II. They tasted the wines and drank in the setting, but they always returned home at night. The result was that
Healdsburg, Geyserville and Cloverdale looked much the same in

1970 as they did in 1930. And the land was pretty much occupied by the same people living their lives in splendid isolation.

One place that exemplified life in the area was Chianti. Established before the turn of the 20th century, Chianti sat alongside the southern border of the Colony property. The area formally came into being when ISC established a railroad station at the southern end of their ranch and named it Chianti. Chianti is a small place with no formal boundaries, no business district and no post office. Encompassing possibly four hundred acres, it sits primarily on a gently sloping portion of the hills facing Alexander Valley from the west. The land climbs almost two hundred feet before reaching an elevation of four hundred feet, when it disappears into the rough crags and gnarly manzanita that crest behind Chianti before receding into the upper regions of Dry Creek Valley.

In 1886 the Italian Swiss Agricultural Colony was five years old. It was in this year that two young men arrived from Italy to work in the Colony's vineyards. They were Edoardo Seghesio and Francisco Baiocchi. The two, just a few years apart in age, met at Asti. They would live the rest of their lives in houses just a few hundred yards from each other. Seghesio was the first to acquire land in Chianti, when he purchased 56 acres with a small house in 1895. Baiocchi would acquire his ranch in 1899, the same year Giuseppi Mazzoni and Abramo Trusendi acquired their ranches on the southern half of the ridge. Mazzoni and his fourteen-year-old brother-in-law, Trusendi, had arrived from Italy in 1898, when they also went to work at the Colony.

Five houses and three wineries were built on the slope or at the base of the hill before and shortly after the turn of the century. The five houses (but not the wineries) of Chianti are still there, still alone after nearly one hundred years. The Trusendi house, from its lofty perch on the upper reaches of Chianti, still looks out on one of nature's most beautiful vistas, the vineyards of Alexander Valley. A row of trees outlines the path of the Russian River. Beyond the river, the land rises quickly to the ridge of the Mayacamas Mountains flanked by Mount St. Helena, once home to Robert Louis Stevenson on the south, and the highest peak in Lake County, Cobb Mountain, rising 4,722 feet to the north.

The Trusendi house, built by Mazzoni and Trusendi around 1900, was the second house built at Chianti. Giuseppi's wife, Rose Trusendi Mazzoni, arrived at Asti around 1902 with their five-year-old daughter, Lena. It was the first time Giuseppi had seen his daughter since he left Italy shortly after her birth.

In 1905 Mary Pigoni arrived from Italy. Still in her teens, she had come, or been sent, to America to marry Abramo Trusendi. Years later, Mary confided to her daughter a story she had never told anyone before. Before leaving Italy, Mary had never seen Abramo. As we close out the 20th century, women can only imagine the turmoil that enveloped the young Miss Pigoni as she made the nearly six-month journey to a strange land to marry a man she had never laid eyes upon. Mary's fears are evident in the plans she made. Mary would stay in Santa Rosa, working at a small hotel owned by friends of the family. She would not notify Abramo of her arrival until after she had seen the man.

The plan almost cost Mary her life. On April 18, 1906, unable to sleep, she got up early to prepare breakfast for the hotel's guests. Within the hour, the San Francisco earthquake struck. It did extensive damage in Santa Rosa. Mary's bedroom, where she would normally have been sleeping, suffered extensive damage. The early-rising Mary escaped severe injury, possibly death, by leaving her bed early that morning.

Mary did have the opportunity to surreptitiously evaluate Abramo Trusendi. She liked what she saw and in 1906 they were married. The marriage was, as they say, made in heaven. Their first child, Allan, was born in 1908. Melvin (Mike) arrived the following year. The youngest of the three Trusendi children, born over 85 years ago, Midge Trusendi Pelanconi, still lives in Geyserville, less than two miles to the south. Her two brothers each lived over eighty years in Geyserville before passing away. Josephine Rovere Fredson, stepsister to the Trusendi kids, was the last of Mary's children to be born in the big house at the top of the hill. Widowed once again and with the kids grown, Mary sold the house in 1953.

The Mazzonis lived with Abramo and Mary until Allie Trusendi was born. The Mazzonis then decided they needed more room and built another house at the bottom of the hill. By 1910 Giuseppi had built a winery alongside the house. The Mazzoni house, no longer in the family, is still occupied, although the winery closed in 1977.

The third house to be built at Chianti belonged to Francisco Baiocchi. Refusing to give in to oppressive poverty and an empty future, Francisco had left his wife and two young children in Italy to make a new start in America. He arrived in San Francisco in 1886. He told acquaintances from the old country, now living in North Beach, "Vado alla Colonia" (I'm going to the Colony). It was a cry frequently heard in North Beach and one the city would continue to hear in the years ahead. Baiocchi worked in the Colony's Remington Tract vineyards along the Russian River. He would work nine years for the Colony before leaving to work for Edoardo Seghesio. In 1893, Francisco was finally joined by his wife and two children. The youngest, Nello, had been only a few months old when his father had last held him seven years earlier.

After thirteen years of hard work, Baiocchi acquired forty acres of bare land from Thomas Finnerly. The property was located immediately behind Seghesio. Baiocchi had two years to pay off his note for $300, payable semi-annually, with interest at ten percent. By 1901 the land was his, and Baiocchi planted grapes. Within a few more years he built a house, and the Chianti Winery proudly bore the sign "Baiocchi & Sons." Baiocchi, as was the custom, kept adding to the house as he added to his family.

Granddaughter Bernice Baiocchi grew up in the house with her two sisters and brothers, mother and father, uncle Guido, his wife Lena (Mazzoni) and their kids. For Francisco, it was God's plan, but he never forgot the early years, the hard work, the separation from his family. Never again would the family be apart. Francisco would beam when, at one point, fourteen people would sit down to his table for dinner. The family patriarch passed away on January 26, 1932. It was Bernice's first wedding anniversary.

Pete and Rachel Ann still live in the house father Edoardo Seghesio

First Asti, next the world. Perennial candidate for high office ("I've upped my standards, now up yours") and comedian Pat Paulsen stands ready to clean up city hall at Asti village. Photo by Demi Prentiss, courtesy of Terri Paulsen.

acquired in 1895, adding one room at a time as the children came. The view has changed little since the days, sixty years ago, when Angela Seghesio sat sewing on the porch. The one change Angela would notice if she were to visit Chianti today is that the railroad station no longer sits alongside the tracks. A few years ago, Pete and Rachel Ann moved the structure to their backyard. The building has been fully restored and serves the family as a museum.

Before the age of automobiles, California communities built grade schools not more than four miles apart. This way, no student had to walk more than two miles to school each way. The walk to school became an important time in a child's life. There would be no adults present or domineering teenagers. It was the only time the five-year-olds were accepted in the older children's world, and while the talk was mostly frivolous, it was a time of mutual learning and growing up at a grade-school pace.

By the twenties, the families of Chianti were settled. While the nation behaved as if the twenties were to be the world's last decade, for the people of Chianti life was just beginning. For the children it was a wonderful time. The Trusendi children would be the first to head out for school, since they lived furthest away. When they reached the bottom of the hill, they were joined by the Baiocchis. The group swelled with the Mazzonis and when the band reached the highway, Josephine Brignoli and the Zanzi and Tamborini children joined the growing ranks for the roughly two-mile trek to the Washington School.

The walk took about half an hour. On rainy days the kids piled into the Baiocchi wagon for a ride to school. Had the kids walked along the gravel-covered highway they would have walked north to the Rossi house, turned right at Washington School Road and walked down the hill to the schoolhouse. But of course the children took the shortcut through the vineyards. Not only would they thus avoid the hill on Washington School Road, but they could walk the railroad tracks. Anyone who has ever been a child knows that railroad tracks were made for two purposes: trains and children.

In 1921 it had already been fifty years since the SF&NP surveyors and rights-of-way men had arrived in Alexander Valley. In November

Asti village: the original home of Dr. De Vecchi, once owned by the Pellegrini family, is on the right beneath the landmark oak tree. Pat Paulsen's tasting room is in the center. Circa 1986. Courtesy of Cloverdale Reveille.

of 1871, Miers Truett deeded the railroad a right of way across his land. Less than a year later, Donahue's rail gang laid the tracks around which the lives of the people of Asti and Chianti would center for the next three quarters of a century. The kids weren't supposed to walk the tracks, but it was generally understood to be okay if they were careful. The couple of trestles made crossing ravines easier, but they did pose a potential danger of getting caught on the trestle when the train came through. Nevertheless, the tracks were a magnet and it was fun to return the wave from the engineer of the passing freight train.

As the years changed so did Asti. In 1966 the schoolhouse closed. Abandoned, the schoolhouse became a home to transients. In 1974 it burned to the ground, leaving not a trace. The ebb and flow of industry fortunes changed the winery as well. Gone was production of America's finest champagne. The Colony House no longer belonged to the Colony. The Prati family, long out of ISC, owned the big house or the castle, as the neighborhood kids called it. The state-of-the-art bottling line was gone. Tipo was only a memory, and the flow of visitors to Asti slowed to a trickle before it too stopped. The Lucca Ranch was empty. No one lived in Colony housing because there no longer was any Colony housing.

The Asti village has undergone several changes of ownership since Dr. de Vecchi built his summer home there before the turn of the century. Comedian Pat Paulsen acquired the village in 1986. In keeping with his comedic routine, enjoyed by millions of viewers of the Smothers brothers' television program, Paulsen declared himself mayor of the town of Asti. He opened a tasting room in the old Pellegrini grocery store. Paulsen, whose sad, drawn face was known to Americans across the country, was in fact an upbeat man who thoroughly enjoyed life. He found humor everywhere. Paulsen was proud that his wine made it to the White House even though he had never been invited to the President's residence. Above all, he loved Asti and its grapevines. For an instant, all seemed well for Paulsen. But the moment didn't last. Burdened with personal problems, Paulsen left Asti in 1989, the dreams gone, his holdings in bankruptcy, his family life shattered.

The tasting room is gone but not Paulsen's winery across the river. Acquired by Chris and Kris Williams in March 1994, the winery produces high-quality Chardonnay and Sauvignon Blanc under the Wattle Creek label. Transports from Australia, Christopher and Kristine have fallen in love with the Asti area and they are investing that love in building a larger and better winery than was there before. Whereas Sbarboro brought Italian vines to Asti in the 1880's, the Williamses have planted Sirah vines brought to the area from Australia. And of course, by the closing years of the 20th century, all of the founders of ISC were gone. Andrea Sbarboro, Pietro Rossi, Enrico Prati, the twins Bob and Ed Rossi, Edoardo Seghesio, all were now memories.

Ed Prati celebrated his 81st birthday in 1998 but passed away just one year before the millennium. From the house he shared with Billie atop the hill, Ed kept a vigil on Asti 116 years after Andrea Sbarboro

The heart of Asti: the view, looking east from Ed Prati's hilltop. The Villa can be seen in the center of the photo. Toward the foreground, one can see two railcars sitting on a siding, and closer still, the churches. Photo by the author.

climbed the hill for his first glimpse of the Truett Ranch. The sun still rises over the winery now owned by Beringer and it sets behind Gallo's vineyards. The Russian River still flows past Sbarboro's Villa Pompeii, occasionally washing over the footprints of Andrea and Joe Vercelli. But the vineyards around the winery have been replanted. El Carmelo, now past its ninetieth year, rests upon its knees, waiting for the blade of a dozer. The people who came from around the world to marvel at the little church have long passed away or forgotten, and those who were married in the church and had their children baptized in the chapel have been mostly buried from it.

One thing has remained, not smaller or weaker, but larger and stronger. Since Father Meiler said that first Mass in the schoolhouse in 1893, there has never been a Sunday when Mass wasn't offered at

Asti. The church and the faith of the immigrants are as vibrant today as in those days, over one hundred years ago, when the faithful knelt on the hard wooden floor of the little schoolhouse.

But while the families remained strong and vigorous, the little church, the made-over greenhouse, began showing its age after forty years. Major repairs in the fifties failed to stop leaks in the now porous roof. By 1960, a new church, Our Lady of Mount Carmel, was built just a few yards from Madonna Del Carmine. Today, nearly forty years later, Mass is still celebrated at 8:30 A.M., in Our Lady of Mount Carmel Church. Our Lady of Mount Carmel is nearly filled on Sunday mornings, but the old families are thinning out. Frank Pastori and George Domenichelli, both born in Geyserville, are the new ushers. Domenichelli, the younger brother of longtime usher Frank, is ninety years old and still drives daily to the post office, going about life almost as he always has. *[Just days before this manuscript went to the publisher, Domenichelli passed away. He was in his pickup at a vineyard where he "used to work" when his maker decided it was time to give George a rest.]*

Eugene (Pete) Seghesio and his wife, Rachel Ann, still attend the 8:30 A.M. Mass. For fully thirty years, the front ten pews center right were the territory of the old-timers. Herewood and Edith Peterson (she's Italian and he's a "want-to-be") sit in the front right pew just as they have since the church opened 37 years ago. They have the pew to themselves now, their four kids living their lives in other parishes in other towns. And the years have taken a toll on those who used to sit in the pews behind the Petersons. First the children moved out, then the grandparents and finally the parents left on their final journeys, leaving empty spaces in the front pews. There was no reason for others to avoid those pews, but they did. It took years before newcomers began to trickle into the hallowed old-timers' seats. Still, if Hey and Edith Peterson are elsewhere on a Sunday morning it's a good bet the pew front right center is vacant.

The Asti churchgoers must still contend with the little church in the vineyard. It sits there, 92 years old, on its greenhouse concrete pad. Children ask their parents about the strange-looking derelict along the edge of the church parking lot. Many don't know and some try to explain the presence of the old church. But the remaining old-timers know. To them, the church is an old basset hound: too tired to move its head, it seems to roll its loving eyes in response to stares. The church always had magic and it still does. Somehow it continues to radiate. Somehow it still touches hearts.

A group dedicated to restoring the little church founded the El Carmelo Corporation on October 13, 1976. The group was headed by Bob Bogner, president, and Joe Vercelli, secretary. It wasn't easy. As the fortunes of the winery wound down, interest in Asti and all that it used to be wound down with it. But Vercelli persevered. He kept the corporation and the dream alive, even though payment of legal fees often came from his own pocket. Joe was not alone. He was surrounded by dedicated folks eager but frustrated in their efforts to save the old church.

Over the years the officers and leaders of the group changed, but the heart and soul of Madonna Del Carmine was Anne Matteoli. Anne was born in Oakland in 1917. Her father, Giulio Toniatti, led the family to Cloverdale in 1928. She was just eleven years old but remembers going to the winery (this was during Prohibition, so the winery was closed) and gazing at the Villa. Its marble statues, fountains and flowers left vivid impressions.

Anne met Lilio Matteoli, who was a foreman in the bottling department at ISC, and the two were married in El Carmelo on November 19, 1950. Her father-in-law and mother-in-law both worked for the Colony. Anne's two brothers-in-law also worked at Asti, and Anne joined the company in 1951. For years she lived just a few yards from El Carmelo. At least once each week the bells pealed, calling Anne and her family to Mass. She was married in the little church, christened her daughter Julie there, and buried her husband from El Carmelo. For Anne Matteoli, the little church was an important part of her life and she spent years trying to preserve it. Anne Matteoli passed away May 22, 1998, but her spirit persists. The final battle of her life, the preservation of El Carmelo, is still being fought.

When Wine World came in 1988, Anne joined with Bill Knox,

public affairs specialist for Wine World, to save the historic artifacts of ISC at Asti. Together with Alexis Carrey and Peli Pelanconi, they worked to identify, store and catalog the artifacts. But still, they could do nothing for El Carmelo. A chain-link fence was put around the building to protect the curious as well as the decaying church. By now renovation means rebuilding. A builder volunteered to save the structure, fund-raisers were held, but still the money could not be raised. The building, sagging ever lower, will possibly still be there at the turn of the century. Perhaps it will have been bulldozed away. But hope springs eternal. If only La Madonna could arrange for a miracle.

That the members of El Carmelo grow tired is understandable. They have fought indifference, lack of money and, at times, outright hostility. The Catholic Church has no official interest. The pastors of St. Peter's Parish in Cloverdale have focused on repairs and upkeep of the replacement church. In the fall of 1991, the El Carmelo Corporation began yet another drive to raise funds. They approached a local cleric, but he begged off, saying he couldn't help. He was fully engaged in activities stemming from the recent Loma Prieta earthquake. Whereas his position was understandable, his remarks made to a *Santa Rosa Press Democrat* reporter were not. Indeed, they were reprehensible. In describing El Carmelo he said, "It's called a vanity church. It's redundant. It's irrelevant. All that church was, was a potting shed. It just seems that people's needs are far greater than that."[77]

Years later, the cleric would explain that vanity churches could be found in the old cities of Europe, where wealthy patrons of the Church would build unneeded churches for the sole purpose of personal glorification. They were, in fact, edifices to wealth. The cleric admitted that he had spoken too quickly; El Carmelo was not a vanity church. More accurately, it should be called by the canonical term "Chapel of Ease." The term refers to a chapel apart from a parish church that serves a public need or a local interest. He still didn't understand and he was still having trouble with his choice of words. A "Chapel of Ease," indeed!

Nothing man builds lasts forever. Many big churches built in major

County Administration Building
Santa Rosa, California.
August 19, 1976
File 8011

Resolution No. 7749

OF THE PLANNING COMMISSION OF THE COUNTY OF SONOMA,
STATE OF CALIFORNIA, RECOMMENDING THAT THE BOARD OF
SUPERVISORS DESIGNATE THE CHAPEL OF OUR LADY OF MT.
CARMEL AT ASTI AS A COUNTY HISTORIC LANDMARK

WHEREAS, wineries and vineyards are an historic part of the Sonoma County scene, and

WHEREAS, for many years a small barrel-shaped chapel has been located at the Italian Swiss Colony winery and has become known throughout the State, and

WHEREAS, the County Landmarks commission has reviewed and recommended that the picturesque chapel be designated as a County landmark, and

WHEREAS, the County Planning Commission has held a duly noticed public hearing and considered the Landmark Commission's recommendation, now

THEREFORE, BE IT RESOLVED, that the Sonoma County Planning Commission hereby recommends that the Board of Supervisors designate the Chapel of Our Lady of Mt. Carmel as a County Historic Landmark.

Commissioner Realy	Aye
Commissioner Marquardt	Aye
Commissioner McClelland	Aye
Commissioner Torr	Aye
Commissioner Lubas	Aye

Ayes: 5   Noes: 0   Absent/Not voting: 0

SO ORDERED.

Sonoma County Planning Commission votes that El Carmelo be designated a County Historic Landmark, 1976. Courtesy of ISC Archives.

Looking almost like an aging parent with a robust child, El Carmelo sits to the right with Our Lady of Mount Carmel on the left. Photo taken in 1960. Photo by B. M. Gaskill, courtesy of Redwood News Agency.

cities to accommodate the tide of Catholic immigrants that began in the middle of the 19th century find their usefulness waning as time approaches the 21st century. Second and third generations have moved out of the inner cities, leaving a few old folks, who won't or can't move out, to care for now empty churches. For the old ones who are left behind, it is a tragedy. But there are few moist eyes in those who leave to follow their own dreams in the suburbs. With the population flow to suburbia, the little country churches have been plowed under and new, larger churches built. Neither of these socio-religious scenarios describes events at Madonna Del Carmine. The people of Asti built El Carmelo, but they didn't leave. And no wave of newcomers rendered El Carmelo obsolete.

But there was a deeper reason for the people to love El Carmelo. The churchgoer at the huge city church would recognize only a few

FIGURE 2

STEWARDS OF ASTI

1881-1901	Italian Swiss Agricultural Colony
1901-1914	ISAC 50%; California Wine Association 50%
1914-1919	CWA
1919-1920	Edoardo Seghesio
1920-1934	Asti Grape Products, Rossi twins, Seghesio, Prati
1934-1941	ISC, Rossi twins, Prati, Merele, DiGiorgio
1941-1953	National Distillers
1953-1959	United Vintners—Louis Petri
1959-1968	Allied Grape Growers
1968-1978	Heublein 82%, AGG 18%
1978-1982	Heublein
1982-1983	R. J. Reynolds (had acquired Heublein)
1983-1987	Allied Grape Growers
1987-1988	ERLY (The Beverage Source)
1988-1995	Wine World Estates (Nestlé)
1996-Present	Beringer Wine Estates

of the large crowd at Mass and knew even fewer to greet after Mass. The enormity of the churches, and the great size of the congregations, prevented a feeling of community within most city parishes. These houses of God, many very beautiful, were in a sense factories of God. But not El Carmelo. Seating capacity was about one hundred. The church was seldom more than half filled with adults, although many children sat on the concrete ledge around the periphery of the church. In a secular as well as religious sense, the feeling was one of a large family get-together. Each family sat in its own pew just as family members sat around the dinner table at home. There was no assigned seating, the delegation of seats just seemed to happen and once established, the seating arrangement could last for years. Most of the congregation played an active role in the church, the boys as altar servers, the girls in the choir. The women washed linens and set flowers on the altar. The men passed the collection plate and repaired leaky roof staves. It was the continuity of the families that gave rise to a strong sense of tradition uniting the congregation to their little church. Members of the fifth generation of those families still worship at Asti.

Today's grandparents can recall stories told by their grandparents of scraped knees and assorted bruises acquired in helping to build the little church. They told of glass panes breaking into lethal shards no matter how carefully they were removed from the frames of the old greenhouse roof. They spoke of the spring, now covered beneath the floor of the sacristy, that supplied water to the old greenhouse. The hidden spring, guarded by thorny blackberry canes poking out from beneath the church, was a magnet for the young boys, who imagined all sorts of evil creatures living in the soft, wet soil that would swallow them up if they got too close. The women reminisce about their St. Mary's Guild meetings in the building the community built immediately behind the church. Later the building would be moved across the street to be used as housing.

They tell the story of the beautiful ceramic holy water font that was missing after one Sunday Mass. The font, a white porcelain bowl, was nailed to the side of the confessional behind the last pew. The mystery of the missing font was solved with its return some weeks later in the mail at the Asti post office. The postmark was someplace in Oklahoma. There was no note.

They laugh at the memory of little ones who forgot before church doing their "business" in the vineyard outside. And time has softened the memories of a cold, unheated church in winter, and unpadded kneelers that stung bare knees in summer. It wasn't until the 1930's that a kerosene stove was installed, its ugly smell fighting the burning incense of High Mass. The acoustics were poor, but the music from the pump organ filled the church and spilled out into the vineyard, disturbing the stillness with its spiritual airs. To the organ were added the voices of the choir, at times substituting enthusiasm for talent, but always with fervent piety.

The Sunday morning sun, only hours since passing over Paris and New York, now rose to feather touch the Asti hilltops. Eagles soaring in the pale sky of a new day, grapes turning color as they closed on fullness, all enveloped the strangely shaped little church with its people in worship. It was God's crowning achievement, this little colony of people living their lives, working and worshiping in Asti. Cold in winter, knee-killing kneelers, poor acoustics and a leaking roof: a humble, obscure house of worship? Yes. A vanity church? Absurd!

El Carmelo has probably lost its chance to be refurbished. Still, the old folks dream of a rebuilt chapel sitting on the same concrete slab poured well over one hundred years ago. Whereas inner-city churches can be surrounded by burned-out buildings and rotting, trash-filled lots in their declining years, the setting around that concrete slab has not changed in 130 years. Vines still surround the site ninety years after the little church was built.

Californians are typically a society of people moved from their birthplace to the Golden State. As such, they tend to be rootless, focused on the future. Some pride themselves on never looking back, always "bravely" facing the perils of life ahead. Indeed, society puts a premium on forward thinking. But man owes his children the past as well as the future, for people are the one constant, present in the past as well as the future. It is the past that exposes man to his foibles, the errors he has already made and is doomed to make again. It is the past that prepares us to deal with the people, rather than the things, of the future.

We owe it to our children to nurture their spirits as well as nourish their bodies. Established, confident societies remember, if not honor, their past. Hopefully it is not a revisionist or selective view of the past, for honesty looking back engenders courage looking forward. Few Americans and fewer still Californians enjoy the rare privilege of a five-generation history. But the families at Asti are willing to share their history with us. It is a proffered gift to treasure.

The people of Asti have given us still another gift, perhaps most precious of all, for they continue to pass the land from generation to generation, the land remaining much as they found it. Gone without a shred of intrusion are the dozens of buildings that once housed the Asti families. Gone too without a trace are the cookhouse and its stone walls, the beautiful barn and the old Truett house. Apart from portions of the winery and the stately buildings of Rossi, Prati and Sbarboro, all of man's vestiges of an earlier era are gone without a trace, leaving only the land as it existed for the Pomos.

There are exceptions. El Carmelo, or at least her concrete floor, still sits upon the land. The magnificent oaks still flourish around the Colony House, and the olive trees planted by Sbarboro's men along the highway over one hundred years ago still produce olives. And Bluxome's carriage lane, for the last one hundred years used exclusively by vineyard workers and their equipment, still runs in a straight line from the highway to the railroad tracks.

But gone are the Indians of Musalacan and the Mexican adventurers of Francisco Berryessa's time. Gone too are the generations of Matteolis, Giampaolis, Mazzonis and Pellegrinis. But of course the land is here, pretty much unchanged through all those years. And our children and grandchildren might take comfort for the future, for the land will remain safe so long as the records show the "I's" have it.

🍎

She sat by the window waiting. It was warm enough to "warm the old bones" but not so hot as to be uncomfortable. She was proud of herself. At her last birthday one of the grandchildren (which one?) had proudly announced that she was four score and six years old. But she still lived alone, still took care of herself. Of course, she had lots of family. Most lived close by and that was a comfort. But she missed her companion of 56 years. He had been a good husband all of those years. He was a quiet man—gentle and loving—always considerate, except during hunting season when some unknown force pulled him away for the hunt. It must have been a "man thing,"

*she thought, built into his genes. Today they play golf. Never did
understand golf. Was that another "man thing"?*

*Two houses past hers, the road ended at a vineyard. She could
see a crew of men working with their hoes. She didn't have to get
close to know they were Mexicans. Mexicans had replaced the Italians years ago. How her husband loved working in the vineyard.
She remembered the walks they used to take, hand in hand along
the vineyard avenues late in the day, the sun's rays cooling as they
changed from red to violet.*

*She thought of El Carmelo, and the days she used to wash the
altar linen in her old washtub. She wouldn't use the washboard,
too rough, but she would put the altar cloth through the hand-op-
erated wringer. All of her five kids had received their sacraments in
the old chapel and everyone had been married there. The new
church wasn't the same. Never would be.*

*Two little girls played in front of the house across the street, un-
aware that a pair of 86-year-old eyes were fixed on them. Would
the vineyards be there when they were 86? She remembered Grandpa
telling her how grapes had grown next to El Carmelo for eighty
years. She could still figure, and she estimated that it must come to
well over 130 years now. For years she had prayed that somehow El
Carmelo could be saved. But as the old people died her hopes died
with them. She no longer prayed for the tiny church in the vineyard, but that didn't mean she had forgotten...*

*A car pulled up. It was her sister's car. At four score and three
she shouldn't be driving, but as long as she did, the two would be
independent. Today was the Altar Society lunch and meeting. Election of officers! She got up to go.*

A good land, a land of brooks of water, of fountains and depths that spring out of the valleys and hills; a land of wheat and barley and vines, of fig trees and pomegranates; a land of oil, olive and honey; a land wherein thou shalt eat bread without scarceness, thou shall not lack anything in it; a land whose stones are iron and of whose hill thou mayest dig gold.

—Andrea Sbarboro, 1910, from
scriptural description of
the Promised Land

Symbols of a Forgotten Past

Italian Swiss Colony wine labels, symbols of an almost forgotten past.

Afterword

They are not long, the days of wine and roses
Out of a misty dream
Our path emerges for a while, then closes
Within a dream
                                    —*Ernest Dowson*

I N 1976 AN INFORMAL WINE TASTING was held in Paris to celebrate America's bicentennial. The best of California's wines were
matched against their French counterparts. The French judges
proclaimed a Napa Valley Cabernet Sauvignon and a Napa Valley
Chardonnay as the best wines in the blind tasting. The Californians
were euphoric. Their wines had come of age. At last the world would
have to acknowledge that California wines were in the league of
their European counterparts.

How quickly we forget, or is memory selective? Some three quarters of a century earlier, Italian Swiss Colony was producing world-
class wines, competing with and often beating the legendary European
wineries. To be fair, during the early decades of the 20th century,
European vineyards had only recently emerged from the dark days
of phylloxera-induced devastation. In 1900, the Colony was awarded

a silver medal at the Paris Exposition. Sbarboro had attended the competition and upon returning to America he reported that the French were "frightened out of their wits" by the quality of California wine. By 1913, ISC had won six top awards, i.e. gold, Grand Prix, etc., in major European wine competitions. Yet the ISC brand is remembered disdainfully, if at all, by today's wine industry.

How did the world's largest producer of table wines fail so completely? To the people in Geyserville and Cloverdale who worked all their lives at Asti, as had their parents and grandparents, the answer is simple. They watched from up close as Heublein first destroyed the brand name and then incrementally moved equipment and jobs from Asti to the Central Valley. They watched helplessly as their lives and the lives of their unborn were changed forever by business interests a continent away. To every man and woman who ever worked at the Colony, it was Heublein who destroyed ISC. But with objective reasoning more possible at a distance, it is clear that no single owner or single decision failed the Colony.

At Repeal, the American wine consumer wanted high-alcohol, sweet wines. The minuscule dry-wine market was readily supplied by European imports and a few California wineries like Inglenook and Simi. The sweet fortified wines could be produced from lower-quality Central Valley grapes, which were cheaper to grow than coastal grapes. As a result, the California wine industry of the thirties through the fifties was centered in the Central Valley. Great names like Petri, Roma and E & J Gallo grew from the Valley's productive vineyards.

Fortified wines like sherry or port, with up to eighteen percent alcohol, outsold dry table wines three to one. Roughly two thirds of Napa vineyards were planted to Petit Sirah and Alicante Bouchet,[78] grapes with market appeal during Prohibition. For at least 25 years following Repeal, the majority of Napa grapes were transformed into inexpensive bulk wines. Almost eighty percent of California wine made during the 1930's was shipped out of state in bulk, to be aged, blended, bottled and labeled by others. Wine, for the most part, was a commodity offering small profit margins.

It was this market that the Rossi twins and Enrico Prati entered in

1934. In that market, Asti and its premium vineyards were at a disadvantage. When they couldn't compete economically, they jumped at the chance to trade equity for Joseph DiGiorgio's Central Valley grapes. As the decade ended, they acquired the LaPaloma Winery, a huge Central Valley facility that would move the Colony further into the jug-wine business and further into debt. Throughout the thirties, the Sbarboro and Rossi families made modest investments in financially strapped ISC. In the days before Prohibition, Andrea Sbarboro would have gone to his board, and Marco Fontana, et al. would have raised the money needed to assure ISC success. But the twins didn't have access to that sort of financial support and when DiGiorgio and the Bank of America wanted their money out of the Colony, the twins had no choice but to sell the Colony to a large East Coast distiller.

With the sale to National Distillers, the fate of Asti was set. Over the next 47 years the Colony would be held by six owners. Each of the six had a Central Valley mentality, and Asti, in effect, became an anomaly. Of the six, only Louis Petri recognized the unique position of Asti, but Petri followed the market and that made him a "good value wine man." If Petri had not turned the Colony over to Allied Grape Growers and if Petri had stayed in control another fifteen to twenty years, the fate of Asti would most likely have been entirely different.

One can reasonably assume that Petri, like Gallo, would have seen the market shift to premium or super-premium wines and, like Gallo, Petri would have shifted his focus to the north coast. Asti would have been Petri's vehicle to the new wine market. It would have been sheer fun to watch the pair of business geniuses, Petri and Gallo, continue their battles of the fifties into the 21st century. And it would have been a delight to see Asti rise once again to the prominence it enjoyed before Prohibition.

Life is awash in "what if" questions, but it is fun to speculate. Sbarboro built the winery at Asti in a hurry. He needed a facility to crush the 1887 harvest. He was also acting in desperation, to fight off failure at the hands of the California Wine Association. What if he had instead hired Hamden McIntyre to design the facility? McIntyre, having designed the beautiful Inglenook and Greystone wineries in Napa, was working on a winery for John Paxton in Dry Creek Valley at the very time the Colony started their project. A majestic winery the likes of Greystone set in the splendor of the rolling hills of Asti might have altered the mindset of Sbarboro and his board.

Possibly an inspiring building in an inspiring setting would have ever so subtly cloaked management and worker alike in an aura of wine as an art form rather than wine as a commodity, a plebeian beverage consumed by the masses. Had he designed the Colony's winery, McIntyre's genius might have forever changed the essence of the wine business in northern Sonoma County. Cloverdale might have become another St. Helena (or St. Helena another Cloverdale), and Sonoma County might not have played second fiddle to Napa Valley for the next hundred years.

Unfortunately it didn't happen that way. Instead of Louis Petri, the fate of Asti came under the hands of Allied Grape Growers, an organization of grape growers with a Central Valley mentality, and then Heublein. It was Heublein who made the decision to "eliminate" ISC and its brands. Heublein's plan was standard business practice, focused on maximizing profits, ignoring the lives and fortunes of those who produced the profits. With the acquisition of Allied Grape Growers wineries in 1969, Heublein acquired a capacity to produce over fifty million gallons of Central Valley wines. Beaulieu Vineyards in Napa Valley was their super-premium winery with a Napa Valley address. They also had the venerable Inglenook, the only Napa winery after Repeal to stick to production of high-quality varietal wines, ignoring the everyday wine market of the thirties.

But Heublein didn't need two venerable names, and besides, Allied Grape Growers had already started Inglenook on the road to jug-wine status. Allied had acquired Inglenook in 1964, promising to treasure Inglenook and maintain its reputation. They reneged on their promise, or at least on the stated goals of the departed Louis Petri. His seat was still warm when they moved production to a large facility they already owned across the highway. Allied Grape Growers, under the direction of B. C. Solari, increased production, lowered

El Carmelo 1998. Just a shadow of its former glory, the building awaits an almost certain date with a bulldozer. Photo by Barbara Gambon.

quality, and reduced the old Inglenook winery to essentially a bottling plant. Heublein increased production still further, using the Inglenook name that had long been associated with the finest wines produced in California to sell a line of wines made from grapes that didn't even grow in Napa. The sorry story ends on an even more sordid note. On the back label of the Navalle wines is the statement: "Navalle [fill in the varietal] is made by Inglenook. And that's probably the most important information you need to know."

There was no room for ISC in the Heublein scheme of things and so the Colony was left to languish in the farther realms of the Heublein empire. In 1983 Allied Grape Growers and ERLY, still clinging to screw-top wines, watched over the dying Colony until its misery was mercifully ended in 1988 with its acquisition by Wine World, Inc.

If the Colony is a thing of the past, the people of Asti are of the present. California statistics suggest that, on average, Californians move every couple of years. Their insatiable quest for ever more material

El Carmelo on the inside, 1998. Temporary rafters support what is left of the walls and roof. The confessional stands in the corner. Note the concrete floor over 110 years old. A little cleaning would make the slab like new. Photo by Fran Florence.

possessions keeps most citizens on the move, to the general economic benefit of society. But not the families of Asti. In spite of the tumultuous history of their employer(s), the families continue to live in their small but comfortable homes. The houses remain, as always, well kept and attractive, in one of nature's most beautiful settings. Life is not all about money or material possessions, it never has been. It's about lifestyle and values. And here, their "cup runneth over."

But Asti is not paradise. Added to life's little problems that people endure everywhere, the people of Asti must live with the matter of Madonna Del Carmine. The presence of the old church alongside Our Lady of Mount Carmel makes it impossible to forget her. Now, their "simple" lifestyle hurts. To fix El Carmelo, they need money, money they don't have. Can they be forgiven if, while on the now padded kneelers at Sunday morning Mass, they squeeze a silent prayer into their own liturgies?

Lord, you have been so good to us,
Always you looked over Asti.
Somehow when life looked bleak
you provided sunshine.

Lord, you who see and know all things,
why have you abandoned El Carmelo?
Is there something more
you want from us?

I am too old to dig and scrape,
I can no longer wield a saw,
pound a hammer
or raise a wall.

Lord, you know I have little money
and my body is frail.
Send your spirit to he who can help
and may your blessings my God
be upon him.

Notes

NOTE 1 (Chapter 2)
The city of Cloverdale was founded in 1854. Twenty-four years later, on August 17, 1878, the isolated town got its own newspaper, the *Cloverdale Reveille*. It was founded by J. F. Hoadley, Sr., whose son served as editor. Less than one year later, on March 3, 1879, the *Reveille* got its adjudication from the Sonoma County Superior Court. The adjudication, which requires regular publication on the part of the newspaper to remain in effect, allowed the *Reveille* to publish official notices. The *Reveille* has maintained its adjudication for 120 consecutive years. The paper is currently owned by Bonny Jean (known as B. J. to all) Hanchett. B. J., a lifelong journalist, acquired the paper in July 1988, when it was just 110 years old.

NOTE 2 (Chapter 2)
Armand Joseph Dehay closed escrow on the 885-acre property the last week of September, just six weeks before ISAC took title to the Asti property (November 8, 1881). Dehay's land formed part of the northern border of the ISAC parcel. Dehay, representing a commune named Icaria-Speranza, paid $15,000 for the land. The Icarians, who required their members to read and speak French, also planted vines immediately, and in a few years they too would build a winery, just a mile up the tracks from Asti.

The Icarians were the second communal organization in the wine business along the SF&NP tracks in 1881. Less than thirty miles down the line, just north of Santa Rosa, the Brotherhood of New Life had acquired four hundred acres of good farmland in 1875 and named the property Fountain Grove. They planted vines, built a winery and by 1886, a year before the Colony produced wine, the Brotherhood produced 70,000 gallons of premium table wines. The Brotherhood came from New York state, the Icarians from Iowa, and the soon-to-be-formed Colony from Italy. The Brotherhood was a religious group, the Colony was based on ethnic and economic forces, and the Icarians combined all at the center of their community. But they each shared a love for California and the fruit of the vine.

The Fountain Grove community flourished until 1892, when its leader, Thomas Lake Harris, fled home to England under a cloud of scandal. The winery continued in operation until 1951, when an indifferent owner closed down and sold out to developers as the town of Santa Rosa grew to its border. The Icarians, in spite of their hard work and determination, failed much sooner. Under-funded, the Icarians could not survive the low grape prices of 1886. Unable to pay their debts, the Icarians dissolved. But the Colony survived, supported by the deep pockets of North Beach businessmen in San Francisco.

NOTE 3 (Chapter 2)
The two parcels in question totaled approximately 325 acres. Except for a few small hills along their western edge, the parcels were the only flat land within sight from the hilltop that morning. The southern parcel (123 acres) was sold by Hutchinson to ISAC the following spring. It became the site of the winery, the Rossi villa and the Asti village.

The parcel closest to the group lay at the bottom of the hill on which they stood. The hilltop would one day be the site of Edward V. Prati's home. This choice acreage of about two hundred acres has been the site of human activity for unknown centuries. The land consisted primarily of deep, well-drained soil with several good springs. While the western edge consisted of rolling hills, to the east the property bordered on the Russian River.

The Pomo Indians were upon the land well before Berryessa took official title to the land as part of the Rincón de Musalacan land grant in 1846. The Indians harvested sedge rhizomes for making baskets along the banks of the Russian River. Title to the land changed twice before Miers Truett acquired the property in 1859. (Book 8, page 568, Sonoma County Hall of Records). Truett was a land speculator and he eventually divided his land into parcels to be sold off. On November 7, 1865, Truett sold the parcel in question to James Thompson (Book 18, page 190). Thompson built his home alongside the roadway (likely between the highway and today's greenhouse) and farmed the property. Immediately to Thompson's south, Miers Truett had built his own home. (This was the house that eventually served Sbarboro's Villa caretakers.)

The record is sketchy, but the following is the most likely scenario of the subsequent history of the 200-acre property:

On May 15, 1873, the year following the railroad's coming to Cloverdale, Thompson sold out to H. C. Turner. We don't know if Thompson or Turner planted the Zinfandel vineyards near the house, but by 1881 the Turners had about ten acres of grapes planted in two parts. Both of these vineyards were planted west of the road (Old Redwood Highway). The larger of the two vineyard plots is still growing wine grapes, although its southern edge has been usurped by the freeway off-ramps. The second vineyard plot was a few hundred yards to the north. Inspection of the area today would indicate that the plot would be located across from, and slightly south of, Our Lady of Mount Carmel Church. This plot too is planted to grapes as the 20th century comes to a close. Although not the same vines, the land has been planted to grapes a period of about 130 years, spanning fourteen owners—some negligent, a few simply hostile—and thirteen years of Prohibition.

On September 17, 1882, the Turner family sold the property to J. P. Whitaker (Book 78, page 45, Sonoma County Hall of Records). Whitaker held the parcel just five years before selling to G. Ginocchio, an ISAC director, on September 10, 1887. Ginocchio rapidly expanded the vineyards. In just four years he had 115 acres planted to Zinfandel. He was one of the largest grape growers in the county. (See the directory of growers and vintners compiled by the Board of State Viticultural Commissioners for 1891.)

It is likely that during this period Ginocchio built the little greenhouse that would serve to produce cuttings for both his and his neighbor ISAC's vineyards. The greenhouse was located alongside a spring, the same spring that served the Thompson/Turner house. Following the design used by noted horticulturist Luther Burbank, Ginocchio poured a concrete slab with two-foot stem walls to support the glass-paned roof. Ginocchio sold the parcel to ISAC June 11, 1898.

In 1907, the people of Asti converted the building to a church. The church served until 1960, when it was abandoned for a new church. The new church was built just a few yards away, still on the old Thompson place. At the eve of the 21st century the concrete slab is still there, well over one hundred years since it was poured. Since that time, houses have been built on the land, and when vacated the houses were torn down. There have been fifteen different stewards of the land since Ginocchio sold out, including the Archdiocese of San Francisco. Of all of man's activity on James Thompson's land since 1865, three things remain. Catholics still worship at Our Lady of Mount Carmel, Ginocchio's concrete slab is still there, and of course the vines. Always the vines.

NOTE 4 (Chapter 3)
The Lucca Ranch houses had been there at least since 1865, the year Calvin Bosworth moved in to oversee Truett's ranch operations. Calvin's lineage would extend to five generations of Bosworths who would live over 130 years in or around Geyserville. Like the grapevines, the Bosworths proved reluctant to ever leave the area. Harry Bosworth, fourth of the line, owns the Bosworth & Son General Merchandise store in Geyserville, less than four miles from the Lucca Ranch. The Bosworths weren't the only family to surrender to the lure of the area. Not many miles from the Lucca Ranch, a large, well-known winery has been a family operation for over sixty years. One of the current principals has set his desk not ten feet from the corner of the room in which he was born.

NOTE 5 (Chapter 5)
A telling incident many years later shed some possible light on Rossi's state of mind during 1900. At the February 1911 CWA stockholders' meeting, Percy Morgan, leader of CWA during the battle with CWMC, announced his resignation due to poor health. In a magnanimous gesture, Pietro Rossi rose to thank Morgan for his years of service. Without further elaboration, Rossi noted that he himself had been "twice on the verge of a breakdown," and he understood the pain experienced by his old adversary.

NOTE 6 (Chapter 6)
Asti expresses its tenacity in subtle as well as obvious ways. The little chapel, El Carmelo, for example, clings to Asti with a tenacity that belies the derelict it has become. Half of the walls are gone and there is no longer a roof. The furnishings are gone and there are no visible remains of the altar. The wooden floor, which once supported the altar, is eerily spongy and beginning to tilt as the foundation sinks unevenly. The rear wall is standing, probably held up by invisible angels. It was against this wall that the sacristy was situated.

The sacristy is a room where sacred vessels and vestments are kept and where the priest puts on the garments to be worn while celebrating Mass. The last priest to hang up his alb after saying Mass did so in 1960, the last year the church was used for services. In 1998, this author found two lonely wire coathangers hanging in a tiny closet that was all that remained intact in the wreckage that used to be a church. Unless some vagrant who carried his clothes on coathangers used the closet, it is likely the hangers had hung from the closet bar, untouched, for 38 years.

NOTE 7 (Chapter 9)

In his oral history, Perelli-Minetti does not elaborate about this supposed opportunity except to say that the opportunity occurred during Prohibition. If indeed the twins and Prati wanted out, it would most likely have been toward the end of the 1920's, when grape sales plummeted. Perelli-Minetti's view of Asti's vineyards west of the freeway is ironic. In today's world of viticulture, the hilly land would be considered superior to the deep soil along the river. At the turn of the 21st century, the 1100 acres in grapes would be valued in the area of $35 million.

NOTE 8 (Chapter 9)

The Rossi family still holds reunions every five years at the Rossi villa. As the 20th century closes, almost 150 family members attend the reunion. The children of Pietro and Amelia, progenitors of this thriving family, were:

NAME	BORN	DIED	SPOUSE
Albert	1882	1887	
Maria	June 1, 1883	September 4, 1960	Ambrose Gherini
Sophia	1885	1891	
Luigi	1887	1891	
Edmund*	August 7, 1888	May 23, 1974	Beatrice Amie Brandt
Robert*	August 7, 1888	April 15, 1961	Nellie Ellen Mahony
Esther	May 25, 1890	March 29, 1968	Never married
Aimee	January 4, 1892	June 27, 1985	Nun–Order of the Sacred Heart
Ameliea	1893	September 12, 1983	Nun–Order of the Sacred Heart
Beatrice	January 12, 1896	November 19, 1989	James Torrens
Gioberto	1897	1899	
Albia	August 26, 1899	December 17, 1988	Charles Wall
Eleanor	April 22, 1901	December 20, 1991	Vincent O'Donnell
Pietro Carlo	May 30, 1902	August 8, 1992	Jesuit Priest

*Twins

NOTE 9 (Chapter 12)

(Material for this note was taken from the wonderfully entertaining book *Ardent Spirits: The Rise and Fall of Prohibition,* by Jack Kobler, published by Da Capo Press, New York.)

Abraham Lincoln was a man of such noble character that people of all persuasions claimed him for their side. In 1842 the 33-year-old Illinois legislator was invited to address an anti-alcohol group who were staging a monster rally to celebrate their cause on George Washington's birthday. Lincoln was to serve as "orator of the day" at the culminating ceremony at the Springfield Second Presbyterian Church.

The enthusiastic crowd waited eagerly for a moving eloquence extolling the evils of drink from the teetotaler Lincoln. For the crowded church this was to be a pep rally for the cause. What they heard outraged many in the crowd, for with courage granted to few men, Lincoln told them what he believed, not what they wanted to hear. Like others of Lincoln's words, these were timeless and as true in any age as that of 1842. The following are excerpts from Lincoln's remarks that day.[79]

> The warfare heretofore waged against the demon intemperance, has, somehow or other, been erroneous. These champions for the most part, have been preachers, lawyers, and hired agents; between these and the mass of mankind there is a want of approachability... They are supposed to have no sympathy of feeling or interest with those very persons whom it is said, advocates temperance because he is a fanatic, and desires a union of the church and state; the lawyer from his pride, and vanity of hearing himself speak; and the hired agent for his salary...
>
> Too much denunciation against dram-sellers and dram-drinkers was indulged in. This, I think, was both impolitic and unjust. It was impolitic because it is not much in the nature of man to be driven to anything, still less to be driven about that which is exclusively his own business, and least of all where such driving is to be submitted to at the expense of pecuniary inters of burning appetite. When the dram-seller and drinker were incessantly told not in the accents of entreaty and persuasion, diffidently addressed by erring man to an erring brother, but in the thundering tones of anathema and denunciation, with which the lordly judge often groups together all the crimes of the felon's life, and thrusts them in his face ere he passes sentence of death upon him, that they were the authors of all the vice and misery and crime in the land; that they were the manufacturers and the material of all the thieves and robbers and murderers that infest the earth; that their houses were the workshops of the devil, and that their persons should be shunned by all the good and virtuous as moral pestilence—I say, when they were told all this, and in this way, it is not wonderful that they were slow, very slow, to acknowledge the truth of such denunciations and to join the ranks of their denouncers, in a hue and cry against themselves.
>
> "But," say some, "we are no drunkards, and we shall not acknowledge ourselves such, by joining a reformed drunkards' society, whatever our influence might be." Surely, no Christian will adhere to this objection. If they believe, as they profess, that Omnipotence condescended to take on himself, the form of sinful man, and as such, to die an ignominious death for their sakes, surely, they will not refuse submission to the infinitely lesser condescension, from any mental or moral superiority over those who have. Indeed, I believe if we take the habitual drunkards as a class, their heads and hearts will bear an advantageous comparison with those of any other class. There seems ever to have been a proneness in the brilliant and warm-blooded to fall into this vice—the demon of intemperance ever seems to have delighted in sucking the blood of genius and generosity...

NOTE 10 (Chapter 12)
Sbarboro probably didn't know the extent Stanford went to irrigate his enormous vineyard. Immediately after acquiring the almost four-thousand-acre ranch, Stanford hired an army of laborers to construct an irrigation ditch thirty feet wide at the top, at depths ranging from nine to fifteen feet, and about ten miles long.[80]

NOTE 11 (Chapter 13)
Although not a factor during the days of Prohibition, there is still one more aspect to the differences in Central Valley wine grapes and those grown at Asti in the north coast. This disparity would plague the owners of Asti for over fifty years following Repeal. In the relentless, day-after-day, night-after-night heat of the Central Valley, the wine grape ripens fully, but the heat-liable grape acids, essential to fine wine, are dissipated. On the north coast, generally defined as Napa, Sonoma, Mendocino and Lake Counties, hot summer days are followed by cool nights. Thus when the grape has ripened, it still contains the acids which are essential to fine wine.

The consequence of these economic and cultural differences is a Central Valley wine appropriate to the vast market of good but inexpensive wines and a north-coast grape producing costly, premium wines of a quality and price sought by a considerably different consumer. The problem for the owners of Asti was that the market following Repeal overwhelmingly favored wines from the Central Valley.

NOTE 12 (Chapter 14)
Angela's visitor was following in the footsteps of Abe Lachman. In the years before Prohibition, Lachman used to visit the area with thousands of dollars in twenty-dollar gold pieces to buy grapes and wine. Lachman, of course, was the man who brought Sbarboro to Cloverdale at the time ISAC was looking to acquire vineyard land.

NOTE 13 (Chapter 16)
The history of the beautiful Mission Bell winery reflects the history of the California wine industry. Six hundred and forty acres, including one hundred fifty acres already in grapes, were acquired by ISC in 1896. The following year, under P. C. Rossi, the one-million-gallon winery was built. The winery subsequently came under the ownership of CWA (1901), who sold it to Krikor Arakelian in 1920. Under Arakelian, the Mission Bell brand became the biggest-selling wine for several years in New York City. Arakelian sold to Petri in 1949 and Petri returned Mission Bell to ISC in 1953. In 1968, along with ISC, Mission Bell was acquired by Heublein, who sold the venerable winery to Canandaigua in 1974.

NOTE 14 (Chapter 22)
The Scatena Bros. Winery in Healdsburg was one of the oldest in the area. The winery was originally built in 1890 by the Roma Wine Company. Various members of the Scatena family owned the winery until 1944, when Francesco Scatena died and the winery was sold to the Alta Vineyards Company. In 1946 the Seghesio family acquired the winery. A significant part of the 107-year-old winery burned in 1997. The Seghesio family, now operating as the Seghesio Family Winery, rebuilt

the destroyed portions of the old winery, adding a beautiful tasting room and barrel-aging cellar.

NOTE 15 (Chapter 22)
Asti formed a union which became an AFL Warehousemen's union. It wasn't an easy time for the workers or management. Torn by conflicting emotions, the attitude of the day was expressed years later by Alex Carrey: "This ended, the coming of the union, the company's summer barbecues. The closeness between labor and management was broken."

NOTE 16 (Chapter 23)
Several top-quality wine producers have gotten started using a custom crush arrangement. Fritz Cellars custom-crushed wines for several years while it built its own business to the level where sales matched the full production capacity of the winery. The super-premium Dry Creek Valley winery Quivira Vineyards got its start custom crushing at Fritz. In fact, Quivira was at Fritz in 1984, the same year Rossi began his program at the small winery.

The small tanks that gave Fritz flexibility in their own wine program were perfectly suited to small, start-up wineries such as Quivira and Rossi's small batch of late-harvest Riesling. Another small winery at Fritz in 1984 was Charis Vineyards, a Dry Creek winery owned by this author.

References

CHAPTER 1
1. Fredrickson, Vera-Mae; Peri, David. *Mihilakawna and Makahmo Pomo,* U.S. Army Corps of Engineers, 1984.
2. Revere, Joseph. *Naval Duty in California,* Biobooks, Oakland, California, 1947.
3. Ibid.

CHAPTER 2
4. Sullivan, Charles L. "Italian Swiss Colony, The First Half Century, 1881-1933," 1980.
5. Stindt, Fred. *The Northwestern Pacific Railroad–Redwood Empire Route,* 3rd Edition, 1978.
6. *History of Sonoma County,* Lewis Publishing Co., 1889.
7. Clar, C. Raymond. *Quarterdecks and Spanish Grants,* Felton, California, Glenwood, 1971.
8. Finley, Ernest Latimer. *History of Sonoma County, California: Its People and Resources,* Press Democrat Publishing Co., 1937.
9. Baxter, Marcelle. "Icaria-Speranza: A French Utopian Experiment in California," *The Journal of the Sonoma County Historical Society,* August, 1989.
10. Sullivan, Charles L. "Italian Swiss Colony, The First Half Century, 1881-1933," 1980.

CHAPTER 3
11. Jones, Idwal. *Vines in the Sun, A Journey Through the California Vineyards*, W. Morrow, New York, 1949.
12. Peninou, Ernest. "Leland Stanford's Great Vina Ranch 1881-1919," Yolo Hills Viticultural Society, San Francisco.
13. Sbarboro, Andrea. Memoir, The Argonaut, edited by Heather Wheeler, *Journal of the San Francisco Historical Society,* Volume 7, No. 2, Winter 1996/97.

CHAPTER 4
14. Teiser, Ruth and Catherine Harrow. *Winemaking in California,* McGraw-Hill Book Company, 1983.
15. Ibid.
16. Peninou, Ernest and Sidney Greenleaf. *Winemaking in California, III.* The California Wine Association, The Porpoise Book Shop, 1954.

17. *San Francisco Chronicle,* May 14, 1898.
18. Wood, Jim. "All In The Family," *San Francisco Examiner Magazine,* October 1, 1995.
Additional material concerning the Seghesio family came from extended interviews with Peter and Rachel Ann Seghesio.
A small part of the Seghesio saga was created by the author in an effort to give added feeling to the story. These elements are not presented as historical facts and they should be readily evident to even the casual reader.

CHAPTER 5
19. California Wine Association—Library of California Historical Society, San Francisco, Manuscript 300, Minutes of Board of Directors meetings, Volume 2
20. MacKendrick, Paul. *The Mute Stones Speak,* W. W. Norton & Co., 2nd edition.
21. Sbarboro, Andrea. Memoir, The Argonaut, edited by Heather Wheeler, *Journal of the San Francisco Historical Society,* Volume 7, No. 2, Winter 1996/97.
22. Personal communication from Lelio "Ningle" Giampaoli, who shared memories of days growing up at the Villa. In this instance, Ningle remembers the awe inspired by the motorcycles in the eyes of a pre-teenage boy.

CHAPTER 6
23. Sbarboro, Andrea. Memoir, The Argonaut, edited by Heather Wheeler, *Journal of the San Francisco Historical Society,* Volume 7, No. 2, Winter 1996/97.
24. Peixoto, Ernest. "Italy in California," *Scribners Magazine,* July 1910.

CHAPTER 7
25. The story of Father Louisiana and subsequent priests to serve St. Peter's and El Carmelo churches is part of a small collection of parish history kept at the rectory of St. Peter's Church, Cloverdale, CA.
26. "Hallowed Were The Gold Dust Trails." Out of print, available through Diocese of Sacramento, Father William Breault, Diocesan Pastoral Center.

CHAPTER 8

27. Rossi, Edmund Jr. "Italian Swiss Colony 1949-1989: Recollections of a Third Generation California Winemaker," an oral history conducted in 1988–1989 by Ruth Teiser and Lisa Jacobson, Bancroft Library, University of California, Berkeley.

28. Sbarboro, Andrea. Memoir, The Argonaut, edited by Heather Wheeler, *Journal of the San Francisco Historical Society,* Volume 7, No. 2, Winter 1996/97.

29. From a publication by ISC entitled "Italian-Swiss Colony, Producers of Fine California Wines & Brandies," author unknown, published between 1912 to 1915. Copy in Beringer Asti archives.

30. *Pacific Wine & Spirit Review,* Volume 52, No. 7, May 31, 1910.

31. Baxter, Marcelle. "Icaria-Speranza: A French Utopian Experiment in California," *The Journal of Sonoma County Historical Society,* August, 1989.

32. *Pacific Wine & Spirit Review,* Volume 54, No. 2, December 30, 1911.

CHAPTER 9

33. Perelli-Minetti, Antonio. "A Life in Winemaking," an oral history conducted in 1969 by Ruth Teiser, Bancroft Library, University of California, Berkeley.

34. Pinney, Thomas. *A History of Wine in America—From the Beginning to Prohibition,* University of California Press, Berkeley, California, 1989.

35. Pacific Wine & Spirit Review, January 31, 1912.

CHAPTER 10

36. Lapsley, James T. *Bottled Poetry; Napa Winemaking From Prohibition To The Modern Era.* University of California Press, Berkeley, California, 1996.

37. Rossi, Edmund. *Wines & Vines,* April 1938.

38. California Wine Association, Library of California Historical Society, San Francisco, Manuscript 300, Minutes of Executive Committee Meeting Minutes, Volume 7

39. California Wine Association, Library of California Historical Society, San Francisco, Manuscript 300, Minutes of Board of Directors meetings, Volume 3

CHAPTER 11

40. Teiser, Ruth and Catherine Harrow. *Winemaking In California,* McGraw-Hill Book Company, 1983.

41. Rossi, Edmund. "Italian Swiss Colony and the Wine Industry," an oral history conducted in 1971 by Ruth Teiser, Bancroft Library University of California, Berkeley.

42. California Wine Association, Library of California Historical Society, San Francisco, Manuscript 300, Minutes of Board of Directors meetings, Volume 4

43. Ibid.

44. Ibid.

45. California Wine Association, Library of California Historical Society, San Francisco, Manuscript 300, Minutes of Executive Committee meetings, Volume 8

CHAPTER 12

46. Sinclair, Andrew. *Prohibition: The Era of Excess,* Boston, Little, Brown, 1962.

47. Sbarboro, Andrea. Untitled Memoirs, January 1, 1911, *The Argonaut, Journal of the San Francisco Historical Society,* Volume 7, No. 2, Winter 1996/97.

48. "Jefferson & Wine Model of Moderation," edited by R. deTreville Lawrence III, The Vinifera Wine Growers' Association, 2nd Edition, 1989.

49. Kobler, John. *Ardent Spirits: The Rise and Fall of Prohibition,* Da Capo Press, New York, 1973.

50. Gomberg, Louis. "Analytical Perspectives on the California Wine Industry, 1935-1990," an oral history conducted in 1990 by Ruth Teiser, Bancroft Library, University of California, Berkeley.

51. *Respectfully Quoted–A Dictionary of Quotations Requested from the Congressional Research Service,* U.S. Government Printing Office, Library of Congress, Washington, DC, 1989

52. Appears in unpublished work, Beringer archives, Asti, California.

53. *Pacific Wine & Spirit Review,* January 31, 1916

54. Peninou, Ernest. "Leland Stanford's Great Vina Ranch 1881-1919," Yolo Hills Viticultural Society, San Francisco.

CHAPTER 13

55. Rossi, Edmund. "Italian Swiss Colony and the Wine Industry," an oral history conducted in 1971 by Ruth Teiser, Bancroft Library University of California, Berkeley.

56. Sinclair, Andrew. *Prohibition: The Era of Excess,* Boston, Little Brown, 1962.

57. Florence, Jack, Sr. *A Noble Heritage, The Wines and Vineyards of Dry Creek Valley,* Winegrowers of Dry Creek Valley, 1993

58. Matteoli, Anne. Oral History, Beringer Archives, Asti, California.

CHAPTER 14

59. Carrey, Alexis. Oral History, Beringer Archives, Asti, California.

60. *Wines & Vines,* May, 1937.

CHAPTER 15

61. Sbarboro, Andrea. Memoir, The Argonaut, edited by Heather Wheeler, *Journal of the San Francisco Historical Society,* Volume 7, No. 2, Winter 1996/97.

62. James, Marquis and Bessie Rowland James. *Biography of a Bank: The Story of Bank of America N.T.&S.A,* Harper, New York, 1954.

63. Sbarboro, Andrea. Memoir, The Argonaut, edited by Heather Wheeler, *Journal of the San Francisco Historical Society,* Volume 7, No. 2, Winter 1996/97.

CHAPTER 16

64. Rossi, Edmund. "Italian Swiss Colony and the Wine Industry," an oral history conducted in 1971 by Ruth Teiser, Bancroft Library, University of California, Berkeley.

65. Crawford, Charles. "Recollections of a Career with the Gallo Winery and the Development of the California Wine Industry, 1943-1989," an oral history conducted in 1989 by Ruth Teiser, Bancroft Library, University of California, Berkeley.

66. Petri, Louis A. "The Petri Family in the Wine Industry," an oral history conducted in 1969 by Ruth Teiser, Bancroft Library, University of California, Berkeley.

67. Ibid.

CHAPTER 18

68. Rossi, Edmund Jr. "Italian Swiss Colony 1949 1989: Recollections of a Third Generation California Winemaker," an oral history conducted by in 1988–1989, Ruth Teiser & Lisa Jacobson, Bancroft Library, UC Berkeley.

CHAPTER 21

69. Material relating to the Little Old Winemaker commercials was provided in personal communications with the last creative director for the commercial, Mr. Ron Berman from Marin County, California.

CHAPTER 23

70. Petri, Louis A. "The Petri Family in the Wine Industry," an oral history conducted in 1969 by Ruth Teiser, Bancroft Library, University of California, Berkeley.

71. *Wines & Vines,* November 1964, Page 23.

72. Petri, Louis A. "The Petri Family in the Wine Industry," an oral history conducted in 1969 by Ruth Teiser, Bancroft Library, University of California, Berkeley.

73. *Wines & Vines,* October 1969.

74. Petri, Louis A. "The Petri Family in the Wine Industry," an oral history conducted in 1969 by Ruth Teiser, Bancroft Library, University of California, Berkeley.

75. Teiser, Ruth and Catherine Harrow. *Winemaking in California,* McGraw-Hill Book Company, 1983.

76. Berger, Dan. "Despite Label, Colony Wine Excellent," *Santa Rosa Press Democrat,* September 17, 1986.

CHAPTER 25

77. *Santa Rosa Press Democrat,* November 25, 1991.

AFTERWORD

78. Lapsley, James T. *Bottled Poetry, Napa Winemaking From Prohibition To The Modern Era,* University of California Press, Berkeley, California 1996.

NOTES

79. Kobler, John. *Ardent Spirits: The Rise and Fall of Prohibition,* Da Capo Press, New York, 1973.

80. Peninou, Ernest. "Leland Stanford's Great Vina Ranch 1881-1919," Yolo Hills Viticultural Society, San Francisco, 1991.

Acknowledgments

I OWE MUCH TO MANY for the help I received in writing the story of the people of Asti and ISC. The San Francisco Historical Society, particularly Deanne Kestler and Romney Lange, was especially helpful to an unknown researcher.

Many people were supportive and provided important information but the book could not have been written, certainly not in its present form, without the extensive help of a special few. To Bob Rossi, Rachel Ann and Pete Seghesio, Gloria Stryker, "Auntie Bea" (Baiocchi) Trusendi and Joe Vercelli, I owe a special thank-you.

And the list goes on. Nello Baiocchi, Alex Carrey, Lelio (Ningles) Giampaoli, Mae Giampaoli, Jim Mazzoni, Bob Myers, Andy Vasconi, each had a hand in building the story.

Dave Hastings and Bob Del Sarto's contributions were valuable and appreciated. Fr. William Breault provided substantial contributions, moral support and encouragement.

To Malcolm Margolin, a caring man who didn't have to help but did, I extend my sincerest gratitude.

Last but not least, there was Bob Locher, a friend whose genuine concern enabled our friendship to grow even as he critiqued and helped shape *Legacy of a Village*.

Finally, I must thank my Creator, who somehow managed to put me in the right place at the right time, providing the opportunity to spend so much time over the past several years with some of His most wonderful creations, the people of Asti and ISC.

To you all, mille grazie!

Index

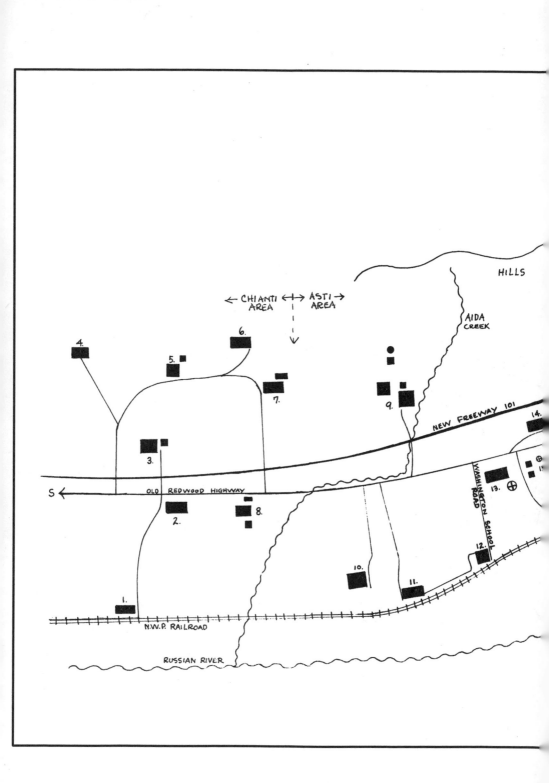